D0900327

# TRUSTBUILDING

# TRUSTBUILDING

*An Honest Conversation*
*on Race, Reconciliation, and Responsibility*

## ROB CORCORAN

With a foreword by Governor Tim Kaine

UNIVERSITY OF VIRGINIA PRESS

CHARLOTTESVILLE & LONDON

University of Virginia Press
© 2010 by the Rector and Visitors of the University of Virginia
All rights reserved
Printed in the United States of America on acid-free paper

*First published 2010*

9 8 7 6 5 4 3 2 1

Library of Congress Cataloging-in-Publication Data
Corcoran, Rob, 1949–
    Trustbuilding : an honest conversation on race, reconciliation,
and responsibility / Rob Corcoran ; with a foreword by Tim Kaine.
        p. cm.
    Includes bibliographical references and index.
    ISBN 978-0-8139-2875-3 (cloth : alk. paper)
    ISBN 978-0-8139-2881-4 (e-book)
    1. Race relations. 2. Reconciliation. 3. Trust—Social aspects.
    4. Conflict management. I. Title.
    HT1521.C638 2010
    305.8009755'451—dc22                    2009024800

*For Neil, Mark, and Andrew*

CONTENTS

I first encountered a small group of people calling themselves Hope in the Cities as a newly elected member of the Richmond City Council in 1994. It was clear from the beginning that they were a dedicated bunch, but it was also clear they were facing huge obstacles. Richmond, after all, had been a major interstate slave trade market and the capital of the Confederacy. It was famous for its Massive Resistance to integration. The city government and the city in general were starkly divided along racial lines. Richmond was congenitally resistant to change of any kind.

Into this atmosphere stepped Hope in the Cities, determined to heal these divisions through conversation and dialogue. It seemed like a tall order. But, fifteen years later, they've pulled it off. They've succeeded in beginning the healing by insisting on honest conversation, demanding reconciliation, making divergent and often divided groups take responsibility. This small group focused on fixing Richmond's racial problems has expanded over the years, taking its message nationwide and to South Africa, France, and the United Kingdom.

This book, using personal narrative and exhaustive reporting by Rob Corcoran, chronicles how Hope in the Cities has moved what looked like an immovable barricade. The job is not done, but Hope in the Cities has provided a map for the future.

In 2007, Virginia became the first state to officially apologize for slavery. Later that year, thanks to the work of Corcoran, Paige Chargois, Ben Campbell, and many others, we unveiled the *Reconciliation Statue* at the site of the old slave market in Richmond. I noted when I participated in that unveiling that the apology was appropriate because Virginia had promoted, defended, and fought to preserve slavery. How we got from there to where we are today is the subject of this book.

Today we have an African American president of the United States. Our population is more diverse than it has ever been in the history of our country. Racial discrimination remains with us, and we will continue to need the help of Hope in the Cities to conquer our lesser instincts. *Trustbuilding* is not a conclusion but a chart, a useful guidebook to that ultimate destination that we know we will someday reach.

Tim Kaine

Governor of Virginia,

2006–2010

At the age of twenty-two, as an unemployed shipyard worker in Green-ock, Scotland, my father encountered an idea that changed his life. In 1935, a student who played on the same badminton team apologized to him for jealousy. Dad was team captain, and the student admitted that he had hoped to be captain himself. He explained that he and other students at Glasgow University had decided to apply their faith practically with changes in their own lives. Curing selfishness in people, they claimed, was a basis for a new social and economic order.

Dad grew up in the poverty that was the norm for working-class families of the era. Despite his skepticism, he found the honesty and strength of purpose that he saw in the students immensely attractive. He was even more impressed to meet three industrialists who were committed to putting people before profit. One of them had moved into a smaller house to avoid reducing his workforce during the Depression.

An unusual alliance of workers, students, and businessmen emerged in the Clydeside region. One of my father's new friends was Archie Mackenzie, who went on to a distinguished diplomatic career. According to Mackenzie, "a culture of teamwork began to challenge the inherited doctrine of class war." For my father, it was the start of a lifelong effort to bring new perspectives to the labor movement. It was also an important stage in the development of an international network for trustbuilding and reconciliation between people and communities now known as Initiatives of Change.

Dad's experience in bridging class differences played an essential part in shaping my own worldview. From him I learned that people of diverse cultures and political backgrounds could overcome divisions to achieve change.

Since 1980, my wife, Susan, and I have made our home in Richmond, Virginia. This book was born out of the practical experience of working with people from many walks of life whose courageous actions are building a new vision for a city scarred by a history of slavery, civil war, and racial discrimination. Our lives were changed by individuals who became our friends and who offered a level of trust far beyond what we had any right to expect. It has been our privilege to accompany them and to learn from them. This is their story.

As the world's cities, towns, and villages—and even our own homes—become increasingly multicultural, questions of identity and inclusion take on new urgency. Richmond's story provides a practical framework of action for concerned citizens everywhere who are anxious to heal divisions and to build healthy, welcoming communities.

## ACKNOWLEDGMENTS

I am grateful to Dick Holway at University of Virginia Press for taking a chance on an unusual book that combines narrative, social commentary, and "how-to." I would like to express special thanks to Mary Lean for encouragement and editorial advice in the early stages of this project, and to Karen Greisdorf for her support and pertinent suggestions. Thanks also to Philip Schwarz, who provided vital data on Virginia's slave history, and John Moeser for his expertise on Richmond's socioeconomic and political development.

I am indebted to colleagues in the Hope in the Cities team: their work provides much of the inspiration for this book. I want to give special mention to Collie and Audrey Burton, our neighbors of thirty years, and whose welcome to the neighborhood set much of this story in motion. Thank you to Don Cowles, Cricket White, Tee Turner, Paige Chargois, Ben Campbell, and many others in Richmond who have shared their reflections with me. Thanks to Niki Toussaint for information on Oregon Uniting, to Frances Trosclair in Natchez, and to Walter Rice and friends in Dayton for taking time to share experiences. Thanks also to Laurence Le Moing and Philippe Lasserre in France, and Gerald Henderson in the United Kingdom, who arranged interviews or read portions of the manuscript, and to Samuel and Virginia Pono and Pieter and Meryl Horn in South Africa, who were wonderful hosts.

Our three sons have traveled with us on this "journey," and they provided invaluable personal insights into the Richmond public schools. Above all, I am more grateful than I can say for my wife, Susan, who has been my companion and collaborator in all the events described in these pages.

# TRUSTBUILDING

# A City in Recovery

On the night of November 22, 2003, three hundred Richmonders gathered at an old gun foundry on the banks of the James River. Once the Tredegar Iron Works had been the industrial heart of the city and its walls had echoed with the sound of hammers and the roar of furnaces. Now a solitary cannon reminded visitors of past glories.

Set in one of America's most historic cities, Tredegar had seen its share of drama. But those who built it could not have imagined the history that would be unfolding on this night.

The first Europeans arrived in Virginia in May 1607, followed by the first Africans twelve years later. Ten days after arriving at Jamestown, Christopher Newport and Captain John Smith, with a small boatload of English settlers, spent several days exploring the river. They made their way up to the fall line, the farthest navigable point, where the city of Richmond now stands. At the time, several Algonquian tribes, united by a powerful chief named Wahunsunacock, or Powhatan, as he was called by the Europeans, made their home there.

The subsequent interactions of Europeans, Africans, and the native population were marked by tragedy and cruelty. The enduring legacy of mistrust, wounds, and inequities represent, as many observers have noted, America's defining moral challenge.

In 1983, L. Douglas Wilder, a Virginia state senator who would become the nation's first elected black governor, underscored the extent to which entrenched racism had hampered the region: "Virginia, having singularly provided significant leadership for the colonies from the earliest years, was also credited, tragically, as the leader in the gradual debasement of blacks through its ultimate institutionalization of slavery."[1]

As the state's capital, Richmond symbolizes America's unfinished business. Few American cities combine such a potent mix of events and memories. Yet, four hundred years after Newport and Smith first ventured up the river, Richmond is the surprising seedbed for a movement of dialogue and trustbuilding that could have far-reaching implications for America—and for a world torn by racial, ethnic, and religious conflict.

In June 1993, this former slave market and capital of the Confederate States during the American Civil War attracted national attention with a bold public acknowledgment of its unspoken history and with a call for "an honest conversation on race, reconciliation and responsibility." Leaders of government, business, nonprofit organizations, and different faith groups joined residents of the inner city and farthest suburbs in an effort to address the "toxic issue of race" and build a vision of justice and reconciliation. Many of these leaders were at Tredegar to mark a decade during which this southern city had begun to free itself from the grip of its past. Reaching beyond Richmond, this effort represented a sustained bid to reframe a national debate on race marked by recrimination, resentment, guilt, and denial.

At the far end of the great foundry, a multiracial chorus quietly began a rendition of "Non Nobis Domine." As the music rose over the oak cross beams to the vaulted ceiling, projected images of a city and its history appeared behind the singers. The crowd murmured as it recognized its heroes.

Dr. Robert L. Taylor, just risen from a hospital bed, was one of the first to arrive, walking slowly but with immense dignity and determination with his wife, Dorothy. A veteran civil rights warrior and cofounder of Richmond's first interracial church council, he had no intention of letting recent surgery prevent him enjoying this moment. He paused to greet Rajmohan Gandhi, a grandson of Mahatma Gandhi. Ten years earlier, as part of Richmond's "honest conversation," Taylor and Gandhi had addressed five hundred people from twenty countries and thirty U.S. cities on the grounds of Virginia's State Capitol at the climax of an unprecedented walk through Richmond's racial history.

In the ensuing years, Richmond's private and public conversations on race shifted perceptibly. New relationships and partnerships began to span traditional boundaries. Gradually (nothing moves swiftly in Richmond) a citizen-led movement known as Hope in the Cities gained strength, creating an environment where tough public policy issues, previously "off-limits," could be examined openly and without blame.

The gathering which brought Taylor and Gandhi to Tredegar would have seemed inconceivable when they spoke together a decade before. Even today many might look askance at the venue. The Tredegar Iron Works had produced more than one thousand cannon for the Confederate army during the Civil War. Without the industrial muscle of Tredegar, the South could not have sustained the long, brutal struggle that resulted in more American deaths than the two world wars, Vietnam, and Korea combined. Many of those who labored here were industrial slaves, and in the early nineteenth century Richmond had grown wealthy as a center of the interregional slave trade that ripped families apart to provide male, female, and child workers for the new plantations in the Deep South. When the great conflict came, the Union and Confederate armies fought forty-three major battles within thirty miles of Richmond. Indeed it could be said that the ground of Virginia was soaked in the sweat and tears of slaves who strove for freedom and the blood of young white southerners who believed they were fighting in defense of their homeland.

After the war and Emancipation, black Richmonders experienced another bitter century of exclusion when a system of segregation replaced slavery throughout the southern states. Virginia led the movement of Massive Resistance against the integration of schools, and when change became inevitable, white Richmonders fled the city by the thousand. Wealth and poverty grew side by side in separate worlds. The interlocking walls of race, class, and political jurisdiction that bedevil many of America's metropolitan regions came to define the limits of opportunity.

And yet here tonight, blacks and whites, city residents and suburbanites, recent immigrants and descendants of "first families," grassroots activists and corporate executives, mingled as if it were the most natural thing in the world.

The chorus had swung into a Negro spiritual, "Walk Together Children, Don't You Get Weary." Ben Campbell, an Episcopal priest and urban visionary, took the stage to describe Richmond's tortured history as a dark cloud hanging over the city. But a hope had been born in his heart that "the place where racism began in its worst form might be the place where healing can begin."

He was joined by Michael Paul Williams, an African American columnist with the *Richmond Times-Dispatch* and a native Richmonder. He had seen his hometown evolve from a place that "discreetly oppressed its black citizens and where race was not discussed in polite company," to a place where serious dialogue was occurring. The conversations had not always

been calm or coherent, conceded Williams, but they had seldom been triv-
ial. Richmond had struggled to "move the discussion from power, spoils
and misguided nostalgia toward empathy, healing and a better tomorrow
. . . to move from powerful symbolism to transformative change. . . . We
have witnessed our politicians move from stark division and open rancor
toward honest attempts to reach consensus."[2]

Williams highlighted steps to reach a new, shared appreciation of history. As evidence, he noted the erection of a statue honoring the native-
born African American tennis star and humanitarian Arthur Ashe on an
avenue previously reserved for Confederate generals, and, most recently
(and controversially), the honoring of Abraham Lincoln with a sculpture
near the foundry. "Indeed," concluded Williams, "anything is possible."

Some of those present might have been surprised by the unequivocal nature of Williams's statement, his evaluation of the dialogue that was taking
root, and his affirmation of new relationships. Listeners might be impressed
that a hard-nosed journalist could claim that a community still plagued by
racial division, poverty, and violence was moving toward "transformative
change."

Williams was followed by two Virginians whose family stories illustrate
the region's tangled and painful history. Carmen Foster, a member of a distinguished African American family, had been executive assistant to Henry
L. Marsh III, Richmond's first African American mayor. It had been a turbulent time for the city. After centuries of white rule, a black majority won
a majority of city council seats in 1977. "Confederate Capital Finally Falls
to Blacks," headlined the *Afro-American* newspaper. Richmond made national news as one of the first cities in America to elect a black mayor.

Opposition erupted when Marsh led the council in firing the highly capable but opinionated white city manager, an act that one business leader
warned would cause blood to run in the streets. Since Richmond had long
prided itself on its civility and had been spared the violence experienced by
other U.S. cities in the 1960s and 1970s, this seemed unlikely; but the scene
was set for several years of confrontational politics on a council which tended to vote along racial lines.

All this Carmen Foster had seen. In 1990, she left Richmond and headed
north to attend graduate school, living in the Boston area for almost ten
years. She hoped the move would fulfill a need to redefine herself outside
the context of the black-white racial tensions of her hometown.

For a decade she lived and learned alongside Americans of every conceivable racial and ethnic background. She traveled in Europe, Asia, Africa, and Latin America. But although she relished her sojourn in Boston, she also discovered that racism comes in many flavors: "Whether it is southern-fried or northern-baked, it's always bitter, hard to swallow, and the aftertaste lingers a long, long time."

Now she was back in Richmond, and this evening she was escorted by her father, Dr. Francis Foster, a dentist and esteemed local historian. His grandfather was a slave named Jack Foster, the manservant of Christopher Tompkins, a Confederate colonel in the Civil War. After the war, Jack worked at Tredegar for its superintendent, Francis Glasgow. Jack married Virginia Taylor, the daughter of a slave woman and a local white merchant. They named their own son Christopher. When Jack died in 1897, the seventeen-year-old Christopher took over his father's job as a messenger and porter. He can be seen today in a photo displayed at the old ironworks, standing with Francis Glasgow and Arthur Anderson, the foundry owner. Descendants of slaves like Jack Foster who worked at Tredegar after the Civil War helped build Richmond's robust African American middle class.

Carmen remarked on the real differences she had seen since returning to Richmond a few years earlier, particularly "the honest dialogue about our past and our present which builds authentic relationships and challenges us to take responsibility for how we envision and craft our future." She noted that however Richmond chose to reinvent its community life, "we stand on a collective past, a shared heritage, and interwoven roots."

Standing beside Carmen Foster as she spoke was H. Alexander Wise, the great-great grandson of Henry Wise, the governor of Virginia who led his state out of the Union in 1861. He became a general in the southern army and, at the end of the war, surrendered, bitterly, to his own brother-in-law, General George Meade. One of his sons was killed in action, another wounded, and a third died of tuberculosis from sleeping on the wet fields.

Governor Henry Wise also reportedly fathered a son by a slave woman. That boy, William Henry Grey, became a prominent church leader and a politician in Arkansas at the time of Reconstruction, where he fought in vain for equality for his people.

Alex Wise's family story illuminated the pain and sense of betrayal experienced differently by black and white southerners, which "hardened into racial resentments in our society that have lasted for generations." But he said he had found a measure of freedom "in trying to imagine the world from the different viewpoints of William Henry Grey, of his mother, Elizabeth, of George Meade, as well as of Henry Wise."

Carmen Foster, Alex Wise, and others in Richmond who have learned to appreciate each other's stories as they work to heal racial history tread a delicate line. Such work, according to Donald Shriver, requires "a moral-historical discrimination not easily achieved by anyone white or black in modern America."[3] Empathy for individual courage and sacrifice must never imply sympathy for a heritage built on injustice: "Citizens need time to learn hospitality to each other's feelings about their diverse, painful pasts. . . . But suffering itself, whatever its nature and circumstances, can evoke a communal bond."[4] This awareness informs Richmond's reconciliation movement.

Wise described Tredegar as the future home of the first national Civil War center to tell all sides of a bitterly contested history. Through the center, everyone would be challenged to "walk in the other person's shoes." Tredegar might become a place first of dawning awareness, then of civil discussion, and finally of healing.

*Wade in the water, children,* sang the chorus, their conductor, Glen McCune, urging them on. In a city said to have more churches per capita than any other city of its size, it is rare to find blacks and whites worshipping together. One Voice, as the chorus is known, is distinguished by its unusual degree of racial integration and by its repertoire of sacred music from Western classical and African American spiritual traditions.

Glen McCune describes himself as a product of his time and culture: "I grew up in a poor white working-class environment near Shreveport, Louisiana, and I had never experienced any relationships in my life that were not bounded by Jim Crow." A stint in the army in Germany provided the first window onto a wider world and his first experience with black Americans as equals.

For McCune, music became a road to redemption as "a recovering racist." His arrival in Richmond was a surprise. "I had vowed I would never return to the South, and for thirty years I never did—except to visit my parents."

One Voice is an apt metaphor for the community, says McCune. "The chorus is a resource for people who are pursuing the goal of reconciliation. Music penetrates hearts." But it's more than singing: "If we don't infuse it with our stories, it will not be dynamic. When you invest your story and yourself when you are singing, your masks come down."[5]

*God's gonna set this world on fire,* sang the chorus, as colors exploded onto the screen behind them.

A mere hundred yards from the foundry, Abraham Lincoln is depicted seated on a bench in conversation with his son Tad. There is space on the bench for a visitor to join the conversation. Only seven months earlier, the sculpture had been unveiled in the wake of stormy public debate. So deeply did some southerners still feel their loss, so deep was their resentment of the North, that it took 140 years for America's greatest president to find a home in Richmond.

Rajmohan Gandhi asked the crowd to imagine the challenge Lincoln— and his own grandfather Mahatma Gandhi—might have posed today. While praising Richmond's progress, he suggested that the larger purpose was not merely the attainment of American unity, but the healing of a larger global divide: "After 9/11, which joined America to the suffering soil of the rest of our earth, Americans cannot afford to think only of uniting America— though, given today's sharp divisions in the USA, that too is a vital goal. Americans certainly can do with honest and respectful conversations with one another. Yet after September 11, America, and all of us, have to strive to heal and unite the world, and for a just and lasting peace everywhere."

Was it possible that a city divided by a cruel and violent history might, through courage and honesty and a willingness to forgive, become a source of hope and healing not only for America but for the world? This was the vision that Richmond celebrated tonight.

And then it was over. The choir sang the finale from *Les Miserables.* The crowd spilled out into the clear night with the lights of downtown to the east.

Earlier, Carmen Foster had described healing as hope and responsibility in action. Healing is about the future. The question is, "Do we *really* want to be well?" In 1993, a critical mass of Richmonders declared to the world that they wanted to be well. A decade later, on November 17, 2003, the affirmation at Tredegar reflected a community on the road to recovery.

## Repairing the Levees of Trust

........................................................................................................................

In a world of global cities, Richmond may seem relatively unimportant. With a center city of two hundred thousand and a metropolitan population of 1 million, it maintains a small-town atmosphere and a leisurely southern pace that has changed little over the years. Its economic prominence in the region has long been eclipsed by its southern cousins Atlanta and Charlotte. Newcomers from other cities tend to absorb the ambience rather than change it.

Richmond experiences the stresses of economic disparity, violent crime, uncontrolled suburban growth, and political fragmentation found in much larger urban environments. But its modest size and relative stability make it an ideal place in which to nurture innovative approaches to community relations.

Since the early 1990s, Richmond, home to my family for three decades, has been the focus of a sustained and broad-based effort to challenge and change the terms of the racial debate by replacing it with a model of "honest conversation" that includes everyone in a search for solutions.

A friend likened America's racial issue to an old coffeepot that keeps percolating. Every few years something happens to bring the vexed problem bubbling to the surface. Unplugging the percolator requires courageous conversation and honest acknowledgment of the underlying sources of distrust. The Richmond story matters because real dialogue, real healing, and real partnerships are happening daily in a city most thought could never change. Richmond matters because it is the first city in the United States to publicly, formally, and inclusively acknowledge its traumatic racial history. Richmond matters because societies everywhere are confronted with the need for reconciliation between communities traumatized by histories of racial, ethnic, or religious division as well as economic disparity.

The thesis for this book is simple: building trust is the essential foundation for building healthy communities. I believe social action and legislation without accompanying changes in individual lives and relationships are unlikely to be effective over the long haul. The most-needed reforms in our communities require levels of political courage and trust-based collaboration that can only be achieved by individuals who have the vision, integrity, and persistence to call out the best in others and sustain deep and long-term efforts. Without trust, true collaboration is unattainable. Without trust, we can't get to real reform. Without trust—particularly trust across racial divides—it will be virtually impossible to generate the will to tackle the daunting challenges facing America's communities.

John W. Gardner tells us, "building healthy communities is less about structure and more about building relationships. Relationship building is the key to breaking political gridlock and being able to take action in the public interest."[1]

Trust must be built at the personal level and in the public arena. This book describes steps to build trust between individuals—steps of restitution and forgiveness—as well as initiatives to engender civic trust, including public acknowledgment of unjust history and new approaches to public policy.

Change emanates from the bottom up. Despite media focus on racial and ethnic conflict, a grassroots movement is growing in many parts of the United States and across the world. Ordinary people are coming together to do extraordinary things. In hundreds of local efforts, diverse groups of citizens are bridging the traditional boundaries of race, class, and culture. Thousands have engaged in dialogue, symbolic acts of reconciliation, and collaborative problem solving. These hope-giving initiatives appear quietly, like green shoots in a parched landscape. Through careful, sustained work, a process emerges. Tools are tried and tested.

Richmond's story is one striking example of this growing global movement. It illustrates two critical components for real dialogue: Not pointing the finger of blame, but extending the hand of friendship. And insisting on bringing everyone to the table, even those with whom we most disagree. By treating people as potential allies rather than enemies, we can focus on solving problems instead of continuing to glare at each other from self-righteous and isolated positions.

The key to healing is in provoking and sustaining this honest conversation among ordinary citizens. Productive conversation requires readiness by all stakeholders to hold themselves, their communities, and institutions accountable, and to be willing to change where change is needed.

## The Changing Face of America

The extraordinary rise of Barack Obama, son of a white woman from Kansas and a Kenyan who started life herding goats, is dramatic testimony to the advances in race relations and racial equality in the United States. The America of 2008 would have been unimaginable forty years earlier, when Alabama's governor George Wallace ("Segregation forever!") ran for president and Martin Luther King Jr. was gunned down in Memphis. That a black man could live in the White House is a stunning reality that opens new horizons for every young man and woman of color.

And the color of America is changing. Fifty percent of all children under five years of age are from racial or ethnic minorities. African Americans and Hispanics form a majority in nearly half the nation's one hundred largest cities. Demonstrations by 2 million Hispanics in 120 cities in 2006 urged our reluctant political leaders to recognize the changing face of the nation. Thirty-four million Americans were born overseas. A new generation—many of them, like Obama, born into blended families—are embracing a more fluid identity. They are impatient with arbitrary racial categories. This has profound implications for our understanding of race and how we define ourselves as Americans.

A 2004 Gallup Poll of adults eighteen and older found that 78 percent of blacks, 61 percent of Hispanics, and 57 percent of whites said they prefer to live in mixed neighborhoods. Seventy-three percent of Americans approve of interracial marriage, up from 4 percent in 1958, when the question was posed only to whites. Such unions rose from 67,685 in 1970 to 440,159 in 2005, comprising a total of 7 percent of all married couples.

But while America seems more at ease with diversity in general, racial and economic segregation actually *increased* in many urban areas during recent decades. In the years 1994–2006, the number of nearly all minority (less than 5 percent white) public schools almost doubled. Hispanic enrollment increased 55 percent.[2] Children in public schools are much poorer than they were decades ago and more separated in highly unequal schools.[3] An African American baby boy has a one-in-three chance of going to prison in his lifetime. Although the income gap between the races is closing, vast inequities in wealth persist. And, as races and ethnicities mingle and merge, some observers foresee a "Beige and Black" America in which a white-Asian-Hispanic majority is offset by a minority of blacks who are once again excluded from the melting pot.

Obama's victory represents the triumph of the civil rights movement. But the task of building a just and inclusive America where every child has the opportunity of living in a safe and healthy neighborhood and of attending an excellent school will take far greater political will and a transformation of our culture.

Global terrorism, illegal immigration, and economic recession make many of us more fearful and less inclusive. We perceive differences of ethnicity, culture, and religion as potential threats. Today, more than ever, the United States is challenged at home and abroad to live up to its highest ideals.

Hurricane Katrina revealed the shameful reality of two Americas, separate and unequal. In the greatest dislocation of Americans since the Civil War, a major city lost two-thirds of its population. The hurricane showed no respect for race: many poor whites suffered hugely. Yet, in a national poll, 70 percent of African Americans said they believed that help would have come faster to a city with a white majority.

New Orleans reflects trends in the country as a whole: underinvestment in vital infrastructure, greedy development, and a growing disparity of wealth and access to vital services. Richmond contains one of the wealthiest census tracts in a moderate-size U.S. city; but within walking distance lie neighborhoods with some of the lowest incomes in the nation.

Yet, Americans are hugely generous, highly practical people. While politicians argued in the wake of Katrina, ordinary citizens took action and opened their homes and their hearts to strangers. Private donations to Katrina victims exceeded the outpouring of support following September 11, 2001.

Americans understand that sustaining a diverse national community demands shared risk and sacrifice. We are prepared to pay the cost if our leaders have the courage to ask.

New Orleans challenges us to consider our country's still unfulfilled commitment to the proposition that all men and women are created equal. Broken promises over the decades have breached the levees of trust. None of us is responsible for the wounds of the past, but we are all responsible for the acts of repair.

## A Global Challenge

Just eight weeks after Katrina, the streets of Paris burst into flames as France struggled to contain the explosive anger of a generation of young men of Arab and African heritage who feel excluded from mainstream society. The worst urban unrest since the 1968 student protests called into question the very foundations of the French model of integration, which officially ignores ethnic differences in favor of a transcendent French identity.

Trevor Phillips, chairman of Britain's Commission for Racial Equality, noted that the violence in Paris was a warning to the whole of Europe that race issues have become central to politics. Everywhere, "smugness" about the state of race relations is being punctured: "This is big politics on which governments will stand or fall. In the 1970s and 1980s, industrial relations marked a tense dividing line in Western societies. Disputes periodically erupted into dangerous and even violent confrontation . . . that menaced and sometimes brought down governments. Race relations threaten to become a similarly potent battlefront in the first part of the 21st century."[4]

Twenty million Muslims now call Europe home. Unlike in the United States, where the majority of foreign-born Muslims arrived three decades ago and are well established in middle-class society, European Muslims provide a vital manual labor force, performing tasks that native-born Europeans are no longer willing to do. Largely excluded from the political process and often confined to live in ghettos (on the outer edges of major cities in France or the inner cities in the United Kingdom), Muslim youth are easy prey for militants. In the host communities, fear of terrorism combines with a deeper concern about loss of identity to provide fertile soil for demagogy.

Far-right parties in the Netherlands, Germany, Switzerland, Austria, Denmark, Italy, and Russia have gained ground. The United Kingdom has distinguished itself from the rest of Europe by embracing multiculturalism. But bombings on the London Underground in August 2005, the arrest the following summer of twenty-four men suspected of planning to blow up airliners over the Atlantic, and failed car bomb attacks in 2007 led to calls for greater emphasis on assimilation, more in line with continental models, and on patriotism and citizen responsibility.

Claims of discrimination and exclusion by African-Caribbean and Asian British are countered by expressions of resentment at what some white British perceive as institutionalized antiracist brainwashing, or exploitation of the country's generous welfare system by asylum seekers and other new arrivals. Others fear the loss of their culture and values. One leading conservative commentator lamented, "I've lived to see the end of the Britain that I loved."[5]

Around the globe, familiar patterns play out as societies struggle to come to terms with newcomers in their midst. One month after France erupted, five thousand white youths went on a rampage at a Sydney, Australia, beach, assaulting people of Arab and Mediterranean background. "This is our land. Get the hell out of here!" yelled a leader of one drunken mob in frenzied scenes captured by television cameras.

Many community tensions trace their roots to historical events and circumstances that continue to hold enormous emotional power. Often the past is seen through the lens of persistent injustice today. In Latin American countries, where tiny white elites control most of the wealth, issues of ethnicity and economic injustice are closely interwoven. As the native population asserts itself in the political arena and demands greater control over natural resources, new power relationships emerge. Even Brazil, which long portrayed itself as color-blind, is engaged in a debate over racial quotas.

South Africa emerged miraculously from apartheid, thanks to Nelson Mandela's inspired leadership and his commitment to reconciliation. But the yawning gulf between the newly affluent and the desperately poor threatens stability. Notwithstanding a burgeoning black elite, South Africa is still two separate nations—one white and in control of the economy, and the other black and outside the economic mainstream.[6] In May 2007, with unemployment officially at more than 25 percent (but as high as 85 percent in the townships and informal settlements), frustrated blacks vented pent-up rage on immigrants from other African countries. And what about the resentment of white Afrikaners, for whom Africa is home but who feel their contribution is discounted and who are told, "There are no career possibilities for you here"? Very few ordinary South Africans have yet engaged in real face-to-face dialogue with people of another race.

### Steps in Trustbuilding

The challenge of building trust across the divides is universal and inescapable. Can we move from blame and avoidance to an acceptance of shared responsibility for a new future?

We can all think of people whom we regard as being "inside" our circle and others who are "outside." Those we exclude may represent another culture or religion, or a different political viewpoint. They may be people who demand justice, or who hold economic or political power. Living as trustbuilders means going toward those whose worldview is different from our own and who challenge our assumptions, people who irritate us, even people whose very presence threatens our sense of comfort and security. Connecting fragmented communities demands the best of everyone: liberals and conservatives, immigrants and established populations, city dwellers and suburbanites, the young and the seasoned. Each person counts.

The scale and complexity of problems facing communities in transition and the emotionally challenging task of healing historic wounds can appear overwhelming. There are no quick fixes.

The Richmond experience suggests that trustbuilders have at least two things in common: a willingness to move beyond blame to personal responsibility for change and a leadership style that encourages the highest qualities in those around them.

Building trust is not a technique that can be taught; it is a spirit that is caught. It is a fruit of honesty and transparency of motive. This new style of citizen leadership offers a vision of hope and opportunity for everyone.

The stories of individuals in this book are interwoven with social history, analysis, and methodology for honest conversations. The narrative focuses primarily on the evolution of race relations in Richmond during the period from 1980 to 2008, and the emergence of the Hope in the Cities movement in the 1990s. Chapters 7 through 9 examine the Richmond process in the context of the national conversation on race and how the method of honest conversation has been "exported" to other U.S. communities. In chapters 12 through 15, we see its application in the United Kingdom, France, and South Africa.

Honest conversation involves specific steps, which emerge in the narrative of the book. Chapters 16 through 20 are devoted to exploring the philosophy and practice of the following four steps:

1. BEGIN WITH OURSELVES. Those of us who are impatient for change need a consistent set of values that are reflected in our personal lives and our public actions. Without this, there is loss of coherence and breakdown of trust. How can we ask others to make costly and courageous choices if

we are not prepared to look in the mirror and put our own house in order? Put simply, we must model the change we expect of others. I call this *values integration*.

Emphasis on personal responsibility breaks the cycle of denial, blame, and victimhood. It brings moral clarity without sanctimony by relying on what Michel Sentis and Charles Piguet call "the one universal language—a life lived out."[7] Individuals become trustbuilders and creative change makers by being willing to take a fearless look at their own attitudes and behavior. Dr. David Campt, a leading practitioner of racial dialogue, remarks on Hope in the Cities' "robust non-religious spirituality," which finds common ground between different cultures and faith groups, and challenges both conservatives and liberals to turn the searchlight inward rather than engage in accusations. Trustbuilders, whether or not they subscribe to any specific faith, need an inner source of wisdom for guidance and to maintain perspective and equilibrium when the going gets tough.

2. INCLUDE EVERYONE. Open and inclusive dialogue is at the heart of trustbuilding. In honest conversations, all stakeholders come to the table and remain engaged. The unflinching self-examination described above increases our ability to discern underlying factors and concerns. Important discernment questions for any community trustbuilding initiative are: What conversation is not taking place? What question do we fear to put on the table? Who must be part of the dialogue and how might we engage with them? Most of us feel more comfortable interacting with those who share our social background, political views, or values. But little real change can occur if we deal only with those with whom we agree, or demonize those with whom we disagree.

Identifying underlying issues and creating safe space for formal or informal dialogue, where participants can listen deeply to others and ask themselves hard questions, are crucial in uniting divided communities. This deep dialogue moves individuals from simply an exchange of information to an experience of transformation.

3. ACKNOWLEDGE HISTORY. No meaningful conversation about the future could occur in a city like Richmond without public acknowledgment of the pain and suffering experienced by a large section of the population over the centuries. The physical act of "walking through history" is a vehicle

for communities to come to terms with the demons of the past. According to Joseph V. Montville, "Such a walk establishes an agenda for healing. It reveals the record of past hurts and allows the conscience of large numbers of people to give up avoidance and be activated in the most positive sense."[8] The ability to appreciate shared history and to view the story from the standpoint of the other side is key to creating a new narrative for Richmond. Alex Wise describes it as the gift of historical imagination.[9] Other communities have found their own distinctive way of breaking the cycle of denial, guilt, and anger caused by unacknowledged and unhealed history. The "walk" can be done in a variety of ways, but it always involves an accurate, respectful, and inclusive public telling of the story. Hannibal Johnson, author of *Black Wall Street*, says the Richmond experience demonstrates "a model of true community reconciliation in an inclusive, validating way, without sacrificing moral clarity."

4. BUILD A TEAM. A team working effectively for broad community change is constantly expanding its circle and building collaborative networks that transcend the usual boundaries of politics, class, ethnicity, and geography. John Gardner describes "networks of responsibility drawn from all segments coming together to create a wholeness that incorporates diversity."[10]

A team promoting trust must demonstrate authentic relationships in its daily life. With the thousands of books on teambuilding filling the bookstores, we should all be experts by now! But how many initiatives implode because of jealousies, hurt feelings, too much reliance on one charismatic figure, or lack of clearly defined roles and accountability?

Failure to build a genuinely diverse network of trust weakens many worthy initiatives. Racial justice projects are often marginalized because they are driven by well-meaning liberals or dedicated activists who operate in the advocacy mode of the 1960s. Almost invariably when I first consult with a community group, I will ask, "Where is the business community? Where are the conservatives?"

Disconnected efforts, however noble and well conceived, are doomed to failure. David Rusk argues that isolated self-help initiatives by inner-city neighborhoods will not succeed over the long term unless they are supported by regional institutional change: "It is like helping a crowd of people run up a down escalator. . . . The real challenge is to rewire the direction of the escalator."[11] To achieve institutional change we need allies who are willing to share insights, knowledge, and access to key players and centers of power.

Thirty years of work in Richmond have convinced me of the need to build diverse, self-sustaining teams, capable of engaging all sectors of the community. These teams are deeply rooted in open dialogue, acts of acknowledgment and reconciliation, and in relationships that will continue to flourish and bear fruit beyond the life of any specific project.

Richmond is a work in progress. The wounds of racial injustice are still evident. Vast gaps in opportunity and wealth continue to divide the region. But, as Donald Shriver wrote in *Honest Patriots,* "Like few other cities in the United States, Richmond can now host a civic conversation that involves virtually the whole of the American story."[12]

## Catalysts of Change

Our house on Sunset Avenue in Richmond's Carillon neighborhood is less than four miles from downtown. It is a peaceful community of some two hundred homes bordered by Byrd Park to the east, the James River to the south, and the interstate highway and downtown expressway to the west and north.

There were several young families on our street when we arrived in 1980. Everybody knew one another, and before long we had spare keys of at least three neighbors. We came to love the city's distinctive neighborhoods and unsurpassed architectural gems. The parks and the river became daily playgrounds for our kids. A two-hour drive could take us to the museums and galleries of Washington, D.C., to Virginia Beach, or to the Blue Ridge Mountains.

We were awed by the stunning beauty of Richmond's spring as dogwoods and azaleas burst into life. We learned to move slowly during the steamy days and nights of the long summer when the temperature actually appeared to rise *after* the sun had gone down. We relished the crisp, clear skies of fall and enjoyed the inevitable panicked rush to the supermarkets that accompanied the first snowflakes.

Almost immediately, we found ourselves plunged into the life of a city reinventing itself in the wake of the political changes of 1977. And we experienced firsthand the personal choices and challenges confronting anyone who wants to be part of a movement for inclusion in a society in which everything seems designed to separate people by race, education, wealth, or geography.

As the family grew, our three boys enrolled in the public schools, where they were part of a tiny white minority. We joined St. Paul's, an active downtown Episcopal church once known as the "Cathedral of the Confederacy," but now working vigorously for racial reconciliation.

At first glance, Richmond is an unlikely place to pioneer a new approach to race relations—or any other social revolution for that matter. Perhaps because many of its early European settlers were British, Richmond inherits two characteristics of my native land: resistance to change, and a tendency to cloak true emotion in a blanket of politeness. This can be, on the one hand, enormously frustrating, and on the other, deeply misleading. Both whites and blacks often appear to be invested in behavioral patterns destined to keep the metropolitan region locked in structures that perpetuate extremes of poverty and wealth, deny equal opportunity, and nurture violence.

Yet, the problems, though severe, are not so large as to be unmanageable. Richmonders retain a strong sense of place. People who disagree about everything else often share a deep loyalty to their hometown, and those who relocate here tend to stay. More than one person has said, "It's a city that you can get your arms around."

## Transition

In 1981, the *Richmond Times-Dispatch* reviewed the city's shifting social and political landscape in a six-part series entitled "Black and White in Richmond." The newspaper noted that for many decades the city council had been controlled by a white "establishment." With few exceptions, members of this elite group had grown up in Richmond's West End, attended private schools and the University of Virginia, were Episcopalians, and made their money in business, banking, or law. While in power, members of this establishment were "magnanimous" toward their black colleagues, even electing Henry L. Marsh III as vice mayor. However, once removed from power, "the old leadership became the highly vocal, visible opposition, backed by the two daily newspapers' editorial pages and Main Street money."[1]

Several fateful events had taken place during the previous decade that were to prove major stumbling blocks to the region's unity and progress. In 1970, Richmond annexed twenty-three square miles of neighboring Chesterfield County, an action that added some forty-seven thousand new residents to the city. Because most of these Chesterfield County residents were white, this action was widely perceived as an effort to dilute Richmond's growing black vote. A civil rights activist, Curtis Holt, sued the city, claiming that the votes from the annexed area cost him victory at the polls. The federal courts ruled that the annexation was unconstitutional, and the U.S. Department of Justice insisted on a new ward plan to replace the previous at-large elections as a condition for allowing the annexation. During the negotiations with the federal government, council elections were suspended for seven years.

John Moeser, who came from Texas to teach at Virginia Commonwealth University (VCU), describes the racial atmosphere of the time: "It was ugly and explosive. . . . For the first two years if we could have left we would have done it."

"We felt we needed to do something to restore race relations in the city," said Thomas J. Bliley, who became mayor in 1970 after a hard-fought campaign in which the established group turned back a determined challenge by the emerging black leadership. "We felt one way to start was to make Mr. Marsh vice mayor."[2] A civil rights lawyer, Marsh was "a slightly-built, whispery-voiced minister's son" who had represented the plaintiff in more than one hundred school desegregation cases in Virginia.[3]

Marsh's calm demeanor may have been deceptive. In 1977, when blacks finally won a majority on the council as a result of the new electoral arrangement, many in the white establishment found the reality of a strong and determined black political leader who would not bow to convention a bitter pill to swallow. Some of the old guard complained that Marsh and his colleagues were not treating the new minority fairly when it came to making political appointments. However, they conceded that in the past Marsh had on occasion been allowed to fill a position or two, but not when it threatened white dominance. Suddenly white leaders seemed to discover the issue of race as if it had magically appeared as a result of the 1977 election.

At the same time, there was a disingenuous attempt to downplay the racial aspect. In fact, several people interviewed by the newspaper said they would not mind if all nine council members were black, provided they were "responsible people." "I believe we should be represented by the best people available," said one white leader. "If you're saying that a person has a right to be represented by one of a particular race, I say that's wrong."[4] Considering that for most of the city's history African Americans had been allowed virtually no say in the governance of the city, this viewpoint would not appear to have a lot of credence.

At first, hopes had been high. "Our city can be and ought to be a model for the nation," said Marsh on taking office in March 1977. Despite white fears, the new leadership, while assertive, was notable for its restraint and lack of racial rhetoric in the face of criticism by some of the old guard, threatening phone calls, abusive letters, and slurs by the media. Margaret Edds, in her essay "The Path of Black Political Power," notes that the editorials of the *Richmond News Leader* called the new black majority "monkey-see, monkey-do leaders of a banana republic" and "a bunch of clowns in a Chinese fire drill."[5]

One community activist said it was important that black leaders assured whites that when they took power they would not "do to them the same way we have been done to." If not, he said, "then we're not ready for it. We're no better than they are."[6]

But some members of the establishment never forgave Marsh for the abrupt firing of the city manager, Bill Leidinger. And when he and his colleagues blocked the construction of a Hilton hotel because it threatened their own downtown development priorities, the anger of the business community knew no bounds. Some were ready to move out.

Willie Dell, who served with Henry Marsh as one of only two blacks on the council before the 1977 election, says, "I never felt the white community wanted to give us credit."

Class as well as race was—and still is—a social barrier in Richmond, among blacks as well as whites. Dell, who, with her sharp mind and colorful African dress, brought energy—and sometimes sparks—to council meetings, recalls a sense of loneliness and exclusion when she arrived from Rocky Mount, North Carolina. She recalls her early encounters with Richmond snobbishness: "Racism was nothing new to me. What was new was to have black people look at you as if you were a zero. They would say, 'You aren't from here. This is the way we are.' Even on the city council I was an outsider with my North Carolina accent. People told me, 'You've got to learn to speak proper.' I thought it was more important to think proper. I was 'too black'; I did not belong to any social groups. Although I was a Baptist, I joined All Souls Presbyterian Church because someone was kind enough to invite me."

A more conservative African American, Roy West, unseated Dell in 1982. He then garnered the support of the four white council members and cast the deciding vote for himself to become mayor. West was seen by some as a bridge builder who could relate to the business community and to the suburban leaders.

Meanwhile, the white population was rapidly deserting the city and pulling investments from the urban center. The downtown retail core was struggling. Vast new shopping malls proliferated in the suburbs while the city saw a steady erosion of jobs.

Following the 1970 annexation, the Virginia General Assembly had prohibited all Virginia cities from engaging in any future annexations, thereby removing the possibility of significantly increasing the tax base. In 2007, the city represented only 5 percent of the metropolitan region's total land mass, but contained 43 percent of the population living in poverty.[7]

Virginia had pursued a policy of Massive Resistance to school integration in the mid-1950s following the 1954 Supreme Court *Brown v. Board of Education* ruling that racially separate schools were inherently unequal. Richmond's painful slowness in integrating its public schools in accordance with the ruling finally led District Court Judge Robert R. Merhige to order cross-town busing in 1971. One year later, an ultimately unsuccessful attempt to consolidate the city and county school systems led to near hysteria. A large percentage of the white population migrated across county lines or chose to place their children in private schools and academies. A student population of 47,988 students in 1970 had shrunk to 35,412 by 1978, and the percentage of white students had plummeted from 36 percent to 18 percent and was still falling.

Relations with the majority white suburbs soured, and the sense of "city-county" separation increased. "There was just no willingness to cooperate at all, or to cross jurisdictional lines for shared services," says John Moeser, who chaired the Department of Urban Studies at VCU. "The annexation incident had created very bad feelings." Construction of new federally financed highways encouraged, and indeed subsidized, the exodus from the urban center. While the surrounding counties experienced explosive growth, the city stagnated.

According to Moeser, in Richmond, as in other U.S. cities, three factors fueled suburban expansion in the postwar years: (1) the federal government developed the FHA mortgage, which caused a rapid increase in construction of suburban houses, while pursuing an explicit policy of denying mortgages for home ownership in minority or integrated neighborhoods and to minorities seeking homes in white suburban neighborhoods; simultaneously, federal public housing programs concentrated predominantly black low-income housing projects in the central city; (2) federal highways promoted and subsidized automobile transportation to the suburbs; and

(3) technological changes revolutionized warehousing and took entry-level distribution employment out to the fringes of the city.

The media frequently spotlighted acrimonious exchanges on the city council. At the same time, the newspaper noted with unintended irony that "race is not a factor in the suburbs since no blacks are on the board of supervisors there."[8]

Some relationships held firm, and Richmond's traditional civility helped to avoid major confrontations. Lewis T. Booker, a white lawyer, and Rev. Miles Jones, a prominent black pastor, served together on the Richmond School Board during the difficult arguments over consolidation and the introduction of busing. Both credited each other's leadership qualities in building bridges across racial lines as a key factor in maintaining a degree of harmony on the board.[9]

One significant development was the emergence of Housing Opportunities Made Equal (HOME), which successfully challenged segregationist practices and worked for open housing through education—and, where necessary, through litigation. A well-connected interracial board leveraged contacts in churches, influential social circles, and social services agencies. As early as 1973, HOME had filed fourteen federal suits—more than any other organization in the country.[10]

But on the whole, open and honest conversation about race was rare. Polite silence was the norm. The 1981 *Richmond Times-Dispatch* series illustrated the depth of the divide and the extreme reluctance to engage around the core issues. "Race relations is the kind of topic that many people in the Richmond area simply avoid," led one story. Fifty-one percent of those asked to answer questions for a study on race relations declined to do so. It was something they did not want to talk about, even anonymously over the phone. "The reasons for refusing can't be determined," said the writers, "but one strong inference is that many of them simply found the topic too sensitive."[11]

## Unexpected Allies

It was late afternoon on a sultry September day. On the front doorstep of our new home was a strikingly handsome African American woman. "My name is Audrey," she announced. "I've come to welcome you to the neighborhood." We'd only moved in a few hours earlier.

"Is your wife home?" inquired Audrey. Within seconds, she was picking her way past packing boxes in the hallway and climbing the stairs to where Susan was bathing our nine-month-old son. As Neil splashed happily, the two women chatted.

Thirty years later, Audrey Brown Burton and her husband, Collie, are still our neighbors. Audrey's simple gesture of welcome, a decision to walk across the street to greet unknown newcomers, persons of a different race, led to friendship that changed four lives and formed the basis for a network that now spans continents.

Audrey grew up in New Orleans and is proud of her African, European, and Native American heritage. One of her aunts spoke only French. Her grandfather was part Cherokee and lived to almost one hundred. Collie is tall, slim, and dark-skinned. His mother was still driving to church in her mid-nineties. The Burtons make an elegant, regal couple. Their devotion to each other, their deeply rooted faith, and their love for the community are evident in their relaxed, embracing attitude to all who cross their path. Words of wisdom alternate with frequent laughter.

Collie, now in his late seventies, prepares breakfast every third Thursday of the month for a group of clergy of all backgrounds and denominations. The idea formed in his mind after a discussion with his pastor: "It occurred to us that there would never be transformation in Richmond until the spiritual leaders began to work together. We have a two-hundred-year problem in this town. We've been dysfunctional so long that we think it's normal."

Several years earlier, he and Audrey had joined St. Giles Presbyterian Church, a predominantly white congregation in Richmond's West End. Why choose a church where they were a distinct minority? "I no longer believe in the concept of race," says Collie. "Why perpetuate a myth? If there is no such thing as race, you can't talk about a black church or white church." Before long they were both respected elders and both served on the presbytery.

Up to forty pastors gather at 7 a.m., starting with thirty minutes of prayer followed by Collie's excellent food. There is no formal agenda, just people getting to know each other. They linger and talk for as long as they want. It has led to the creation of a prison ministry and exchange of pulpits, but, above all, to a web of relationships, friendship, and respect.

Audrey, a former prison administrator, spends most of her days ministering to the community, counseling and encouraging emerging leaders. She has also led a roundtable for women, created a program for young people caught up in the juvenile court system, and helped start a nonprofit organization to train former offenders in business skills. With Don Cowles, a former senior executive with Alcoa Corporation, she launched an initiative to examine public school integration. She has decided, she says, not to speak about racism but about healing.[12] "I am on a rescue mission for the healing of African American children," she says, "to save them from hating themselves and hating white people."[13] Willie Dell says she thinks of Audrey as "fertilizer": she "helps you to grow."

It was not always so. "My tongue was a two-edged sword," recalls Audrey with a glint in her eye. Willie Dell remembers Audrey publicly calling the mayor a liar at a city council meeting. The daughter of a Pentecostal minister, Audrey grew up living in a shotgun house with an outdoor privy. She earned degrees in business and sociology; worked with Chrysler, the Urban League, city and state government; and started an organization for African American women to enhance personal development. She also won a struggle with cancer, went through a divorce, and fought racial discrimination on the job. Beneath the warm exterior, the pain, anxiety, and frustration caused by racism sometimes overwhelmed her: "I was angry for many years." Her confrontational approach won some battles but also left scars.

In 1971, Audrey married Collie, a former associate director of the Richmond Urban League and a single father of three small children. Collie had left Richmond in 1954 "because it had not changed," and when he came back, "it still had not changed enough." He learned organizing skills from friends in Youngstown, Ohio, "who were alleged to be communist." At the time we got to know each other, he was leading a community development project in Richmond's East End.

A few days after our first encounter, we invited the Burtons over for dinner. I do not recall the details of that evening, the first of many shared meals over the years, but the four of us connected immediately. The Burtons had organized and led the voter registration drive that empowered Richmond's African American community and made new political leadership possible. They were also active in the local civic association. The Carillon neighborhood is justly proud of itself as one of the first and best examples of racial and economic integration in the city. White residents refused to be panicked by real estate agents who warned them that property values would drop when the first blacks moved in.

In retrospect, there was an element of challenge in Audrey's welcome: she was coming to check us out. The Burtons were founding members of the Richmond Urban Institute, a newly formed interracial organization focusing on research on housing investment patterns, transportation, and racial tensions. The fact that I had attended the first retreat of the organization during an exploratory visit to Richmond six months earlier probably counted for something.

The Burtons were also intrigued by our backgrounds. My father is a Scottish trade unionist who grew up in a Marxist environment and married the daughter of a conservative London businessman. They devoted their lives to the international labor movement, spending years in the United States, India, and Japan. Susan's mother was a New Yorker whose father worked on Wall Street, and who spent her youth partying, making gin in the bathtub during Prohibition, learning to fly, and even standing in as a vocalist in Ozzie Nelson's band. She surprised herself by marrying an Oxford don and Anglican clergyman-turned-playwright who pioneered modern faith-based theater. His industrial drama *The Forgotten Factor* was described by Senator Harry Truman as the most important play to come out of World War II.

As products of the 1960s, Susan and I were swept up in the idealism of the era, and in the years before our marriage we both worked with the international programs of Initiatives of Change in Europe, Asia, and Australasia. Shortly before coming to Richmond, we had spent several months with a multiracial team in South Africa just after the brutal repression of the 1976 Soweto student uprising, and in Rhodesia at the height of its violent independence struggle. In all these places, we found remarkable individuals who were taking courageous personal action to address racial or ethnic conflict, resolve industrial disputes, or tackle corruption.

The Burtons probed us with questions. I told how forty-five years earlier, my father had found a practical philosophy that spoke to his deepest passion for justice, based on a radical linkage of personal and social change. This had enabled him to play a role on many continents in the resolution of intractable industrial disputes and the growth of responsible trade union leadership, which ushered in fairer labor agreements and new work practices that saved industries. My own entry into this kind of activity was in 1966, when I worked with a team of students and young professionals to support trade union leaders in their effort to build improved relationships in the docks of Britain.

I told the Burtons that my later experiences in Asia and southern Africa had impressed on me the consequences of British arrogance and racism on the lives of so many people. I could not shoulder blame for the actions of my ancestors, but I should accept responsibility for working to correct those wrongs now. I also recognized that the fault could not be attributed solely to governments: most Britishers, myself included, carry inherited attitudes and cultural assumptions that, if left unchallenged, can perpetuate the wounds of the past.

It is surprising that the Burtons and others took us seriously. We had come as unpaid volunteers to support emerging efforts for racial reconciliation in a city with a three-hundred-year history of racial oppression. How naïve! We were young (thirty) and looked even younger. Mamie Kenney, the wife of our former mayor, often claimed that I was a teenager. Perhaps because we appeared harmless and obviously in need of help, people were particularly kind to us, and shared confidences more readily than they might have with native Richmonders. I discovered early on—through necessity—that willingness to admit ignorance is often an effective way to engage others.

Whatever the reason, Collie and Audrey became our closest friends. After many years in the trenches, they were ready to try a different approach to community action. The issues of poverty, unemployment, lack of affordable housing, and inadequate education that face a city like Richmond are familiar to many urban centers. But in Richmond and elsewhere, the biggest challenges are not technical or even intellectual. We have the knowledge and resources to succeed if the courage and will are present. The real problems are rooted in human relationships.

Collie, a veteran of the civil rights movement, was to say, "We spent so much effort in changing structures, but we had to keep going back and doing it again because we did not change the hearts of people."[14]

**Whatever You Fear**

In the midst of the malignant racial atmosphere of the 1970s, a small but determined group of citizens was already at work. Motivated by a vision that Richmond might be a beacon of hope instead of a stereotype of division, they felt compelled to reach out to the new political leadership and to extend a hand to those who were disgruntled.

This unelected group of some thirty individuals organized themselves to hand-deliver letters to each of the nine newly elected city council members that stated: "We are a group of ordinary Richmonders who want to thank you for your effective service on the Council. Your leadership, courage and tenacity, we feel, will help to make Richmond a city where everyone is needed and can play a full part. . . . Though diverse in our backgrounds and occupations, we too hold the conviction that Richmond can demonstrate to the nation and the world answers to racial division."[15]

With the letter was a copy of a small publication called, appropriately enough, *The Black and White Book*.[16] It described individuals whose willingness to accept change in their own lives had made them effective agents for social change. Of special interest was the story of Mrs. T. W. Wood, a member of one of Virginia's oldest families. In 1957, when she was well into her eighties, she attended a conference at the Shoreham Hotel in Washington, D.C., where she made a startling public apology to Mary McLeod Bethune, the pioneer African American educator, for her own "superiority and arrogance." The encounter between these two women was later featured in *The Crowning Experience*, a musical starring the renowned African American mezzo-soprano Muriel Smith. The play ran in Atlanta for five months in 1958, and, for the first time in Atlanta's history, blacks and whites entered a theater by the same door. A leading black lawyer, Colonel A. T. Walden, remarked that Atlanta would "never be the same again."[17] The play went on to break a 123-year box office record at the National Theatre in Washington. My father-in-law, the playwright Alan Thornhill, wrote much of the script and lyrics, and my wife as a girl of six traveled as part of the play's school—"the first integrated school in Atlanta," as she likes to say.

Two of the signatories to the letter to the Richmond City Council members were Mrs. Wood's daughter, Lillian, and Muriel Smith, who lived in Richmond for the last years of her life. Another was Helen Rumple, a retired secretary. She invited Walter Kenney, the new councilman for the Sixth District, and his wife, Mamie, to tea. It was the first invitation the Kenneys had received to a white home in Richmond. Sixteen years later, as mayor of Richmond, Kenney was to invite the world to join the city on its journey of healing.

Meetings of an emerging Richmond reconciliation network were frequently held in the home of Virginia and Tom Sanders. Virginia was head of the Richmond Parent Teacher Association (PTA) in the turbulent 1970s, and Tom taught at the University of Richmond. Virginia says, "People I had known for thirty years at our church would step out of the way if they saw me coming because they had just put their child into private school."[18] She recalls speaking at a regional PTA conference: "I said, 'If we had had open housing, we would not have had busing.' The audience hissed and booed. But as I left the hall, my vice president, who was black, put her arm around me and said, 'Now I know you are not the fake I suspected you were.'"[19]

Tom Sanders noted the crippling effect of fear: "We have a saying in our family," he told me. "Whatever you fear, draw near. It will probably disappear."

Many of those involved in the network drew inspiration from the principles of Moral Re-Armament, now known as Initiatives of Change, which had been active locally for decades. In the 1920s, Frank Buchman developed a practical philosophy linking change in the lives of individuals with change in society. His work, which led to a global movement known as Moral Re-Armament (MRA) and then Initiatives of Change, pioneered new approaches to local, national, and international reconciliation.[20]

An early activist was Dr. J. Levering Evans, pastor of Weatherford Memorial Baptist Church. With Dr. Robert Taylor, he led Richmond's first interracial ministerial alliance, founded in 1953. One Sunday morning, when Taylor appeared unannounced at Weatherford, Levering spontaneously invited him to serve communion with him. While the bold partnership with an African American pastor cost Evans some church members, he and Taylor began to lay a foundation for new race relations. Evans's daughter Elizabeth recalls that at her father's funeral, Taylor paid tribute to his friend and observed that without his leadership, there might well have been violence in Richmond.

Two congregants, Bill and Marge Clarke, were influenced by Evans's commitment to racial reconciliation. Working as a school librarian in the early 1970s, Marge met Winston Jones, a black postal worker who was mentoring several boys with behavioral problems. Impressed by his persistence, she invited him and his wife, Janene, to her home.

In the mid-1960s, Winston had been one of the first blacks employed at a DuPont chemical plant, where he faced threats and insults from white workers who refused to call him by name or sit with him at the lunch table. Undeterred, Winston and Janene led the integration of the Woodland Heights neighborhood on Richmond's Southside, overcoming fear and suspicion among their white neighbors.

The Clarkes introduced the Jones family to their friend Cleiland Donnan, the leader of the Junior Assembly Cotillion. (For those unfamiliar with southern culture, cotillions may best be described as a combination of a dance school and manners class for the children of the white elite.) "Miss Donnan," as she was known to generations of her pupils, wore heels with lights that flashed on the dance floor. In a career spanning four decades, she taught the foxtrot and social graces to ten thousand budding leaders of Richmond's business, political, and cultural life. One observer wrote that parents "sought her attention as avidly as they would an admission counselor to an Ivy League school."[21]

In 1972, Cleiland had decided to "be part of the answer for the problems of Richmond." She often compared her personal journey of change to peeling an onion "layer by layer." Sometimes, she would say, "pride gets in the way and I do not want to change today's layer." Listening to an African American explain how he felt about the history of racism, she said: "I saw clearly my own false pride in my ancestors and all those beautiful plantations along the James River. Standing out like a bolt of lightning was the hurt and pain and suffering of slavery. But most of all, the seemingly small hurts stood out—my own arrogance, slights, my thinking that 'they,' the blacks in the East End, had their place and I deserved my place in the West End of town."[22]

Cleiland opened her home to people of all races. She sold her prized tobacco stock to help finance a center for racial reconciliation in Richmond—a radical step for a Virginian. And, although a proud southerner, she tells of visiting a cemetery where thousands of Union soldiers lie buried to say "thank you for saving my country."

Cleiland grew up close to the Country Club of Virginia in Richmond's West End. But there was always a strong social conscience in the family. As Catholics, they knew something of discrimination in Virginia's tight society cliques. Her grandmother Janet Randolph was an early leader of the United Daughters of the Confederacy and launched a fund to support widows and orphans of Confederate veterans. During the Depression, the family business faltered, and Cleiland was thrust from the comfort of a prestigious private school to join children from very different economic backgrounds in a public school. Her mother was shocked to see children coming to school hungry and launched a fund to remedy the situation.

In the days before the regular use of antibiotics, repeated ear infections left Cleiland with severe deafness—a challenge that did not prevent her from making the small cotillion started by her mother into a highly successful business. Perhaps this personal challenge encouraged her deep empathy with others who were facing hurdles or discrimination based on race, class, or physical ability.

But Cleiland's confidence on the dance floor and as a businesswoman did not immunize her from the initial fear of breaking social taboos. When she first invited black Richmonders to her home, she felt it would be more acceptable to tell her neighbors she was expecting some "African guests." Indeed, since black Richmonders usually only ventured to the West End as paid domestic help, Janene Jones had her own reservations as she and Winston approached the front door. But before long Cleiland was throwing regular parties for diverse groups and working with Janene Jones at her day care center.

Her evolution as a risk taker began when she observed young people, including her own neighbors, experiencing the turmoil of school integration. Her friends Dick and Randy Ruffin, both descendants of prominent Virginia families, were actively engaged in supporting the school system. Randy Ruffin volunteered at an almost all-black elementary school. The Ruffins became close friends of Richard Hunter, the first African American superintendent of the city's public school system, and his wife, Margo. They also came to know Melvin Law, the president of Citizens for Excellent Public Schools. Law, an African American from West Virginia, was an early member of Housing Opportunities Made Equal and later became chairman of the Richmond School Board.

Beyond the desire to help address immediate needs, the Ruffins were motivated to support efforts to build partnerships in the new political and social environment. They pursued a deliberate strategy to raise the level of discussion by placing Richmond's problems in a global context and inspiring a vision of "how a city, still rooted in its past, might contribute to needs for healing in America and the world."[23] Dick, a former Rhodes scholar, had resigned from a promising career at the Pentagon to give his time as an unpaid volunteer with Moral Re-Armament's work of community building and reconciliation.

This was the context in which Susan and I came to live in Richmond, at the invitation of the Ruffins and their colleagues. The members of the eclectic group with whom we found ourselves working were, for the most part, without power or political influence. In some cases, they appeared ill-suited for the task of organizing a movement for new race relations. Such giants of the civil rights movement as the Virginia hero Oliver Hill had done the heavy work of breaking down legal barriers, working for voting rights, and making it possible for a new political structure in Richmond to emerge. Activists had led sit-ins at the local department stores and restaurants to press the cause of integrated public spaces. But as Henry Marsh, by then a state senator, was to remark in a 1993 interview, "We have to build the relationships that go beyond what the law can do."[24]

Dick Ruffin put it this way: "For too long we have wanted leaders who would somehow do the job for us while we went our own ways, pursuing private goals. What we need personally and nationally is the leadership that bridges differences, turns enemies into friends and brings out the best from opponents as well as from those in one's own group."[25]

By the fall of 1977, the informal network had gained enough momentum to organize a public forum, "Richmond: A Model City." Two hundred and fifty people took part, including elected officials and leaders of education and civic organizations.

### Potlucks and Partnerships

The expanded network that evolved from the forum dedicated itself to building relationships across the racial and political spectrum. But the dynamics of the core group were heavily influenced initially by the conservative background of the dominant white culture. African Americans were still a minority and were usually too polite to voice disagreement publicly or to admit to hurts caused by unintended slights, paternalism, and assumptions born of ignorance.

The arrival of Audrey and Collie Burton created a new paradigm. Undeterred by the inevitable lingering effects of racialized thinking, they embraced their unlikely teammates as "family." They were also willing to express their true feelings and convictions. Some, who imagined a gentler path to reconciliation, found the direct talk on race too much to handle and drew back. Others stuck. The Burtons themselves paid a price with some of their peers. "I lost some friends, some colleagues. People I had been close to all my life," says Audrey. "A couple of sisters said, 'You are hanging out too much with white folks.'"

A turning point for the Burtons was a visit to the international conference center run by Initiatives of Change in Caux, Switzerland. Since the postwar years, when it played a pivotal role in the reconciliation efforts between France and Germany, Caux has enabled people from many conflict situations to find new perspectives. Run by volunteers, its magic is found not in formal meetings but over leisurely meals, chopping vegetables in the kitchen, or walks in the forest. At a forum with Africans from such countries as South Africa, Uganda, Zimbabwe, and Ethiopia—many of whom had suffered terrible personal loss—they exclaimed, "The problems in Richmond don't look so big after all!"

The Burtons were impressed by the spirit of community, expressions of hope, open dialogue, and freedom from competition and stress that they found in Caux. "There was a buildup of pain, anxiety, and frustration caused by racism, by the way I had been socialized and shaped by society. . . . There had been a need in myself to release a drowning spirit," Audrey explained.[26]

She and Collie began to experiment with regular times of reflection. Many years later she told a group of community leaders: "I had to reconstruct my model, to become free of hostility, anger, hate and frustration. The people we meet at the community level are full of these things. It was a spiritual transformation, not an intellectual one. Rather than constant confrontation, I learned to be quiet, to reconnect. My behavior and language changed. Way down deep inside, God called me by name."

The Burton home at 3002 Garrett Street rapidly became a place of welcome, refreshment, and inspiration for people of all backgrounds. The emphasis on the home as a context for community building proved crucial. While Richmond was rapidly desegregating in the workplace, social interaction between races remained minimal, and it was rare, even in the well-integrated Carillon neighborhood, for black or white people to visit each other's homes. The Burtons, Cleiland Donnan, the Sanders, and the Clarkes broke fresh ground by welcoming diverse groups for good food and fellowship. By the end of the 1980s, potluck dinners for thirty or forty people were taking place regularly in homes across the Richmond region. Over fried chicken, spaghetti, or ham biscuits, prejudices dissolved and friendships formed. Sometimes a community leader—a police chief, school superintendent, or county supervisor—would join the group for informal, off-the-record conversation and a rare opportunity to meet with people who were not pushing an agenda. In unexpected ways, potlucks led to new partnerships.

At a typical meeting held in the Burtons' home in February 1983, the Richmond group began to identify fundamental issues and strategic goals:

1. There is a need for healing and reconciliation between individuals and groups.

2. We don't really know each other; there is a wide gap between those in the cities and counties.

3. Focus on the potential greatness of Richmond if people would relate to each other.

4. The network should be seen not as an organization, but (representing) a philosophy relevant to the needs of the city.

5. People need to know there is a team at work—that there are individuals who have experienced radical change in their attitudes and relationships.[27]

These conclusions provided a framework for understanding and common action. The group dedicated itself to reconciliation at a regional level. Its references to the "city" implied the entire metropolitan area. The porous nature of the network would provide an environment where all stakeholders might feel ownership of the project. Equally important was the bold, positive vision, given substance by the reality of a diverse team learning to work together.

# Influences

## From Liverpool
## to India

You can't export the details. What you can export is . . . the change in attitude that comes to people when they realize that if healing will take place, it must take place within themselves. . . . So am I, so goes the world.
—Alfred Stocks, chief executive, Liverpool City Council, 1973–86

From the start, the Richmond network adopted the approach of thinking globally and acting locally. The emphasis on personal change as the springboard for change in society proved a solid foundation on which to build new relationships. For the Burtons, the opportunity to interface with the world in Caux was decisive. Throughout the 1980s, diverse Richmond teams took part in actions in different U.S. cities as well as overseas. They achieved this without corporate sponsorship, foundation grants, or government support. Individuals devoted their vacation time and dug into their savings. Those who could not take part themselves participated by supporting others.

A partnership begun in the early 1980s with the British city of Liverpool gave impetus to Richmond's reconciliation effort. Exchanges have continued for more than two decades. Liverpool's profound racial tensions, like Richmond's, are rooted in the history of slavery. Both cities accumulated enormous wealth through the horrendous transatlantic slave trade. Many Africans sold in Richmond's slave markets had crossed the Atlantic in Liverpool ships, which made five thousand Atlantic crossings. It was said that during the American Civil War more Confederate flags flew in Liverpool than in Charleston, South Carolina. Liverpool has taken important steps to acknowledge this shameful past, and later in this book I describe a project to establish a Reconciliation Triangle with Virginia and West Africa. But in 1983, honest conversation about race was still in its infancy. Recognizing their powerful historical link, a group of Liverpool leaders invited a multiracial team from Richmond to share their experiences in bridging traditional divides.

## Two City Managers

The scars of riots two years earlier were still evident in blocks of burned-out buildings as thirteen Richmonders drove through the Toxteth neighborhood. On July 5, 1981, black and white youths had fought pitched battles with police who, for the first time, used tear gas to control civil unrest in mainland Britain. One hundred and forty buildings were destroyed, leaving an already deprived neighborhood looking like a war zone. Most observers agreed that race was not the only cause of the violence. Frustration at high unemployment, resentment at police harassment, and sheer criminality all played a part. But at the heart of it was what one college principal described as Liverpool's "unique and horrific" breed of racism.

Collie and Audrey Burton shared the leadership of the visiting Richmond group with Howe Todd, the senior assistant city manager, and his wife, Joyce, recently retired from teaching at a private school. The Richmonders met with senior police officers, Marxist militants, elected officials, and a leading judge. Interviewed on local radio, Collie Burton remarked, "Ten years ago, for Howe Todd and me to come to Liverpool talking about solutions to race relations in Richmond would have been impossible." "In fact we were antagonists," Todd interjected.[1]

In truth, the history of distrust was far more recent. Just six months earlier, I had stopped by the Burtons' home to report on a lunch meeting with Howe Todd. "And what was he trying to put over on you?" asked Audrey accusingly. "Well, he'd like to join our team going to Liverpool," I replied cautiously, suddenly aware that I had stepped into a minefield. As a comparative newcomer to Richmond, I was ignorant of the history of public confrontation between Collie Burton, the community organizer, and Howe Todd, a white city administrator in charge of the allocation of community block grants. Known as "Mr. Richmond" because of his intimate knowledge of the city and his energetic leadership in preserving and restoring Richmond's architecturally distinctive historic neighborhoods and waterfront, Todd had a distinguished forty-year career in local government, ending as the acting city manager. Yet bureaucracy and paperwork can get in the way of human relations; it's easier to restore a building than to establish trust.

The Burtons and others in the African American community viewed Todd as a racist who had little time for them. I left the Burtons house feeling deflated and concerned.

But a few days later Audrey called to say that she and Collie would host a cookout for the traveling group—including the Todds. "If we are going to go to Liverpool together, we'd better get to know each other," she said. However, before the event, Collie warned Audrey, "If that man (Todd) says anything I don't like, you know I'm going to have to put him off our property."

"But Howe had a sense of humor," says Audrey. "We were able to talk about general things, and we began to build a relationship." The Burtons invited the Todds for a second visit, and the two couples rapidly became friends. They agreed to speak honestly. Collie Burton said to Howe Todd, "If you use a racial term, we have the right to give you a lesson."

In the 1970s and 1980s, Liverpool faced crisis after crisis. Economic recession and a change in the pattern of trade led to a dramatic decline in the port. The city lost 100,000 jobs in ten years. By the 1970s, Liverpool was the poorest city in Britain. In addition to racial tensions, political polarization over fiscal policies brought the very existence of the democratic process into question.

The man whose job it was to keep the city functioning through this period—and the primary initiator of the Richmonders' visit—was Alfred Stocks, the city's chief executive (city manager). Stocks believed: "If you can learn to trust others and get them to trust you, you can do almost anything. Conversely, without trust, however good the policies, you can do almost nothing."[2] He was one of the few people who inspired confidence in all parties. Gerald Henderson, who has worked since 1982 to help improve race relations in Liverpool, says that following Stocks's untimely death, leaders at both extremes of the political spectrum could say, "Alfred was my friend."

As a major port, Liverpool attracted large numbers from China, Africa, and the Indian subcontinent. There are also twenty thousand "black Liverpudlians" who have lived in the city for many generations and who often feel excluded and ignored. The city's role as Britain's leading port in the transatlantic slave trade has left bitter scars.

Following the 1981 riots, Stocks invited the chair of the Merseyside Community Relations Council to speak to a meeting of leading employers and executives. He told them, "There may not be discrimination by intent, but there is certainly discrimination by default."[3]

Stocks ordered the first survey to determine the level of discrimination in the city's hiring practices. "Nobody had taken the trouble to find out. . . . In a sense we put it on one side and said, 'Well, jobs are open to everybody, people are appointed on merit, so what?' The thought came to me persistently to find out what the facts were."[4]

The facts, when published, were devastating. The city municipal workforce of 31,000 included just 269 blacks, or, as Stocks put it, "about one-tenth of what we should have been employing." Stocks worried about the effect of publishing the figures—"I thought the heavens would fall"—but the city council agreed.

Stocks was now in a position to challenge other employers. "I wrote to an employer I knew well, and his firm employed 1,400 people. I said, 'How many black people do you employ?' He said, 'Four, and six Scotsmen.' It was his way of making a little joke but the truth is there. . . . And that pattern is repeatable. There are no black people working on the Liverpool docks. . . . The jobs are handed out in families, father to son, son to grandson . . . in this self-perpetuating way. So . . . we began to reveal the truth, and once the truth lay revealed and on paper, we started . . . a process of restoring fairness in an extremely unfair and unjust situation."[5]

Stocks described himself as a timid person who found his greatest source of strength and clarity in early morning reflection. These were moments to bring into the presence of his God "the tensions, the worries, the fears, saying, 'Here they are! They are more than I can deal with.' . . . The stresses and strains . . . may be at work. They may be in the family. They may be with friends. Then specifically seeking leading in the problems and issues and how to deal with them . . . I could not possibly manage without it."[6]

Stocks's religious convictions never led to self-righteousness or rigidity. To the contrary, his willingness to engage in honest self-examination led to greater openness and compassion toward others. He had begun this as a young man.

"I had blamed my father for all the ills in our family life. [But] I was the one responsible. I had deprived my father for years of the love and affection that a son owed a father who had given him so much. And [I realized] that it was deprivation which caused my father in turn to be insecure and to have developed the personality from which I was rebounding. I began to go home, week-end by week-end, and the relationship at home was restored and transformed as a result of the new love and honesty that was born between us. So that was the first lesson I learned: to put things right myself, before I could hope to put things right elsewhere."[7]

As chief executive, Stocks applied this lesson in addressing religious intolerance, which runs as deep as racial prejudice in Liverpool. As recently as 1958, a Protestant mob had stoned the Catholic archbishop. From the mid-1970s, relations between the two rival communities began to improve, but certain groups continued to make Stocks's life difficult. One day, stuck in his car in the Mersey Tunnel for an hour as a procession marched past, he was "absolutely furious that these people had caused this personal inconvenience." Afterward, he felt unhappy with his feelings of prejudice and even hatred toward one particular faction. As was his habit, he reflected on this problem. A surprising thought occurred to him: "Ostracism has no part in public policy."[8]

This insight and a subsequent apology to those he found most difficult resulted in a request to Stocks from this same group to mediate a critical issue, which he helped bring to a satisfactory settlement. He developed a reputation for an ability to approach individuals who might be divided by ideology, race, or class and engage them in respectful conversation. He said, "I want to work in my city to liberate the forces that can build a society based on what each has to contribute and not on the domination of one group over another."[9]

But Liverpool was an ideological battleground. A carefully planned bid by Trotskyite Militant Tendency (a Marxist group within the U.K. Labour Party) to infiltrate the Labour Party gave them control of the city government in 1983. As Stocks recalls: "When they came into power, they looked at us paid officials with some suspicion. We must surely be Conservatives to a man! We had been to university, we had degrees, we had a natural affinity with middle-class thinking, and they were in some doubt about whether they could trust us."[10]

The new council implemented a hugely expensive housing project, creating a budget deficit in direct defiance of legislation set out by the Conservative government in London. By October 1985, the city was close to bankruptcy. The workforce of thirty-one thousand received notice, and the administration made contingency plans for life-and-death services. On the brink of disaster, Stocks remained focused and in dialogue with all parties. He later told a group of young people, "Sometimes it would seem that the whole situation in the city could explode in my face. I did not know what to do. I would lay it down before God, along with all my fears and apprehensions and pray. Then sometimes I would get a thought, I would act on it, and it worked."[11]

In the end, a financial package was arranged. Stocks was reticent about his own role in averting the crisis, but one senior figure told Henderson privately, "If the truth were known, that man saved the city."

Stocks's effectiveness lay in his ability to remain accessible to everyone. He explained that it was not a question of whether "people like me approve of the Militant Tendency," but whether he was willing to walk alongside them—"to walk with my brother."[12] Political opposites recognized a man who would listen and give his opinion honestly.

Stocks thought Richmond might have something of value to share with his city. But the impact on the Virginians was surely greater than the impression they made on Liverpool. This was the first venture outside Richmond for the fledgling team, most of whom had never worked together before. The days in Liverpool and the daily interaction with the Burtons marked a turning point for Howe Todd. He began to speak of the need to "build up people, rather than tearing down or criticizing others." He had learned that "when we talk about problems we must have a spirit of sharing and willingness to hear the other person."[13] This new approach did not go unnoticed back in Richmond, especially among African Americans.

"I've seen Howe Todd grow in terms of his ability to genuinely interact with all levels of the community," Audrey Burton told a reporter.[14] A black executive director of a nonprofit organization remarked to me: "Howe Todd used to be known as someone who never listened. Whenever I went into a meeting with him, I always felt the cards were stacked, that the decisions were already made. Now he really listens to what I have to say." Always the enthusiast, the veteran city manger was so convinced of the importance of his newfound perspective that he called a special meeting of all city government department heads to tell them about it.

The Burton-Todd partnership created ripples across Richmond and set the tone for many other connections across traditional divides. The two couples shared their new insights over dinner with Carolyn Wake, a white member of the city council, and her husband, John. Collie Burton explained, "I've learned that when you get into a position of leadership you have to be responsible for everyone, not just your own group." Later he told a group of black British community organizers: "Each of us needs to confront ourselves, to rid ourselves of self-pity, fear and bitterness. As we do this, we will begin to grow with dignity and as a free people."[15]

## Gandhi and King

Four years later, Richmonders found themselves on the road again, this time in India. Rajmohan Gandhi had met with then-mayor Andrew Young and Leon Sullivan, founder of Opportunities Industrialization Center (OIC), in Atlanta in the summer of 1987. Reflecting on the spiritual link between America's civil rights movement and his grandfather's pioneering work for nonviolent change, the history of suffering of black Americans, and the need to bridge divisions of caste and religion in India, he wrote of his vision that "America's Blacks and India's Untouchables and Tribals may in partnership give something precious to the world."[16] He recalled the 1936 meeting between his grandfather and Howard Thurman when the Mahatma expressed his hope that the message of nonviolence might be brought to the world by African Americans.

In October 1988, again led by the Burtons, twenty-two Americans from Richmond and five other cities joined Gandhi and fifty-five Indians and representatives from other parts of Asia, Africa, and Europe on a *yatra* (journey) to retrace the Mahatma's famous 1933 Salt March. The group traveled by bus, stopping for meetings and ceremonies in towns and cities along the way. The younger Gandhi noted that many of the world's liberation movements claim connection to the Mahatma's marches: "Our march may help restore the true meaning of liberation and may be a contribution towards purifying liberation movements and purging them of hates, jealousies, vendettas and the death wish." Gandhi challenged his audiences to consider that while many Indians settle in the United States, they mix primarily with their own community, to some extent with whites, but rarely with blacks. "Gandhi and Martin Luther King Jr. never met, but their spiritual children are having daily communion in Gujarat," he said.

For the Americans, it was a powerful, often emotional experience. Audrey Burton mused, "Why did Gandhi and King go to prison for liberty, and we have so many locked up for wrongdoing?" Former Richmond city councilwoman Willie Dell was accompanied by her husband, Nathan, a Presbyterian minister. "I had been brought up to believe that the Hindu god was not ours," he told the group on the final day. "Yesterday, I started to read the

Gita, and I heard the voice of my God, as if in stereo where the music comes from different sides to make an impact on the ear."

Richmond also benefited from international visitors who brought new insights and broader perspectives to a community often obsessed with parochial concerns. Conrad Hunte, the former vice captain of the world champion West Indies cricket team, was one such guest. Hunte is revered by cricket fans for his record 446-run partnership with Garfield Sobers in Pakistan in 1958, and for his role in the "greatest cricket match"—the 1960 Test match with Australia, the first ever to end in a "tie." At the height of his fame, he had followed a call to set aside his career and devote his energies to preventing a race war in Britain. Following the assassination of Martin Luther King Jr., Hunte moved tirelessly across Britain, meeting with leaders of the African-Caribbean and Asian communities, including Black Power members.[17]

Hunte asked, "Who are the six blacks and six whites who, if they had a Damascus Road experience, could transform Richmond?" As a lay preacher, Hunte tended to frame his thoughts in biblical terms. But his question illustrated a practical strategy for community mobilization which was not dependent on organizational capacity, financial resources, or even sheer numbers. Rather, it involved careful discernment to identify individuals through whose radical change the wider community might glimpse a vision of entirely new possibilities. These individuals were not limited to the "usual suspects"; they might even appear to represent "the problem." Thus, the demonstration of new relationships between such opposites as Howe Todd and Collie Burton might do more to transform race relations in Richmond than exhaustive analysis, exhortation, or advocacy.

Another influencer was Hunte's U.K. collaborator Hari Shukla, a Ugandan-born Indian who directed the Racial Equality Council in Newcastle upon Tyne, a city with more than fifty racial and ethnic groups. Shukla, who was honored for his leadership in community trustbuilding, says: "I found that I needed to be honest myself before I tried to work with others. As a result people began to trust me."[18] With Shukla's encouragement, the various minorities began to cooperate and to make a fuller contribution to the city. Aided by Shukla, the police were running a successful liaison group with ethnic minorities a decade before Lord Scarman's report on Britain's 1981 riots proposed that such bodies should be set up throughout the country. Newcastle was one of the few British cities with large Muslim populations not to experience communal violence protesting the publication of Salman Rushdie's *The Satanic Verses.*

Visits to Richmond by Shukla, Hunte, and Alfred Stocks gave encouragement to those working to break through entrenched attitudes. Their personal testimonies demonstrated how individual change was an essential basis for building trust among people of diverse viewpoints.

## Long-Distance Runners, Prophets, Bankers, and Builders

........................................................................................................................

### Listening to the Community

Nothing made a deeper impression on the Richmond network in its forma-
tive years than the model of "creative connections" in Pasadena, California.
In 1972, after many years of international work, John and Denise Wood settled in this southern California community eight miles east of Los Angeles
in the foothills of the Sierra Madre Mountains. John was director of development for the Braille Institute while Denise spent several years as dean
of students at a private girls' school. After an active life, they could have
retired in the pleasant California sunshine. But instead of slowing down,
the Woods took on the job of caring for an entire city.

Behind Pasadena's image as a cultured, affluent community, with its
"low-profile elitism,"[1] new realities were pressing in. The "genteel ambience"[2] was eroding as the city felt the impact of its proximity to downtown
Los Angeles. The rapidly growing immigrant population and the increasing
number of people living in poverty were threatening "the comfortable life of
those who were trying to walk on the other side of the road, eyes averted."[3]
Some headed for the all-white suburbs when Pasadena implemented public
school busing in an unsuccessful attempt to achieve a measure of integration and equity in the school system. (In 2006, Pasadena high schools were
70 to 90 percent Hispanic and African American.)

All Saints Episcopal Church was active in the community, under the
leadership of its rector, George Regas. As a member of the vestry, John
Wood volunteered to explore the possibility of a skills training center. This
involved building a partnership between the city government, the school
system, and a community college—all of which guarded their territory jeal-
ously. "I didn't know how to go about it," says John. "I'd only been to Har-
vard, which doesn't prepare you for real life all that well."[4]

In spite of his professed lack of qualifications, John brought two vital attributes to the table: the ability to build trust and a willingness to listen. He

embarked on a careful round of consultations with key community leaders and was elected to lead a fourteen-person task force that met twice a week at 7:30 a.m. for twelve months. John's role was to keep the group on track and to encourage those with differing views to listen to each other. The fact that they never had to take a vote speaks volumes about his leadership style. Within four months of the task force's report, the center opened, enabling more than four thousand people a year to learn skills ranging from data processing to bicycle repair and English as a second language.

In 1983, All Saints commissioned Denise Wood to conduct a survey of the quality of life of Pasadena, as the church's gift to the city in honor of its first hundred years in Pasadena. Denise said: "I set myself the goal to listen to the city, which meant to listen to every strata of life, to every race, to every district. It meant most of all to listen to individuals. . . . The head of the League of Women Voters gave me five names. I went to each of these interviews with no hidden agenda of my own; I went to be taught. These five gave the names of other individuals, who in turn sent me to others. My one-on-one interviews finally totaled 104 people over seven months."[5]

Denise found severe black male unemployment, hunger, homelessness, and rapidly increasing drug use. She also discovered individuals who were giving creative leadership and inspiring others to take action. She called her report *Experiencing Pasadena: The Needs, Promises and Tasks of an American City.*[6] An African American minister said of it, "There is no blaming, no name calling, but you didn't water down the truth." The mayor posted pages of the report in the city hall and asked Denise to speak on his radio program because, he said, "You speak for the whole city."

Denise says she was not the same person after the interviews: "Those people changed me. They revealed to me a city in pain, yet with enormous potential. It was rapidly becoming two cities: a rich city and a poor city." Her description of a meeting with a community activist known as a "troublemaker" is typical:

> Arriving at his ranch, on the outskirts of the city, I found a deserted scene. A couple of broken down cars . . . barking dogs . . . two or three small houses. It was only after I had gotten out of the car that a door opened and Eugene emerged. We sat down under a tree.
>
> That original visit was a test of my courage and resolve. I felt like a fish out of water. Issues of race and poverty were staring me in the face. By meeting him

on his own ground and talking about what interested him, I was able to discover another side of his personality. I discovered he wanted to write an opera!

Over time we came to trust one another. . . . He became a key player in a summer youth employment program for street kids . . . kids no one else would employ.[7]

## Caring for the Caregivers

It was the Woods' style of teambuilding and caring for individuals in the community that was so unusual. "We decided to invite individuals who were knowledgeable or affected by a community issue to come and sit at the same table," says Denise. "It would be an informal group over mid-morning coffee or a simple lunch." Many of those working in the city's 192 social service agencies did not know each other. Often people were meeting for the first time. "The civility of a meal was helpful. We always had flowers on the table! We learned to listen to one another. And so people gained a better appreciation of each other and perceived the problem under discussion in new ways, not only in the one they had earlier championed."[8]

As a result of Denise Wood's report, All Saints decided to sponsor an Office of Creative Connections (OCC) with Denise as its first director. Its mission was simply to "identify urban needs and resources by listening to people . . . and to build on the strengths in our community by bringing together individuals, organizations and agencies."

By its third decade of operation, led by its executive director, Lorna Miller, OCC had incubated several important initiatives. Day One is a citywide, multijurisdictional attempt to reverse the trend toward drug and alcohol abuse. Its motto is, "take charge of your life, take care of your community." More than sixty local organizations sponsor Youth Month programs. Another project, Young and Healthy, provides health care to uninsured and underserved children. It operates in all thirty-two local schools with 270 doctors, dentists, mental health professionals, optometrists, nurses, pharmacists, and others who volunteer their time. OCC sponsors a year-round after-school enrichment and academic program for students from kindergarten through high school. It also convenes "city conversations" for community leaders to identify and address racial and ethnic inequities and the need for cross-cultural dialogue.

John and Denise Wood describe their approach to community building as a four-stage process:

1. Listen to the people of the community one by one and to its public bodies to gain a living picture of its needs, its strengths, and its possibilities.

2. Discern the meaning of what has been heard and the imperatives of what must be addressed.

3. Report to the community—not name-calling or blaming, but not watering down the truth—and speak with a moral voice to the whole community.

4. Connect citizens around common concerns and create coalitions and structures to carry out what needs to be done.

The Woods emphasize that this is not a set formula and that the stages may take place concurrently. They talk about a new "mind-set"—a way of looking at the life of the community that appeals to the best qualities in everyone, thinks for the whole community rather than just one group, and builds lasting relationships. "At the heart of the mind-set," say the Woods, "is our belief that there is something of God in every human being and that we must reach out to it and build on it."

John and Denise are reticent to talk publicly about their faith, preferring to let their lives do the talking. But they are deeply rooted in spiritual practices that enable them to be "long-distance runners." Denise says: "It gets you up in the morning, prevents burn-out, teaches you to listen to other people, to believe that things will happen. I used to play a lot of touch football. I believe my faith gives the courage to make a forward pass and believe someone up ahead will catch it."[9]

**If You Want to Be a Bridge . . .**

Frank F. Mountcastle Jr. was one business leader who heard the Woods' story during their several visits to Richmond. Born into a comfortable middle-class family in New Jersey and the product of a Princeton education, he entered banking early. After a career of thirty-five years with NationsBank (now Bank of America), mostly based in Richmond, he retired as senior vice president responsible for economic development.

Still handsome in his seventies, he is a courteous, gentle man who loves his community avocation almost as much as his game of golf and who believes deeply in the banking profession's responsibility for encouraging healthy, inclusive communities. "A quiet storm" is how Rev. Sylvester "Tee" Turner, an African American community leader, describes Mountcastle. "He has been steady in addressing issues without a lot of comment or fanfare. He probably has a more personal involvement at the grassroots level than any other corporate person I know. But he's unobtrusive. He has the gift of giving back that is unique. Until you get to know what he does he is almost invisible, but it is so empowering."

But in college and the early days of his career, Mountcastle took no part in challenging the accepted norms of a racialized environment. He confesses: "I told minority jokes, and I was a spectator during Massive Resistance. I regret that very much." But the changes he observed in the city—the decreasing involvement by the white community and the increasing level of poverty—concerned him. "I served on the board of the Boys and Girls Club. During a ten-year period it went from being mostly white to almost all black." When he met John and Denise Wood, Frank determined that he too could be a catalyst of change for the city he had come to love.

For several years, Mountcastle had been a member of a group that met every Wednesday morning at 8 a.m. for spiritual fellowship. The group met at the United Virginia Bank, hosted by John Robertson, a senior vice president. A dozen lawyers, investment advisors, and realtors would gather for mutual support and to share stories from their personal journeys. Usually the group read a passage from the Bible, but there was no set structure, and conversation frequently centered on a particular individual's request for advice or prayer. (The group, which moved first to St. Paul's Episcopal Church, and then to St. Stephen's Episcopal Church, continues to meet, with many of the original members.)

Amidst the coats and ties of the business crowd, one figure stood out—both for his physical girth and the breadth of his vision. A black lay preacher named John Coleman brought a different worldview and a refreshingly earthy approach to the buttoned-down group drawn largely from Richmond's West End. Coleman was the director of the Peter Paul Development Center, the Episcopal diocese's city commissioner, who described his "wilderness experience" when "God freed him from excess baggage." Growing up in a segregated city, he dropped out of high school and became an embittered alcoholic. Yet, for many in Richmond, he came to symbolize reconciliation.

I met John at a retreat of the Richmond Urban Institute, the city's first interracial think tank. "So Rob, I hear you are doing some stuff," he said by way of inviting conversation, parking his large frame beside me during a lunch break. He and I joined the Wednesday group together. John opened up his life without reservation and allowed me a glimpse of what it meant to be a black American. Over the next six years, we traveled together on several occasions to cities across the United States and even to Europe.

A familiar figure on Richmond streets, John was friend to bus drivers and to bankers. Although the Peter Paul Development Center, which he founded, serves one of the city's most deprived neighborhoods, his ministry was to rich and poor alike. He was one of those rare individuals who care as much for the "up and outs" as for the "down and outs." John refused to stereotype, saying: "You always hear about the racial gap, the generation gap, the communication gap. But the only gap we have in this society is the people gap." John never shied away from delivering blunt challenges, but he also understood the need to "build a bridge of trust strong enough to bear the weight of the truth you are trying to deliver."

John's approach was a valuable lesson for me as a new arrival from Europe who could be easily critical of the conservative views I encountered in Richmond. As the son of a lifelong warrior in the labor movement, I found myself uncomfortably surrounded by people whose worldview, politics, and life experiences were far removed from my own. Slowly, I came to realize that it was not my job to judge anyone, or to try to convert them to my way of thinking, and that I might even have something to learn from conservative Republican businesspeople! Today, some of the very people whom I was so quick to judge are giving significant leadership in efforts for racial healing and justice in Richmond.

Interaction with John Coleman impressed Frank Mountcastle. The example of the Woods stirred him to action. He got to know Bill Pickens, a senior African American executive with the minority-owned Consolidated Bank.[10] Pickens quizzed Mountcastle about the policy of NationsBank toward economic development in the city. "I was a bit embarrassed by the question," says Mountcastle, "because I had to admit that I did not know as much as I should." He immediately called the city's director of economic development and set up a meeting with representatives of nine banks for a full discussion on the concerns of the city government—the first such meeting to take place.

According to one observer, the great fear in Richmond is of breaking ranks. Mountcastle has been prepared to challenge his peers, even at the risk of losing friendships. John Coleman understood that "if you want to be a bridge you have to be prepared to be walked on." Some blacks saw him as a "sell-out," while whites often embraced his message of reconciliation but preferred to avoid facing the facts of racism. When one well-meaning admirer gushed, "John, I just don't see your blackness," he cracked back, "If you don't see me, big and black as I am, you've got to be blind." Later he told me, "You've got to learn to be comfortable with being uncomfortable."

John Coleman died at age fifty-four of a massive heart attack while crossing the Martin Luther King Bridge, which connects Richmond's business center to his own East End—a connection he strove to make a reality in human terms. More than one thousand people turned out to celebrate his life. Black and white, bishops and businessmen, students and community leaders packed St. Paul's Episcopal Church, where once the leaders of the southern Confederacy worshipped.

## Building Human-Scale Communities

At the other end of the social spectrum, Mary Tyler Cheek, a member of the Virginia aristocracy, was also prepared to break ranks. The daughter of the renowned Richmond journalist and historian Douglas Southall Freeman, and the widow of the director of the Virginia Museum of Fine Arts, Cheek played a prominent role in launching such organizations as the Richmond Urban Institute, Richmond Renaissance, the city's first interracial public-private partnership, and the Richmond Urban Forum, which gathered black and white leaders in social settings. Perhaps her most lasting contribution to Richmond was in recruiting T. K. Somanath to lead the Better Housing Coalition (BHC).

"T.K.," as he is known to everyone in Richmond, is a civil engineer from Mysore, India, who arrived on a Greyhound bus from New York in 1971. Twenty years later, Mary Tyler Cheek lured him from a secure job at the Richmond Redevelopment and Housing Authority (RRHA) to launch what was to become one of the nation's most innovative and highly regarded nonprofit housing corporations. As development director for RRHA, Somanath had gained a reputation for creating dialogue between city authorities and the communities they served. Cheek's vision was to create a vehicle to restore some of the city's most deprived communities by building high-quality affordable housing and creating environments where people felt secure and connected with their neighbors.

In 1990, BHC undertook its first major project in an African American neighborhood dislocated by the construction of the downtown expressway. "Housing conditions were deplorable; there were drug dealers and gangs," says Somanath. "People couldn't borrow money or get homeowners' insurance. Pizza companies wouldn't deliver."[11]

After extensive consultation with the community, BHC bought up properties from absentee landlords and renovated eighty-six rental apartments and townhomes and eight single-family homes. The coalition secured grants to subsidize rents of the long-term residents. BHC built a community resource center where children can do homework and have access to computers. The center also provides financial and budget counseling for residents. The holistic approach is shown in BHC's focus on creating "walkable, human-scale neighborhoods."

The growth of the BHC represented one of the decade's most significant developments in Richmond. By the mid-1990s, entire neighborhoods were being revitalized in the suburbs as well as the center city. Somanath's skill in building a regional coalition and engaging unlikely partners made him an important player in the emerging reconciliation network. His work epitomized the decisive contribution of the nonprofit community in challenging Richmond to confront issues of racial and economic justice. "Building trust is central to everything we do," he emphasizes, "particularly where trust has broken down between institutions and the grassroots communities they are supposed to serve."

Somanath and other local change makers built important linkages through Leadership Metro Richmond, a regional leadership development and community service program. From its inception in 1981, hundreds of emerging and established leaders created friendships and developed new visions and practical projects to increase the capacity of scores of social service agencies and nonprofit organizations in such areas as affordable housing, health care, and education.

## Launching Hope in the Cities

One block west of St. John's Church, where Patrick Henry helped ignite the American Revolution with the words, "Give me liberty, or give me death," the Richmond Hill retreat center commands a view of the city's downtown. As Richmond lay in ruins at the end of the Civil War (most of the commercial district burned when the retreating Confederate troops set fire to the tobacco warehouse and bridges), the Sisters of the Visitation of Monte Maria, a cloistered order of nuns, chose this spot to build their convent and to pray for the city. Today the 130-year-old building is home to an ecumenical community dedicated to the healing of metropolitan Richmond through prayer, hospitality, racial reconciliation, and spiritual development. A metropolitanwide network of volunteers helps prepare meals and welcome guests in support of a small staff and resident community.

The visionary at the heart of this enterprise is Ben Campbell, an Episcopal priest, journalist, and community organizer who, in the words of one observer, "has a habit of making people squirm." I first encountered Campbell at St. Paul's Episcopal Church, which had just "birthed" the Richmond Urban Institute (RUI) with a five-year challenge grant. RUI was the city's first interracial think tank where black and white came together on equal footing to search for solutions. It conducted a survey of race relations in the city and examined lending patterns by local financial institutions in minority neighborhoods. Its membership was a veritable who's who of Richmond's most dedicated, well-informed, and well-connected social activists.

But trouble was brewing early in the life of the young organization. Ben and his "co-missioner," an African American woman, found it impossible to work together and the RUI board had to fire them both. Added to this was the difficulty of raising funds for an organization that challenged the status quo. Within a few years, the loss of visionary leadership and failure to generate support doomed the institute that had begun with so much promise.

After leaving RUI, Ben worked for a while with a nonprofit housing corporation. Then, emotionally exhausted in the wake of the breakup of his marriage, he went on retreat in New Mexico. He returned to Richmond with a deep sense of calling to the practice, preaching, and teaching of spiritual direction. Sensing the potential of the former convent, he galvanized Richmond's faith community in a campaign that, by November 1987, had raised $650,000 for the down payment. After a $7 million renovation of the building, which can house up to forty-five people, Richmond Hill is in constant demand for retreats by church groups, nonprofit organizations, and even government agencies.

The creation of Richmond Hill coincided with the emergence of Hope in the Cities as a distinct network. The name was first used in June 1989 in connection with an event at city hall sponsored jointly with the Human Relations Commission. The mayor, the city manager, and fifty representatives of government agencies and community organizations packed the largest conference room to hear Hari Shukla from Newcastle, in the United Kingdom, and Bernard Gauthier, a former prefect of police for northern France, give evidence of how new attitudes and motives had increased the effectiveness of their work.

During the spring of 1991, Ben Campbell and I convened a nascent Hope in the Cities steering committee in the recently opened Richmond Hill center. The group included Howe Todd, Frank Mountcastle, T. K. Somanath, Cleiland Donnan, Sylvester "Tee" Turner, who had taken over the Peter Paul Development Center after John Coleman's death, Sam Davis, a business consultant, and Paige Chargois, an articulate African American Baptist pastor who was to play a crucial role in developing a vision for new race relations. New members would join from time to time; some stayed, others dropped out. The committee spent hours in seemingly unfocused discussions, searching for a common vision. But a core group of about a dozen came to know and to have confidence in one another.

Hope in the Cities resisted creating a membership or structure, believing in the power of its informal, nonterritorial nature. Its modest budget (largely to support the home in which Susan and I lived as a center for "building community") was funded by local supporters of MRA/Initiatives of Change and by the national organization. Behind our reluctance to become institutionalized, or to be drawn too quickly into programmatic activity, lay a perception that Richmond needed a network that would be inclusive in its approach, free of the pressure to protect "turf" or claim credit for results achieved. Among Richmond's many excellent nonprofit organizations, there was no serious, sustained effort to address the underlying distrust, rooted in racial issues, which was proving a stumbling block to many constructive initiatives. Hope in the Cities called for "a capital investment of time" in this vital area. Some might feel insecure in dealing with such a loosely organized group, but according to Ben Campbell: "The things that are most needed are not in anyone's job description. No one's paid to be an honest broker." The group pursued a strategy of engaging "hard-to-reach" people, including senior corporate executives and government officials, building a level of confidence with them and developing a shared vision for the Richmond community.

The missions of Richmond Hill and Hope in the Cities complemented each other perfectly: one dedicated to providing a place of hospitality and prayer, rooted in the history of the city; the other pursuing a strategic outreach into public and private sectors with a tested methodology of personal and social change, and drawing on a global perspective and network. Both were dedicated to the healing of metropolitan Richmond through an inclusive, open process to address the historic wounds of the community.

A series of downtown lunch forums featuring such speakers as John and Denise Wood, and John Perkins, founder of the Christian Community Development Association, involved 150 political, business, religious, and nonprofit leaders. Jim Ukrop, whose family-owned chain of Richmond supermarkets donates 10 percent of pretax profits to the community, was a participant and supporter, as was Richard Tilghman, head of United Virginia Bank.

These forums became a meeting space for unusually open dialogue, and the visitors provided an opportunity to gather diverse groups in a nonthreatening environment. People of different viewpoints began to see each other in a new light. Of course, as Ben Campbell noted, "People tend to be on their best behavior when folks from out of town are present!"

Hope in the Cities found an important ally in Richmond's mayor, Walter T. Kenney, who had served as the first African American national vice president of the American Postal Workers Union. When I introduced Kenney to my father, we joked about our labor sympathies in an ultraconservative city.

In a 1991 conversation with Ben Campbell and me, Kenney observed that four major studies on Richmond had been completed that year: "The studies have been done; it is time to take a bite of the apple." Campbell responded, "I guess you have to start by changing some people."

Later, Kenney was to say in a statement to a press conference, "If I change, if I learn how to care more deeply, or listen more intently, then I bring that to virtually everything I touch, whether it is regional discussions, the national agenda, or settling a neighborhood dispute."

In my visits to Kenney's office, I got to know his executive assistant, Carolyn "Cricket" White. Kenney had determined that he would not have an all-black staff, and selected White, a European American, to the surprise of some colleagues. In our early encounters, she did an efficient job of protecting her boss from what she probably regarded as unwise involvement in controversial matters, but as momentum built, she became a key member of the Hope in the Cities team.

In March 1992, Hope in the Cities convened a twelve-member working group from Chicago, Atlanta, Portland, Washington, D.C., and the Twin Cities. The group agreed to work toward a conference in Richmond the following year. According to Ben Campbell, America was in an advanced stage of disintegration caused by a materialistic binge and divisive "urban feudalism." He also believed that diverse, but tightly integrated groups tackling specific local issues, while maintaining an international vision, could have a significant impact.

Events were to push us more quickly than we anticipated. On April 29, 1992, Los Angeles exploded in four days of burning, looting, and shooting. The violence that claimed more than fifty lives and destroyed 1,100 properties followed the decision of a largely white jury to acquit four white police officers who were caught on videotape beating a black motorist, Rodney King, as he attempted to escape arrest. In the ensuing mayhem, ten thousand people were arrested. Throughout the 1980s, tensions were building as Los Angeles's growing Latino population competed for jobs with the long-established African American community. Virtually all black unionized janitorial staff lost their jobs to Latinos willing to work at much lower wages. Blacks and Latinos both complained at what they felt was racially discriminatory treatment by Korean store owners who had moved into their neighborhoods. The Los Angeles Police Department faced accusations of racial profiling and excessive use of force. All these resentments were inflamed by the high levels of unemployment caused by the nationwide recession.

Once again a major American city was engulfed in violence. Once again the chasm of racial antagonism split the country. Twenty-four years earlier, the Kerner Commission Report, published in the aftermath of the urban riots of the 1960s, warned that America was "moving towards two societies, one black, the other white—separate and unequal."[12] The events in Los Angeles indicated the accuracy of that prediction.

Although he did not live to see much of the fruits of his work, John Coleman had accurately diagnosed the nation's difficulty in dealing with race: "White people are walking around with a social disease of guilt, and black people are walking round with a social disease of bitterness." For Coleman, the solution was clear: "The white man has got to repent, but the black man has got to forgive and to repent for a long history of negativity. I can't tell you how much my life has changed since I stopped being bitter against white people."[13]

While Los Angeles smoldered, the Hope in the Cities committee in Richmond prepared for a bold public step. As Ben Campbell was to say, "Perhaps because racism started in its worst form in America, here on this ground, this is the place where the beginning of the end should take place."[14]

Suddenly Richmond found itself propelled onto the national stage, launching a movement for "honest conversation on race, reconciliation and responsibility."

## Breaking the Silence

An Honest
Conversation
on Race, Reconciliation,
and Responsibility

It all began at the river. From earliest times, it was a source of nourishment and an important means of transportation. When the Europeans arrived, the flourishing villages of the Powhatan Confederacy on the surrounding hills overlooked waters that teemed with sturgeon. Today Ancarrow's Landing on the south bank and Rocketts Landing on the north side are again favorite fishing spots for Richmonders. Ralph White, the naturalist who manages the James River Park, calls it "the most cosmopolitan place in the city." On any given Saturday you are as likely to hear Vietnamese, Russian, or Spanish spoken as English.

With the advent of slavery, the James came to symbolize the agony of family members separated from one another at Richmond's auction blocks and sold "down the river" to southern plantations. Up to 300,000 women, children and men may have passed through the city's infamous holding pens.

Philip Schwarz, a history professor at Virginia Commonwealth University, developed a detailed chronology of the slave trade in Richmond and Virginia. During the first part of the seventeenth century, approximately 33,000 Africans were brought to the English colonies of North America. Between 1700 and 1775, the number increased to 280,000; of these, about 100,000 came to Virginia. Very few slave ships actually brought Africans to Richmond; sandbars and other obstacles prevented large vessels from navigating beyond the Bermuda Hundred naval district port about twenty-five miles downriver. Between 1698 and 1774, some 16,000 Africans were unloaded at Bermuda Hundred. They were brought by foot or by smaller boats to markets in Manchester (now part of Richmond) on the south side of the James, and to Richmond itself. By 1782, Richmond's population was 1,031, of whom 428 were slaves.

The Revolutionary War interrupted British importation of enslaved Africans to Virginia. In 1778, the Commonwealth of Virginia prohibited all importation of Africans. This act did not represent a weakened commitment to a system based on forced labor. With the state's growing slave population—due partly to natural increase—wealthy Virginia planters realized that they could make huge profits from the sale of slaves to developing areas to the south. Virginia's enslaved population stood at 292,000 in 1790. By 1860 it was 490,865, the largest of any state.

Thus Richmond emerged as a depot for the interregional trading of slaves. In 1835, forty thousand slaves were sold for export from Virginia.[1] By 1840, partly because of railroad growth, Richmond dominated the trade in Virginia. Between 1790 and the outbreak of the Civil War, an estimated half million slaves were relocated—"sold down the river"—or marched overland from Virginia to the Deep South in a vast forced migration.

"For newly arrived slaves, Richmond must have been a place of astonishing dread; a vision of hell for which no folk tale could have prepared them," writes Selden Richardson in *Built by Blacks*. "For the slave being trans-shipped to the American interior, Richmond must have appeared like a plantation writ large: impossibly industrious and grimly purposeful."[2]

By 1860, fifteen slave-trade companies, nineteen auctioneers, and fifteen "general and collecting agents" operated in Richmond. In 1857 alone, sales at Richmond auctions totaled $3.5 million.[3] Many slaves worked in the Tredegar Iron Works and other industries that built the city's wealth. Yet despite the enormity of their suffering and their contribution to Richmond, not a single historic marker indicated their passage.

The "invisibility" of African Americans and the ability of white southerners to deny their humanity and to weave "brutal acts into the fabric of their daily lives"[4] is reflected in the diary of William Byrd, who owned 179,000 acres and laid out the original plan for Richmond on one of his plantations. The magnificent park a few yards from our house bears his name.

8 February 1709. I rose at 5 o'clock this morning and read a chapter of Hebrews and 200 verses in Homer's Odyssey. I ate milk for breakfast. I said my prayers. Jenny and Eugene were whipped. I danced my dance. I read law in the morning and Italian in the afternoon. . . .

10 June 1709. I rose at 5 o'clock this morning. . . . In the evening I took a walk about the plantation. Eugene was whipped for running away and I had a bit put on him. I said my prayers and had good health, good thoughts, and good humor, thanks be to God Almighty.[5]

Two hundred and fifty years later, one of Byrd's descendants, Senator Harry Byrd, dominated state legislature meetings and made Virginia a center for "Massive Resistance" to school desegregation. Yet, in parallel with this dark side of history, Virginia played a leading role in the founding of the nation and the creation of its democratic institutions. The state prides itself in producing more presidents than any other state. Washington, Jefferson, Madison, Monroe, Harrison, Tyler, Taylor, and Wilson were all born in the Old Dominion. The State Capitol, designed by Jefferson, and Monument Avenue, lined with statues of Confederate generals, are major tourist attractions. According to Donald Shriver, "If there is a city in the United States whose local culture combines memory and amnesia about this ambiguous history, it is Richmond, Virginia."[6]

## The Walk

On a sweltering June afternoon in 1993, Richmonders of all backgrounds came together in a dramatic public act of acknowledgment that would finally break the silence on the city's racial history and open the door to honest conversation about the past and the future. Mayor Walter Kenney and Jack McHale, a Chesterfield County supervisor, led Richmonders from the city and suburbs on a two-mile walk to mark sites previously too painful or shameful to remember. The crowd of five hundred, undaunted by the broiling 95-degree heat, included representatives from thirty U.S. cities as well as Africans, Asians, Latin Americans, Australasians, and Europeans who had come to lend their support.

The walk began, appropriately, at "Indian Hill" with a prayer by a Native American elder to "lift the veil of ignorance from our eyes and see that we are all brothers and sisters." Nearby, an actor recited Patrick Henry's famous lines, "Give me liberty or death"; but moments later those words would be slashed by irony and the anguished shrieks of another actor's story of a slave who hurled herself and her two babies into a well after losing twenty-two children to slavery.[7] History came together at the foot of a monument to

Confederate soldiers and sailors on Libby Hill as Rev. Earl Bledsoe marked the spot where "Indians had watched my African ancestors being taken off boats in chains." Following the route taken by Abraham Lincoln at the fall of Richmond, just ten days before his assassination in Washington, the walkers reached the site of the notorious slave jail complex operated by the brutal slave trader Robert Lumpkin and known as the Devil's Half Acre.

At every stop, an African *grio* (storyteller) led the crowd in claiming their shared history: *I come today to claim my roots; to open my heart; to affirm my deeds; to say that Richmond belongs to me.* From Libby Hill, the walkers watched as carnations were cast on the river in memory of those who had died during the Middle Passage. The voices of a choir wafted across the water as the flowers drifted slowly with the current. For a Jamaican woman, a moment in time stood still: "Today I have mourned members of my family whose funerals we never attended."[8]

Could these acts begin to convert a river of pain into a healing stream for all races? Mayor Walter Kenney said later: "It is often the thing from which we hide that eventually fatally wounds us—from the inside out—and such had been the case in Richmond. . . . We did not highlight these places in an effort to hand out guilt or vent anger. We wanted to acknowledge their existence so that we could close the door and move forward."[9]

For many it was emotionally overwhelming. Ellen Lee Meigs told the documentary filmmaker Karen Greisdorf: "I grew up in the west by the country club and I had never been to any of these places. I'd never heard any of this history. It was all coming at me for the first time. And somehow we were invited by blacks and whites to do this together. . . . It was a tremendous opening of the heart . . . to lose my stinking superiority for ever."[10]

Wayland Baker, a former gang member from Los Angeles, said, "I have heard people say things I didn't ever think I would hear."[11]

Robert Taylor, dean of Richmond's Baptist clergy, told the crowd as it gathered at the steps of the Virginia State Capitol: "When you can see the descendants of slave-masters joining hands with descendants of slaves . . . it is enough to give us hope and to make us rejoice."[12]

A Cambodian who lost a brother and sister in the "killing fields," an Englishman from inner-city Liverpool, a Sudanese diplomat—many who came from overseas were also finding things to relate to. A black South African told a reporter, "Here is all the material for us to make out of the ashes of apartheid a very inspired democracy."[13]

Richmond's first "walk through history" was the highlight of a four-day conference hosted by Hope in the Cities, the City of Richmond, and Richmond Hill. Entitled "Healing the Heart of America," it called for "an honest conversation on race, reconciliation and responsibility." The words were deliberately chosen to describe an approach to race relations quite different from most contemporary dialogue efforts in America. Hope in the Cities and its allies identified the inability to talk openly about race as the underlying obstacle to progress, but they were insistent that honest conversation could not occur without the participation of all sectors of the community. They held up a vision of reconciliation as an achievable goal. And, most significantly, they called for individuals of all racial backgrounds to accept the challenge of personal responsibility as the means to attain that goal.

Harry Jacobs, chairman of the Martin Agency and a prominent leader of the corporate community; Grace Harris, provost of Virginia Commonwealth University; and Mayor Kenney headed a seventy-five-member sponsoring committee comprising the entire city council and boards of supervisors of the surrounding counties, the heads of major religious denominations, senior corporate executives, and directors of grassroots organizations. In recruiting this committee, Jacobs, Harris, and Kenney had asked for "a very personal commitment to the theme and objectives of the conference":

> The deepening crisis facing Richmond and other central cities is becoming nothing short of a national disaster. Neither the laissez-faire workings of the marketplace, nor traditional government solutions are going to avert this disaster. . . . We personally are convinced that issues of race, class, economics, and geography constitute fundamental roadblocks to constructive efforts on nearly all fronts. We will not find cures to our urban problems until we can honestly work through these issues and deal forthrightly with each other—without mistrust, misunderstanding, and resentment.
>
> The issues we face defy purely rational or political approaches. Of necessity, reconciliation must be a moral and ethical, even a spiritual process. . . . It is the intent of the conference to enable Richmonders and our national and international guests to forthrightly express the pain and frustration of the past. We will celebrate the many gains we have made and look forward to the unfinished business which can make our cities whole. . . . We envision the conference as a major, visible event which can be a catalyst for action and have lasting impact in the Richmond area.[14]

The statement which the sponsoring committee agreed to support was notable for the frankness with which it stated the problem and the vision it held out for Richmond and America:

America represents the world's boldest experiment in multicultural living. At a time of rising ethnic tensions around the world, what happens here could give hope to millions mired in conflict. But the American experiment is not finished. In important ways we have failed to build bonds of respect, affection and community between all Americans. Distrust, resentment and fear dwell in the heart of this nation and often frustrate our best efforts to address the crises in our cities.

The toxic issue of race seeps through the national agenda, a continuing agony which stems from an original sin in the soul of America: two people—Native and African American were denied the freedom and dignity we cherish. We are still dealing with that legacy.

Richmond, a birthplace of American democracy, and an early source of leadership, is one city where that legacy lives on. A city built on the graves of Native Americans, and a port to which Africans were shipped in chains, it became the Capital of the Confederacy, a separate nation founded in part to preserve slavery.

The document went on to state the bold vision of the organizers:

Richmond could become a gateway to the spirit of healing and partnership that America needs. . . . We want to unmask our history together and renounce whatever evil effect it has on us so that God can help us bring justice and healing to our city. We are all responsible for our common future. Blame, guilt and hostility will not produce what is needed. The energy for constructive change can only come through a transformation in the human spirit, starting with each one of us, not with the other person, the other race, the other group. Might we be given powerful evidences of true repentance and forgiveness which would give a new birth of hope for other cities?[15]

Carolyn Leonard, the coordinator of multicultural and multiethnic education in the public schools of Portland, Oregon, summed up her Richmond experience: "No one of us can fix [the problems] by ourselves. We each have to link arms with people who are different. We have to be able to listen to people with ideas we think probably should not even be mentioned. It will not be our idea, but the synthesis of what we all bring to the table that will help us move forward. These days in Richmond have helped me erase another line I have found within myself—the line between me and a white man of privilege. It has helped me to reconcile and to erase the line I drew between the north and south; to feel sincerely that I can embrace the United States as one nation made up of many diverse people who *must* work together."[16]

## Breakthroughs

It was Ben Campbell who first imagined the whole of the Richmond metropolitan region coming together in a literal walk through history from the river to the State Capitol. He was adamant that "healing cannot be done in general, it must be specific." Through Nancy Jo Taylor, a teacher who had pioneered Black History education in Richmond's schools, he came to know of Manchester Docks and other sites, some of which were known only through oral history.

Margaret Palmer, a Chicago member of the national planning committee, emphasized the power of a collective ritual: "Every person has his or her own grief and suffering. Each needs to be honored or acknowledged without comparison. . . . Our brokenness has shaped each of us in a unique way and it is part of the gift we bring each other. We need to find a collective ritual that acknowledges this and binds us together."

From Palmer came the inspiration of placing flowers in the water. The artistic director of the Walk, Janine Bell of the Elegba Folklore Society, brought dance, music, and storytelling to the event. Finally it was all made possible by the extraordinary efforts of Melanie Trimble, a drama graduate from South Carolina who volunteered to come to Richmond two months before the event and organized multiple police permits, the closing of city streets, and the erection of five stages.

Campbell's vision gave legs to ideas that had been germinating for some time in the mind of Joseph V. Montville, a former diplomat and researcher on racial and ethnic conflict in the Balkans and the Middle East. Montville's starting point was that unacknowledged historic loss perpetuates a sense of victimhood in those who have suffered. These ongoing resentments due to the divisions of history and decades of inequity poison today's policy debates and public discourse. "Time does not heal wounds. Only healing, actively pursued, heals wounds."[17]

In Montville's view, "walk" is the operative word. "This does not suggest an exchange of accusations and vigorous defense. Any group can do that, and they often do." What began in Richmond was "an honest conversation about the past where informed, intellectually respectable and morally courageous men and women squarely faced their symbolic or genuine responsibilities for past injustices." Montville says that a walk through history establishes an agenda for healing: "It reveals the record of hurt and allows the conscience of large numbers of people to give up avoidance and be activated in its most positive sense."[18]

Montville believes that much of white America's inability to respond to the moral challenges made by the painful situation of African Americans is due to the "strong residual resentment" of the white North by the white South:

> Since the condition of Africans from slavery to freedom has been the most visible contentious issue between North and South, white America has been essentially paralyzed psychologically in its capacity to deal with it openly and honestly. This burden of history is a major impediment to serious study and political collaboration between liberal and conservative/Northern and Southern politicians and leaders of other social and economic sectors of the country. These labels can be challenged on many grounds but there is an underlying logic to their use. The Southern feeling of resentment against the North long predates the Civil War, but it was powerfully amplified by the loss of the war. And much of this loss, this historic wound, has not been healed. This relationship is further complicated by the fact that Northerners do not remember their own history of anti-black racism and record of systematic insult of and disdain for almost all that was southern.[19]

The organizers of the Richmond walk understood that black and white could not heal separately: they needed each other's presence and support in acknowledging the pain of their shared history, and in accepting responsibility for building a new future. In this sense, the walk was much more than a "black history" experience: it was a step in creating a shared narrative owned by the entire community.

Remarkably, it was African Americans who understood most quickly the need for healing on all sides. As he stood at the foot of the monument to Confederate soldiers and sailors, Tee Turner said, "When I first saw that monument I saw pain, the pain that I had suffered as a black man." But then he began to look at it "from the perspective of grief," because the Confederates "built the monument out of grief, and they need to be healed as well."[20]

That it was possible for the walk to honor Confederate dead as well as kidnapped and enslaved Africans was a stunning breakthrough, due largely to my colleague Rev. Paige Chargois. In a courageous decision to go toward that which she most hated and feared, she extended a hand to those who still clung to the Confederate flag as a symbol of pride and loss. "Just seeing the flag whiz by you on the interstate hung across the back window of a pickup truck can send chills down the spine of many African Americans," says Chargois. Determined to "broaden the table" where people with vastly different experiences and perspectives could come and be heard with respect, she sought to engage the United Daughters of the Confederacy (UDC). A friend was acquainted with a very senior woman who had served as a regional president of the UDC and offered to arrange a meeting. "I had no real clue of what the visit to her home would bring, but I was willing to try," Chargois recalls. This is her description of the encounter:

> Excitement stirred strongly in my heart as she greeted me and my colleague so warmly; I believed a breakthrough loomed on the horizon of our meeting. Within seconds of entering her living room, I saw the flag. It had been carefully placed behind pictures of her parents. I almost froze in my tracks. The hatred was deep. We launched into gentle conversation sharing with our hostess the reason why we had come. She immediately stated, "You folks (referring to black people) just have to get the facts straight!"
>
> How I wanted to scream out to her, "Lady, I've got your facts on my back!" But I said nothing, using all of my strength just to fight back the tears. Her words and my feelings immediately focused for me the two dramatically different perspectives on the war; not between historians, not between politicians, not between Americans living in different parts of this country, but between two southerners living out the shared legacies of pain in the soul of this nation.
>
> She began to recount her family's history, sharing about their losses during the war. She even shared how her grandfather had worked to "save black babies," as well as white babies. As she shared her pain, the symbol of the war began to be transformed for me from a symbol of white hatred of blacks to being more a symbol of white pain and loss. Having intentionally selected a chair that would place my back to the flag, after listening to her I turned my face towards the flag and for the first time saw it as their symbol of their pain. That I could accept. No hatred was left.[21]

The willingness of Paige Chargois and other African Americans to recognize the humanity in those who symbolized their oppression enabled white southerners to see and feel history from new perspectives. Dick Ruffin, whose work in Richmond in the 1970s had built some of the relationships from which Hope in the Cities grew, is the direct descendant of the firebrand who reputedly fired the first shot of the Civil War. Edmund Ruffin was a vocal proponent of the southern way of life, including slavery. Known for his experiments in soil improvement and his passionate commitment to the South's rural economy, he threw himself into the secessionist cause. At the end of the war, he wrapped himself in a Confederate flag and shot himself.

Despite this inglorious end, Dick Ruffin says that his ancestor's life was celebrated in his family and by many others throughout the South: "His legacy lives on."

> To understand why, it must be recognized that the defeat of the South was a deep humiliation. In its wake came hatred, anger, insecurity and fear. One effect was for Southerners to define themselves in terms of the north. We were the victims, they the villains. In stories passed down in the family—especially those which contrasted the idyllic quality of life in the pre-war south with the crass materialism of the north—black families hardly figured.[22]

Just before the war, mysterious fires broke out on several Ruffin plantations. Edmund Ruffin could not believe that his slaves were involved. Nor, according to diaries and family lore, was he conscious of the evil of slavery and the catastrophic effect on those who live under its yoke.

Following his participation in Richmond's walk through history, Richard Ruffin wrote of three ways in which his relationship with African Americans was shaped by his family legacy:

> The first is an often unrecognized insecurity, derived mainly from the southerners' wounded sense of self after the war. To compensate, myths about the past flourished. Heroes became larger than life, and many sought to connect themselves with these heroes and with illustrious forebears in the Old World.
>
> Equally, people tried to keep down those of lower status whose rise might threaten their sense of self. This accounts for the shameful indignities imposed on African Americans after Reconstruction. This insecurity persists and also accounts in part for a tendency to cling to our own kind and to feel threatened by the advancement of people different from ourselves.
>
> A third legacy, and perhaps the most persistent, has been the minimalist view of African Americans' potential. Those who saw blacks as property did nothing to pass on to their children a positive idea of what blacks could contrib-

ute to American thought, politics, business and culture. Much as the impressive accomplishments of African Americans have forced reassessment, there is room for attitudes to change further.[23]

In a commentary written for the *Richmond Times-Dispatch*, Ruffin concluded: "People like myself need nothing less than a revolution of rising expectations. . . . Perhaps as white Americans like me put an end to denial and find new visions for what African Americans will give to the world, hope will be born that a new beginning can be made in race relations."[24]

## Repercussions

A comparatively small number of Richmonders took part in "Healing the Heart of America." Attendees at the events totaled 1,500, of whom 150 were participants from other cities and countries; despite the leadership of Harry Jacobs, Walter Kenney, and Grace Harris, few corporate, political, or religious leaders participated in the events. Honest conversation was still risky territory. But the repercussions in the region were widespread and lasting. "Healing the Heart of America" gave expression to a citizens' movement that had been building for at least a decade and in which many organizations and individuals played a part. The impact of this movement was seen in several ways.

### A Rebirth of Collective Memory

Within a year, the city council, at the request of Mayor Kenney, approved the creation of a "Unity Walk" commission to establish the history walk as "a permanent national educational resource, as a contribution to the healing of Richmond's racial history, and as an inspiration to all the people of this metropolitan area and of other communities."[25] For the first time, Richmond's racial history received official, accurate, public recognition. Soon students, faith groups, and community organizations were discovering history in new ways. Organizers of national conventions requested tours. Participants in a family reunion came from as far away as Mississippi. James River Park manager Ralph White mobilized hundreds of volunteers to clear a path, enabling walkers to retrace the steps of slaves. Eagle Scouts built bridges over gullies. Service organizations collected trash or raised money for signs.

Kenney's election loss in 1994 hindered progress, but Ralph White, Hope in the Cities, Richmond Hill, the Elegba Folklore Society, and the historian Philip Schwarz continued to conduct research, place markers, and lead walks. In July 1998, Councilman Sa'ad El-Amin built on the former mayor's initiative to create the Slave Trail Commission and secured city funds to support its work.[26]

Regular events now include an annual night walk along the historic Slave Trail in which walkers with lighted flares make their way silently from Manchester Docks, through the woods along the south bank of the river, then over Mayo's Bridge to the site of Lumpkin's slave jail. In a hopeful twist of history, after the Civil War the building became a school for former slaves and later the birthplace of Virginia Union University, which produced the country's first elected African American governor, L. Douglas Wilder.

The process of research and public acknowledgment continues unabated. Henrico County dedicated a park in honor of Gabriel Prosser, close to the spot where he planned the country's first major slave rebellion. In 1800, Prosser and one thousand men armed with clubs, scythes, homemade bayonets, and a few rifles marched toward Richmond, only to be foiled by a freak flood.

As a result of the initiative of the Defenders of Freedom, Justice and Equality, a local organization leading a "sacred ground historical reclamation" project, a historic marker on Broad Street commemorates the courage with which Prosser and at least twenty-five coconspirators faced execution as freedom fighters in the spirit of George Washington and Patrick Henry. In 2007, Governor Tim Kaine issued a pardon recognizing Prosser's "courage and devotion to the fundamental Virginia values of freedom and equality."[27]

After shunning her memory for 140 years, Richmond honored Elizabeth Van Lew, a Union spy who employed her black servant (Elizabeth Draper, mother of Maggie Lena Walker) to gather crucial information from Confederate officers while serving at their dinner tables. When the conflict ended, Van Lew became Richmond's postmaster. A few years after her death, the city razed her house.

A high school student inspired area residents to raise money for a marker at Bellevue Elementary School where the Van Lew house once stood. The Virginia Department of Historic Resources then picked up the ball. Its director, Kathleen Kilpatrick, who is overseeing a "marker diversity initia-

tive," said, "I decided that we really needed to make sure that those big stories are being told. . . . History has the power to inform and inspire. . . . And
it fosters pride and understanding by focusing on our steps and missteps,
our shared paths and our separate paths we've taken, and therefore guides
us into the future."[28]

In 2007, former Virginia Commonwealth University professor Maurice
Duke and Selden Richardson, a leader of the Alliance to Conserve Old
Richmond (ACORN), produced *Built by Blacks*, a book documenting the
major role of slaves and free African Americans in building the city's fine
homes, churches, and even the State Capitol.[29]

In an event involving thousands of people, the *Reconciliation Statue*,
marking the creation of a "reconciliation triangle" in place of the former
slave trade link between Richmond, Liverpool, and Benin, was unveiled in
March 2007 near the former slave market (see chap. 18).

The following year a full excavation of the Lumpkin's Jail complex began
as a collaborative effort of the City of Richmond and the Slave Trail Commission, the Virginia Department of Historic Resources, and ACORN. A
250-year-old burial ground for slaves and free blacks lies under an adjacent
parking lot. A drive to research and memorialize the cemetery gained momentum after Virginia Commonwealth University bought the three-acre
lot and began to repave it. A grassroots protest including preservationists,
politicians, and the president of Virginia Union University was even supported by the Sons of Confederate Veterans, which declared: "Richmond
needs to understand, preserve our history. It is part of our civic mosaic."[30]
After conversations with community groups, VCU agreed to donate a 50-
by 200-foot area for a public memorial, but activists say all of the site should
be dedicated to honoring the African Americans on whose backs the city
grew and prospered.

*Honoring All Heroes*

A statue of Arthur Ashe, the Wimbledon and U.S. Open tennis champion,
author, and humanitarian, graces Monument Avenue, a location previously
off-limits except to Confederate heroes. Sculptor Paul DiPasquale depicts
Ashe surrounded by children; in one hand, he holds aloft a tennis racquet,
in the other, a book, symbolizing his passion for education.

Ashe had left Richmond as a high school senior with no intention of
returning. As an African American, he was barred from playing on most

of the city's tennis courts. But on his death in 1993, the city's most internationally admired son lay in state in the governor's mansion, the first to be
so honored since General Stonewall Jackson. State flags flew at half-staff.
More than five thousand mourners filed past to pay their respects. Standing in line for more than three hours was Thomas N. Chewning, a senior,
white corporate executive who was to lead the campaign to place the Ashe
monument on the city's most famous street.

A contemporary of Ashe, Chewning was also a tennis enthusiast. He first
met the future champion at an out-of-state tournament. Ashe was seeded
above him, but Chewning had never heard of him since blacks and whites
did not play together in Richmond. It was the start of a lifelong friendship.
The two men kept in touch as they pursued their different careers. Beyond
his success on the tennis courts, Arthur Ashe authored the definitive three-
volume *History of the African-American Athlete*, and became a spokesperson for human rights. He contracted AIDS through a blood transfusion and
died at age forty-nine.

Throughout his life, Ashe maintained a grace that often concealed the
fire within. When he said that the burden of being an African American
was greater than being a victim of AIDS, some of those who knew him were
shocked. It did not surprise Chewning, who understood the deep pain that
his friend felt, starting with the rejection by his hometown.

"In 1994 a woman called me out of the blue as I was driving," says Chewning. "Her name was Marty Dumitt, and she was calling on behalf of a group
called Virginia Heroes, a nonprofit organization founded by Ashe to expose
Richmond public school students to outstanding Virginia role models.[31]
She told me, 'We want you to lead the group to put the statue of Arthur
Ashe on Monument Avenue.' I told my wife I was uncertain; this was a big
subject and I needed to think about it. She said, 'This is ridiculous. You
know you are going to do this. Call her back and tell her you are going to
do it!'" As a member of First Baptist Church (a predominantly white, conservative congregation) and a pillar of the business establishment, Chewning was an unlikely champion for the cause. He stepped forward, he says,
because it was the right thing to do.

The proposal to place Ashe on Monument Avenue prompted "a conversation on race relations that few will forget." Although the national media
played up the differing viewpoints, hoping for a public brawl, "to call it a
controversy is to sell it short," wrote a Richmond journalist. "Something

changed here, if only a little, and old scores over race and rights came that much closer to being reconciled."[32]

In fact, opinions about the appropriate setting for the statue divided blacks and whites equally. Some die-hard Confederates were appalled at the threatened incursion on their sacred avenue. A group called Citizens for Excellence in Public Art criticized the work of sculptor Paul DiPasquale. Some African Americans had no desire to see a black hero on an avenue they saw as glorifying the cause of preserving a slave-based society. One civil rights leader in Virginia has referred to the avenue as a place where "monuments to traitors of the Union are maintained with tax dollars."

Others thought that a spot near the tennis courts would be most fitting. Many of both races believed the symbolism of a Monument Avenue site would properly honor Ashe and signal to the world that Richmond had changed.

For months, commissions and committees debated different options. John Charles Thomas, the first African American to be appointed to Virginia's Supreme Court, hosted a pivotal meeting with political leaders. According to Chewning, it was Robert Bobb, the city manager, who played the key role in determining the actual site. In their first conversation, he said, "Tom, there will be a lot of people who posture, but no one will be more supportive than Robert Bobb." At a crucial stage in the process, Chewning arrived late for a presentation to the city's planning commission. The backers of the Monument Avenue option had agreed to propose a site just west of the historic district, thinking it might provoke less controversy. Robert Bobb told Chewning as the meeting concluded: "We got what we wanted. It's going to be on the Roseneath intersection." Chewning was startled. No one had ever mentioned this location, which was just *inside* the historic district. "Trust me," said Bobb, "that is where it should be." Chewning believes Bobb had the spot picked out from the start.

The matter was settled in the early hours of the morning of July 18, 1995, at an extraordinary meeting of the Richmond City Council. More than one hundred members of the public spoke in a six-hour public hearing, after which the council went into closed session. To the surprise of the media, the hearing was a model of civility—one Richmond columnist called it "our finest hour." In a 7–0 vote (one councilman abstained, another was absent), the council approved the Monument Avenue site. One year later, on a clear July day, the twenty-eight-foot monument was unveiled. A few protesters

hung around the edge of the crowd. The *Richmond Times-Dispatch* headline read, "An Avenue for All."

"If an African American had put the statue there it could have been
perceived as racial," said Chewning later. "But I could look my Caucasian
friends in the eye and say, 'Arthur was just better than most of us.'"

Ben Campbell wrote of the unusual sense that something had shifted in
the city. "Perhaps it was the spirit of Arthur Ashe himself," he said. "Perhaps there was a suspicion that there were memories that really could be
redeemed. Perhaps it was a hint that, with work and yielding, the future
might hold more than continued despair and conflict."[33]

The Ashe decision and the civil conversation surrounding it may have
encouraged other steps toward greater inclusivity in the public telling of
history. In 2003, Abraham Lincoln, long reviled by die-hard southerners as
a symbol of northern repression, finally found a place in Richmond near the
ironworks that made cannon for the Confederate army. The first American
Civil War center to portray the stories of Unionists, Confederates, and African Americans under one roof opened in October 2006 at the Tredegar
Iron Works (see epilogue). And on July 2008, the *Virginia Civil Rights Memorial* was unveiled in the grounds of the State Capitol in honor of Barbara
Johns, who, in 1951, led fellow black students in a protest against unequal
and inferior conditions in Virginia's segregated schools (see chap. 18).

*Public Acknowledgment Opens a Door to Dialogue*

Many of those who walked together began to work together. With the "polite silence" broken, Richmonders felt liberated to enter into honest conversation in public as well as private. Race was no longer a subject confined to
meetings of community activists.

An annual Metropolitan Richmond Day, launched by Hope in the Cities
in 1996 at the suggestion of Walter Kenney, draws up to six hundred leaders
from the public and private sectors to a breakfast forum where such sensitive topics as mixed-income housing and school integration are discussed
in a spirit of open inquiry. At least forty nonprofit organizations and area
businesses cosponsor this major regional event. "There has been lack of
trust. This process can be a major step to reaching common ground for all
of us," said Councilman John Newell of Ashland at the first event.

Three hundred people signed up to take part in small-group dialogues
throughout the metropolitan region. Partners in the effort included Lead-

ership Metro Richmond, the YWCA, the Richmond Peace Education Center, the Office of Justice and Peace of the Catholic Diocese, the National
Conference for Community and Justice (NCCJ), and the Urban League.
   Dialogues paired the NAACP and the Jewish Community Federation,
and congregations of different racial backgrounds. The Museum of the
Confederacy and the Black History Museum hosted a dialogue between
black and white women to coincide with an exhibition on women in the
Civil War. Youth from public and private schools explored new areas of
the city together. African American and European American pastors in
Chesterfield County, an area known for racial tensions, built relationships
of appreciation and mutual support. Many dialogues took place in private
homes.
   Specially trained facilitators led the conversations using a curriculum
developed by Hope in the Cities that announced a "Season of Dialogue."
Over time they began to address specific issues of public policy. Later chapters describe the structure of these dialogues and their regional and national outreach.

*Regional Conversations*

The tone of public discourse in the Richmond region changed markedly
from the rancor of the 1970s and 1980s. A controversial report by consultant James A. Crupi, who interviewed fifty business leaders in December
1993 and January 1994, criticized the "Balkanized" government structure
of the Richmond region. Crupi noted that cooperation was hard to achieve
because of a history of animosity caused by battles over annexation, school
consolidation, and the central role that racial politics played.[34]
   In March 1993, a first "regional summit" brought together top administrators and elected officials from the city and surrounding counties. "The
feelings of all the jurisdictions are that it's time to begin to heal the wounds
and work toward the common interest of building co-operation," said Chesterfield County Board of Supervisors chairman Art Warren, who chaired
the first meeting.[35] The summit was almost stillborn. Henrico County officials pulled out following a suggestion by Roy West, Richmond's former
mayor, that regional cooperation was "the type of coded racism about which
informed black leaders across the country are cautious."[36] But they joined
a second meeting later that year. In September 1994, after years of squab-
bling over water rights and a water purification plant, the city and Henrico

County reached a milestone agreement that would enable the two localities to meet water needs until the middle of the twenty-first century.

The Greater Richmond Chamber of Commerce led the business community to make regional cooperation a priority and organized visits for business and government leaders to examine best practices in other cities. County leaders acknowledged that for the region to flourish, the center city must thrive. "This region will never be a successful venture unless the city is successful," said R. J. "Buddy" Klotz of Hanover County.[37] Changing demographics in the counties undoubtedly helped. Frank Thornton won election as Henrico County's first African American supervisor in 1996, and three years later John Gordon became Hanover County's first African American chairman of its Board of Supervisors.

Larry Chavis, Richmond's vice mayor, had created something of a media stir at the "Healing the Heart of America" conference by suggesting consolidation of the city and county governments within ten years. Although his proposal got mixed reviews (one Henrico supervisor called it "sheep dip"), it did give impetus to conversations that were long overdue.[38] The city and three adjacent counties created the Greater Richmond Partnership in 1994 to promote regional growth. Chesterfield supervisor Jack McHale and Richmond city councilman Tim Kaine even began talking about "growth sharing" or "gain sharing."[39] Under this scheme, 40 percent of local tax revenue on a new business coming to the region would stay in the locality in which the business was located, while the remaining 60 percent would be shared equally among the other jurisdictions. The idea proved too bold, but the fact that it was being discussed on the front page of the newspaper indicated a significant improvement in the political climate. Richmond's expert on urban issues, John Moeser, of Virginia Commonwealth University, commented, "You would not have had a (county) supervisor using that language five or six years ago."[40]

In another sign of the times, Tim Kaine became Richmond's mayor in 1998, with an 8–1 vote of the majority black city council. Afterward he expressed his appreciation for this demonstration of trust by the African American community, but remarked that he wished whites had been gracious enough to take the first step in breaking the pattern of racial voting: "It is remarkable that an African American council will let a white be mayor. I wish the white majority would have exercised this type of leadership but they weren't able to. If African-Americans can do it, it is a remarkable thing."[41] In July 1998, Kaine (who went on to be elected governor) became the first Richmond mayor to publicly apologize for the city's history of slavery.

## A Quiet Revolution

By the end of the 1990s, the expanding network of Richmonders who shared a common experience of walking through history and open dialogue was creating a quiet revolution. In unexpected ways and through unexpected people, the movement bridged traditional cultural, economic, and political boundaries. The distinguishing feature of the movement was a commitment to personal responsibility and a willingness to move beyond denial and blame. As Mayor Walter Kenney put it, "The mentality of victimhood or guiltridden shame anchors us in inaction. . . . Regardless of past or present injustices we are all responsible for shaping our common future."[42] Reflecting on the new possibilities symbolized by the decision on the Ashe monument, Ben Campbell wrote: "It has been happening for some time; people just didn't know it. Where racial brokenness is accepted in Richmond—not papered over—there are good conversations taking place."[43]

Christopher Edley, who directed the White House review of affirmative action, described the Richmond experience in a lead commentary in USA Today: "Most of us have felt history tugging at our souls. Stand on a once bloody battlefield . . . meditate in a cemetery, visit the Vietnam Veterans Memorial or the Holocaust Museum and something indescribable forces you to try to understand, to find meaning. A few people in Richmond are harnessing that force to tackle something huge. . . . [They] have discovered that appreciating shared history can be a catalyst to connect communities long divided."[44]

Sustained work over more than a decade, culminating in the "Healing the Heart of America" conference, confirmed four key principles for Hope in the Cities and its partners:

1. Model within the core group the change and the new relationships that are needed in the wider community.

2. Be inclusive. Take the risk of approaching as potential allies even those who are difficult to work with.

3. Hold up a vision of what the community can become. Difficulties, if faced honestly, can become assets.

4. Recognize that real change occurs when the hearts of individuals are changed. The problems are so intractable and the emotions so deep-seated that only a spiritual impetus can generate the necessary will and persistence for sustained common action.

The Corcorans with Audrey and Collie Burton in the Carillon neighborhood. (Photograph by Karen Elliott Greisdorf)

Neil Corcoran and friend at John B. Cary Elementary School, 1985. (Photograph by Rob Corcoran)

Dr. Robert L. Taylor, pastor of the Fourth Baptist Church, and Cleiland Donnan at the Initiatives of Change conference center in Caux, Switzerland, 1992. (Photograph by Rob Corcoran)

Richmond's first "walk through history," June 1993. (Photograph by Robert Lancaster)

Rob Corcoran with Walter T. Kenney, Richmond's mayor, 1990-94.
(Photograph by Karen Elliott Greisdorf)

Frank F. Mountcastle, who served as senior vice president for economic development
with NationsBank (now Bank of America), with Sister Norma Bourdon from Selma,
Ala. (*left*), and Vivian Paige from Norfolk, Va., at a training weekend for Hope in the
Cities affiliates. (Photograph by Tony Anthony)

A dialogue. (Photograph by Cricket G. White)

Delegation from Liverpool, United Kingdom, walking the historic Slave Trail, led by Rev. Sylvester "Tee" Turner of Hope in the Cities, March 2007. (Photograph by Guy Woodland)

A statue of Abraham Lincoln and his son Tad was unveiled near the Tredegar Iron Works (*right*) in 2003. Lincoln visited Richmond on April 4, 1865, the day after it fell to Union forces. Ten days later, he was assassinated in Washington. (Photograph by Rob Corcoran)

Mural on floodwall depicting General Robert E. Lee. (Photograph by Rob Corcoran)

(Left) The unveiling of the *Reconciliation Statue,* March 30, 2007, with city Slave Trail commissioners Rev. Sylvester "Tee" Turner (*right*) and Ralph White, James River Park manager (*center*), who mobilized Richmond volunteers to clear the trail and fund the first markers. (Photograph by Karen Elliott Greisdorf)

(Below) Groundbreaking for the *Reconciliation Statue* at the site of Richmond's former slave market, with members of the city's Slave Trail Commission; Virginia's secretary of administration, Viola Baskerville (*center, behind podium*); and Virginia state senator Henry L. Marsh III (*with hat*). (Photograph by Rob Corcoran)

H. Alexander Wise, founding president of the American Civil War Center at Historic Tredegar. (Photograph by Mark Gormus; courtesy of *Richmond Times-Dispatch*)

A statue to the Wimbledon tennis champion and humanitarian Arthur Ashe stands on Monument Avenue, a venue previously reserved for Confederate generals. Tom Chewning, a business executive, led the campaign to place the statue. (Photograph by Mark Gormus; courtesy of *Richmond Times-Dispatch*)

Mark, Andrew, Rob, Susan, and Neil Corcoran. (Photograph by Ariane Reis)

# A Call to Community

At this particular moment in America's history, meaningful action at the societal level is virtually impossible. As a nation we lack a consensus concerning how to deal with the problems that bedevil us most. We seem unable to take sustained action for very long. And we don't trust anyone to let them lead. We are, in short, politically paralyzed. The reasons for this paralysis are several but chief among them is our failure to engage each other openly and honestly around race.

—Harlon Dalton, *Racial Healing: Confronting the Fear Between Blacks and White*

Two years after the "Healing the Heart of America" conference, the national debate on race reignited. In the O. J. Simpson trial, a famous black ex-athlete stood accused of the brutal murder of his wife and was acquitted after evidence of police bias nullified seemingly overwhelming evidence of his guilt. The verdict further divided a country already polarized around perceptions of race.

That October, the Million Man March brought hundreds of thousands of African American men to Washington to assert their sense of personal responsibility. Its full significance was obscured by media focus on its controversial leader, Louis Farrakhan, and his verbal assault on the Jewish community.

These two events opened a "Pandora's Box," in the words of Michael McQuillan, one of the architects of the Crown Heights Coalition in Brooklyn, N.Y., formed to defuse tensions between blacks and Jews. "With House members calling for a study commission on race because, as one lawmaker said, 'no one knows what to do,' and the President urging Americans to 'talk frankly about race' but not showing how," he wrote, "Hope in the Cities was ahead of the curve—having launched honest conversations on race, reconciliation and responsibility in Richmond, Cincinnati, Los Angeles, and Philadelphia in that past year alone."[1]

## "I Was Born with the Segregation Gene"

In Cincinnati, Bob Webb, a former editorial writer for the *Cincinnati Enquirer*, had convened a forum in the spring of 1995 in collaboration with Chip Harrod of the National Conference for Community and Justice (NCCJ). Webb grew up in Gulfport, Mississippi, where he absorbed the racial attitudes of the time. "It was as if I was born with the segregation gene," he says. As a student he supported Strom Thurmond in his 1948 presidential bid, running on a segregationist states' rights ticket. Then, as a young journalist, he became a conduit for the forces fighting to preserve the status quo. "The White Citizens' Councils would feed me material, and I would use it in my commentaries."[2]

A surprising encounter led him to first question his attitudes, and then to apologize to a black man who happened to be an African. The African responded, "After the apology, what?" Webb says he has spent the rest of his life trying to answer that question. He began to use his pen "to heal rather than to hurt" as his way of restoring for wrongs of the past. By the time he retired from the *Enquirer* four decades later, he had become the trusted friend of people of all backgrounds in a city known for racial antipathy.

Webb invited U.S. Appeals Court Judge Nathaniel R. Jones, general counsel to the NAACP during the momentous years from 1969 to 1979, to address the forum. Jones told the group: "Institutional racism insulates individuals from having to make ugly personal decisions. Laws are important because they put people in situations where they see things differently."[3] But he recalled King's words that "the ultimate answer to the racial problem lies in our willingness to obey the unenforceable." Later he suggested that the next great advance in race relations would come not in the courtrooms but in the living rooms of America. Mayor Roxanne Qualls, then–state treasurer Ken Blackwell, Rabbi Robert Reiner of the Jewish Community Relations Council, and Episcopal Bishop Herbert Thompson joined the discussion. Thompson's call for a racial summit two years earlier had resulted in three hundred volunteers taking part in ten task forces.

Ideas expressed during the forum led to the first draft of "A Call to Community." The document went through many drafts in the following months, but the essence was clear from the start: "America is at a crossroads. One road leads to community; the other to the chaos of competing identities and interests. . . . [America's] experiment remains incomplete because the original promise of equal opportunity has not been fulfilled. . . . We must demonstrate that our diversity is our greatest strength and that out of this diversity will arise a new American community, a community that could be the best hope for a divided world" (see the appendix for the full text).

### Dealing with Unfinished Business in the Windy City

Hope in the Cities tested the call that fall in Chicago as the Million Man March converged on Washington. Chicago is sometimes described as the most segregated city in America. When Harold Washington was elected as the first African American mayor in 1983, breaking the hold of the old Democratic machine, he was bitterly opposed by more than half the city council. During three years of "council wars," no department heads were confirmed and legislation was blocked. Washington died of a heart attack while in office. One of those who had resisted the mayor was the powerful alderman Richard Mell of the Thirty-third Ward, a working-class, blue-collar community. Mell, who in 2008 celebrated thirty-two years on the city council, served as vice mayor for eight years. When Washington became mayor, he removed Mell from this position. Mell became part of the group of aldermen who, in a parliamentary coup, voted themselves in charge of every council committee. In the debate over Washington's successor, Mell was seen on national television standing on his desk and shouting for attention.

Meanwhile, Margaret Palmer, who had provided creative ideas for Richmond's history walk in 1993, was nurturing a dream of a different Chicago. Palmer was a former legislative aide and a speechwriter for Harold Washington. She and her husband, Henry, a medical doctor, persuaded Mell to view *Healing the Heart of America*, a documentary film about Richmond's walk through history.[4] The veteran alderman was so impressed that he purchased copies to present to Mayor Richard Daley and to all fifty aldermen.

At the February 9, 1994 council meeting, Mell introduced a resolution that called the events in Richmond "a remarkable time of healing of the heart and a message for the whole country." The resolution concluded, "If this type of courageous conversation can be done in Richmond, other cities, including Chicago, could begin honest conversation to heal historic wounds."[5]

It was an unexpected change of heart for the alderman. In October of that year at a Hope in the Cities symposium in the historic Palmer House

Hotel, fifteen other aldermen joined a host committee chaired by Richard Mell and Margaret Palmer to welcome 150 civic leaders from Chicago and other cities. Ray Bakke of International Urban Associates moderated a panel with John Gilligan, a former governor of Ohio; Bliss Browne, an Episcopal priest, community activist, and former banker; Dick Chrysler, a Republican congressman from Michigan; and soon-to-be congressman Jesse Jackson Jr. Margaret Palmer told the audience: "At the end of the Civil War Lincoln had a vision to heal the nation but he was cut down. The vision was not shared by his successors. Now we must take up where he left off, to heal the nation."[6]

Some residents of the Windy City were incredulous at Mell's role. One Chicago leader said that he was stunned when he read the council resolution: "I couldn't believe what I was reading."

In preparing for the symposium, Rev. B. Herbert Martin, who had given the eulogy at Washington's funeral, shared his analysis of race relations with Hope in the Cities leaders. "We are more divided, segregated and hostile than ever, because healing of the heart has not happened," said the pastor who grew up in the all-black town of Mound Bayou, Mississippi. "At some level we did not speak to the real issue. We did projects. We did not do the inner work."[7] Martin was a Chicago organizer of the Million Man March and is a former chairman of the Chicago Housing Authority and executive director of the city's Commission on Human Relations. He leads interracial and interreligious dialogues. "We realized that healing had to be done in dialogue with white men, since white men define to a great extent for black men the male paradigm and what it means to be involved in the whole socio-economic reality of America."[8]

Martin's reconciliation work would be severely tested in 1997 when a black teenager was viciously beaten by three white youths in the city's South Side. Many African Americans criticized him when he appealed to the courts for leniency and mercy for one of the accused youths, whose father had worked with him for years to develop local economic partnerships. Martin, who had himself been attacked by white thugs as a high school student, said he had learned firsthand of the power of forgiveness.

The Chicago forum culminated with Mike McQuillan and other representatives of Hope in the Cities, by now an active network in twelve U.S. cities, reading "A Call to Community." No theoretical treatise, it represented real experience of people in cities across the country who were initiating *honest conversations* and had chosen *to move beyond blame and guilt, beyond hatred and fear, and to face the past with courage and honesty.*

**"We Will Never Again Think in Terms of Them and Us"**

Writing in the *Washington Post,* the columnist William Raspberry suggested that the "Call" was "just what is needed—at least for starters: Listening carefully to each other and to the whole community; bringing people together, not in confrontation, but in trust, to tackle the most urgent needs of the community; searching for solutions, focusing on what is right rather than who is right; and building lasting relationships outside our comfort zone."[9] Raspberry, a persistent voice for rational racial dialogue, linked the "Call" to President Clinton's speech at the University of Texas on October 16, in which he urged Americans to do the hard work of bridging racial divisions that stemmed in part from "the fact that we haven't learned to talk frankly, to listen carefully and to work together across racial lines."[10]

The "Call" was launched formally at the National Press Club in Washington, D.C., on 23 May 1996. Study Circles Resource Center (now Everyday Democracy), the YWCA, the Faith and Politics Institute, and the National Conference for Community and Justice (NCCJ) partnered with Hope in the Cities in sponsoring the event. The organizers described it as "an effort to encourage political leaders to engage in open, honest conversation about race and its impact on national life."

Blacks, whites, Jews, Muslims, Christians, Republicans, and Democrats sat and talked. They had different ideas about the appropriate role of government, about the efficacy of affirmative action policies, even about the nature of the problem itself. But they were united in their belief that through honest conversation, a healing for the nation might begin.

The mayors of Atlanta, Baltimore, Cincinnati, Jackson, Austin, and Louisville sent messages. Earlier that year all attendees at the winter meeting of the U.S. Conference of Mayors had received a copy of the "Call" accompanied by a letter from Kurt Schmoke, the mayor of Baltimore.

Imam W. Deen Mohammed, spokesperson for the Muslim American Association, and Dr. Sidney Clearfield, the international vice president of B'nai B'rith International, spoke in support. Jim Wallis of Sojourners, Raul

Yzaguirre of the National Conference of La Raza, Republican congressman Rob Portman from Ohio, and Kweisi Mfume, president and CEO of the NAACP, were among more than one hundred national endorsers.

A message from Senator Bill Bradley saluted the leaders for coming together to build "the bridges of understanding we need to move forward in our pursuit of a spiritually transformed community in which reconciliation is possible."[11] Bradley is one of the most thoughtful public figures calling America to confront its racial dilemma. He terms the quest for racial unity "the defining moral issue of our time."[12] That year on the floor of the Senate, he proposed a comprehensive urban community-building initiative. In a speech in 1995, he had said that a new language was needed, the language of civil society: "The language of community is about receiving undeserved gifts. What this nation needs to promote is the spirit of giving something freely, without measuring it out precisely, or demanding something in return."[13]

At the National Press Club, Hope in the Cities continued a pattern begun in Chicago by inviting "unlikely" combinations of national leaders to speak to the theme of the "Call." The organizers eschewed political litmus tests in selecting speakers but looked instead for genuine "seekers after truth." Harlon Dalton, a law professor from Yale, chaired a panel of such polar opposites as Jesse Jackson Jr. and Paul Weyrich. No remarks had been vetted. As founder of the Heritage Foundation, Free Congress Foundation, and National Empowerment Television, Weyrich would often provoke strong responses as an icon of the conservative movement. When he rose to speak, many in the audience held their breath.

Surprisingly, Weyrich began with a personal confession that for a long time he had ignored protest in the black community about prejudice and racism, particularly among police: "My attitude was, 'Well, this is just a bunch of criminals probably trying to evade their just dues.' I simply didn't hear those cries. But I must tell you that one of the most profound events in my political life was the revelation of the comments made by the detective Mark Fuhrman during O. J. Simpson's trial. I was astounded and outraged. . . . And so I began to look more closely, and I've taken a particular interest in Philadelphia where certain bad white cops have targeted a lot of innocent black people to advance themselves by enhancing their record of arrest."

As Weyrich continued, there was complete silence in the room. "I now find that in many cases these cries have a great basis of legitimacy, and they are cries that the conservative community . . . needs to take seriously. . . .

And because of our own view on the subject of government power, and the need to keep government in check, we conservatives should have a natural sympathy for these cries and be able to start a dialogue. . . . My own experience is that once you begin a dialogue and you earn the trust of people . . . although you may come into the conversation on a very narrow basis, you will end up expanding that conversation and will continue, hopefully, to build trust on both sides."[14]

By now his audience knew it was witnessing something highly unusual. But, as Jesse Jackson Jr. reminded everyone: "Our children are watching us. They are not watching what we say: they are watching what we do. Our challenge is to rise above [race politics] and the hope that we have is this call to the community for hope in the cities." Congressman Dick Chrysler, a Republican who had attended the Chicago forum, asked for "a bona fide attempt to open our hearts, listen to the anxieties and fears that people feel, the opinions of others, the cries for help."[15]

The national media ignored this public demonstration of honest conversation involving leaders of diametrically opposed political views. But as Martha McCoy of Study Circles Resource Center (Everyday Democracy), a leading promoter and practitioner of dialogue, said: "The good news about our Call to Community today is that this is not a cold start. It is happening already." She emphasized it was "not a call for a utopian dream." To the contrary, it was "a very concrete call for real, actual, face-to-face, personal conversation between people all over this country, between people of all kinds of backgrounds, coming together to really address the public problems in that inclusive, democratic way. In these conversations people listen respectfully to each other and tackle together the most urgent needs of the community. It does not stop with talk. It brings healing, it brings new connections in the community, it brings a new understanding of each other's perspective and views, it brings a new will to work together on public issues and new ideas for solving problems. . . . Most importantly, we will never again think in terms of them and us."[16]

## Running against the Grain

The "Healing the Heart of America" conference and the launching of "A Call to Community" prompted a spate of requests to Richmond for assistance and collaboration from communities throughout the country. *Heal-*

*ing the Heart of America*, a documentary film of Richmond's "walk through history" by filmmaker Karen Greisdorf, encouraged similar action in other cities. Launching Baltimore's local "Call to Community," Kweisi Mfume of the NAACP endorsed the initiative on behalf of the organization's 1,700 branches: "I want to personally pledge to work with any individual, any group, any organization, any elected official, any government agency that endorses this non-partisan vision with us."[17] Groups met and planned activities in Minneapolis–St. Paul, Atlanta, and Cincinnati. At a Hope in the Cities forum in Philadelphia, Mayor Edward Rendell cautioned participants not just to talk to the like-minded: "Just because someone is conservative doesn't mean we should not approach them. We need to talk to the people who can help us." The former mayor W. Wilson Goode also encouraged bridge building, but told his audience, "What you are doing is running against the grain."

A diverse group in Los Angeles worked to heal rifts between the Koreans and blacks. A Korean Presbyterian minister told an African American congregation, "I want to make a true apology for the wrongs the Koreans may have done." Richmond's Mayor Walter Kenney met with community leaders in Brooklyn. In Hartford, Connecticut, people of Asian, Caribbean, African, and European descent, as well as Native Americans, shared meals in each other's homes and discussed how to heal wounds in their city. Seventy local and state leaders took part in a two-day workshop in Rocky Mount, North Carolina, in response to church burnings.[18]

The launch of the "Call" coincided with the rapid expansion of a variety of small-group-dialogue models led by several national organizations in different communities. Practitioners generally agree with the definition of intergroup dialogue as an open and honest forum that brings diverse people face-to-face with the aid of trained facilitators to share personal stories, express emotions, affirm values, ask questions, clarify viewpoints, and propose solutions to community concerns.[19] The growing body of literature reflects a consensus about effective structures and methodology. Dialogue is a process, not an event, and the best dialogues continue over several weeks or months. Dialogues are about relationship building and thoughtful engagement on difficult issues. For this reason, they are best restricted to small groups. Twelve is ideal, with an upper limit of fifteen and a minimum of eight. However, Hope in the Cities has demonstrated that weekend residential dialogues for up to twenty-five people can work well if properly structured.

Everyday Democracy provides support for grassroots dialogue efforts in many parts of the country. Funded by the Topsfield Foundation, it produces high-quality dialogue curricula and trains citizens to come together around shared concerns in a process of deliberative problem solving. By the end of the 1990s, Everyday Democracy had organized 110 dialogue projects; the number grew to 300 by 2004. "From the beginning of our work we have seen the extent to which people want to be part of something that would help them solve their problems," says executive director Martha McCoy. "Problem solving draws the most diverse groups of people. This is important because no one group can recruit the people who are needed."

According to McCoy: "A huge question is how to connect dialogue with institutional change. How to move to policy change when you have been building relationships for a long time." Reflecting on the vast range of dialogue activities that have emerged, she says, "It's a big tent, and I am uncomfortable calling it a movement." She notes a tendency for many dialogue practitioners to work in a "closed universe." "Some see dialogue as an end in itself. Some are there simply for personal growth."

McCoy believes that dealing with race is critical for effective citizen democracy. But she adds, "I was on a conference call with funders talking about the response to Katrina, and the issue of race did not come up once." Changing demographics add to the challenge: "Because Latinos are not a racial group, they may say, 'What does racism have to do with me?' We need to frame it so everyone says, 'That's my conversation too.'"

The specific dialogue model first implemented by Hope in the Cities in Richmond and adopted by other communities provides a frame within which to explore the ideas expressed in the "Call to Community." In this scenario, a group of individuals from diverse backgrounds meets together for six sessions of two or three hours. Two trained facilitators, also racially or ethnically diverse, guide the conversation. They start by eliciting ground rules from the participants with the purpose of providing an environment where all feel safe to express their experiences, feelings, and opinions. These ground rules might include: we will start and end on time; we will ensure the full participation of everyone; we will respect confidentiality; we will acknowledge anger but not express thoughts that are aimed at specifically hurting or demeaning one another.

The six-session series follows this sequence:

1. Beginning the conversation: Why are we here?
2. Our experience of race and community: Who are we?
3. Our experiences and history: Can we come together?
4. Forgiveness and atonement: Can we forgive? Repent?
5. Building hope for the future: What should our city look like?
6. Looking within: Who are we now?

In the first session, participants introduce themselves, express their hopes for the dialogue, and agree on how they will conduct the dialogue. The second session begins with simple questions: In what kinds of neighborhoods did your grandparents and parents live? Were they racially or ethnically mixed? The questions encourage storytelling, and as people recall their childhood experiences, they begin to relate to each other at a human level. Later, they reflect on good and bad experiences with people of another racial or ethnic background.

The third dialogue addresses history: Do you feel enough has been done to redress past injustices? Is there some aspect of your personal group history or current reality that you feel is not being heard or acknowledged? Often the first two sessions are polite and restrained. The third provokes more emotional interventions as people become comfortable with the group and are ready to talk more honestly. The fourth, which probes the role of forgiveness and repentance or atonement in the process of reconciliation, is often the most difficult but most important session. In a broken relationship, does the injured party need to take the first step toward reconciliation?

By the fifth meeting, the participants are starting to envision a reconciled community and to identify obstacles and potential allies. The dialogue concludes by returning to the question of personal responsibility: What have I learned? What will I do? Participants write a personal statement of commitment.

Throughout the dialogue, the facilitators strive to steer the conversation away from intellectual posturing and toward sharing of personal experience. The facilitator's role in setting an example of personal storytelling and honesty is crucial. For this reason, Hope in the Cities insists on intensive training for facilitators, all of whom participate in a dialogue themselves before leading a group. "Even professional facilitators who are trained in diversity issues may not have the experience and sensitivity to lead a group toward reconciliation," says Cricket White, who left a secure job with city government to join Hope in the Cities at a dramatically reduced salary and now directs its training program. "They need an opportunity to become participants in the dialogue as a means of looking at their own conscious and subconscious attitudes about race."

The sixteen-hour training focuses on spiritual principles as well as an understanding of personal styles and group dynamics. The curriculum for the dialogue guide states Hope in the Cities' belief that "the energy for fundamental change requires a moral and spiritual transformation in the human spirit." Participants may or may not express their thoughts through the lens of any formal religious faith, but there is usually agreement (at least by the end of the dialogue) that the problem of racism cannot be solved by education or social programs alone. A change of heart is required.

Cricket White says: "At first we explored training models of other organizations like the National Coalition Building Institute and Study Circles [now Everyday Democracy]. Later, as the program progressed, we saw the need to design our own training, which would place more emphasis on personal responsibility and forgiveness." White believes that creating a cadre of skilled facilitators may be the longest-lasting contribution to the community. Ultimately, the goal is not to create race relations experts but to develop leaders who can sustain a team.

Underlying the Hope in the Cities model is the assumption that people can only build trust with others when they are in relationship with them, and that trust cannot be built in an atmosphere of blame. White observes: "Blame is so destructive because the assumption is that the *intent* of the other person is to do you harm. Whether it is spoken or unspoken, the other person always knows—feels—the blame is there. This assumption of intent is especially hard to overcome if the person has hurt you more than once. In America, we have a societal axiom for self-preservation: 'Hurt me once, shame on you. Hurt me twice, shame on me.' The instinct for self-survival is very strong; this causes us to hold down or step on others. Trust is built in a dialogue when people are able to assume non-negative intentions on the part of others. When people anywhere transcend blame, it is transferable; in this sense, the experience is universal."

White has facilitated numerous dialogues and trained scores of facilitators. She says that the most powerful moment occurs when someone takes responsibility for what their group has done to create or perpetuate a problem and can claim this in front of the other group. "It changes the whole dynamic because the other side knows already. It's not news to them!"

Within a few years, more than four hundred people in the Richmond area had taken part in the "Call to Community" conversations. One dialogue involved fourteen business and professional men, evenly balanced between black and white, and including a Chinese and a Lebanese American. At the conclusion, a conservative business leader commented: "We were raised to regard independence as the great American goal. Maybe we should be thinking more about interdependence. Interdependence requires respect." A retired banker said he would talk to the president of his club about moving beyond token integration. Another said he was ready to put himself at risk with his colleagues by speaking out on racial issues. The Chinese American asked searching questions of the African Americans. He surprised them by saying: "We admire African Americans so much because you get together. We are like sand. We are called the model community. This is not good. What it means is we don't make a fuss, we don't get involved."

Jane Talley, an African American facilitator, says that the learning in the dialogues is as important for blacks as for whites. One black man said he came assuming it would be yet another occasion when he would have to "educate white people." To his surprise, he found himself telling the group how fifteen years earlier he and his brother had been stopped in their car by a police officer who completely humiliated them. The experience was so traumatic that the two brothers had never spoken to each other about it. Later he told Talley, "That dialogue changed my life."

Often the dialogues extend beyond the allotted six meetings. Participants will say, "We are just getting started!" As the network of relationships spreads, people develop long-standing friendships; they spend social time together, support each other in moments of personal need, and collaborate on creative responses to crisis or opportunities in the community.

I will return to the further evolution of the Richmond project later in the book. The next two chapters place the "honest conversation" model in the context of the national dialogue on race. We will also see how three very different cities implemented the Richmond method.

# 8

## One America

A National Dialogue

In December 1997, a call from the White House requested that Hope in the Cities join five other organizations at a meeting to discuss a special project for a race initiative launched by President Bill Clinton. Two months earlier, Clinton had announced his intention to lead the American people in a "great and unprecedented conversation on race" and the implications for the twenty-first century of Americans of so many diverse backgrounds living and working together. Calling for a "candid conversation," he said: "We have talked at each other and about each other for a long time. It is high time we began talking with each other. . . . Racial dialogue will not be easy at first. We will have to get past defensiveness and fear and political correctness. . . . We have torn down barriers in our laws. Now we must tear down barriers in our lives, our minds and our hearts."[1]

With the encouragement of the former governor of Mississippi, William Winter, Clinton launched his initiative by forming a blue-ribbon advisory board, headed by John Hope Franklin, the renowned African American historian. The board's mandate was to use dialogue to raise the issue of racial reconciliation onto the national agenda, to recruit leaders and encourage efforts aimed at bridging racial divides, and to develop recommendations for national policies to bridge opportunity gaps.

"One America," as the president's race initiative was named, gave significant exposure and validation to a dialogue movement already at a high level of development. A survey conducted in 1997 estimated that there were 181 dialogue efforts in the United States. Eighty-five could be said to be truly multiracial and actively engaged in dialogue. Of sixty-five surveyed in thirty-five states, over half had been formed between 1992 and 1997. The Center for Living Democracy reported that "thousands of Americans are now involved in conversations with people of different racial and ethnic backgrounds. . . . With nurture and exposure, these dialogues could become an important national movement."[2]

"One America Conversations" took place in thirty-nine states and eighty-nine cities. "Days of Dialogue" in April 1998 involved 110 communities, governors of thirty-nine states, and twenty-five mayors. Students, faculty, and administrators on six hundred campuses took part. The initiative published a further directory of 124 "promising practices."[3]

A few days after the call from the White House, Paige Chargois and I joined representatives of five other organizations at the New Executive Building. Michael Wenger, deputy director of the initiative, welcomed us and introduced Jonathan Chace, associate director of the Community Relations Service (CRS) of the U.S. Department of Justice. Chace explained that CRS was seeking our assistance in creating a public dialogue guide for the initiative. He said that the White House did not intend to duplicate the work of existing organizations or to promote one group's materials or methodologies over another. Rather, we were to collaborate to craft a publication that would outline key principles and offer basic guidance and options—a tall order for seven strong-minded people who had not worked together before!

The group rallied to the task, and at this first meeting we quickly agreed on the necessary components for the dialogue guide. The drafting team consisted of Manny Brandt, National MultiCultural Institute; Theo Brown, National Days of Dialogue; Sally Campbell, Study Circles Research Center (Everyday Democracy); Carmen Rivera, YWCA; Wayne Winbourne, NCCJ; and Paige Chargois and me from Hope in the Cities. The team's work was ably facilitated by Marty Walsh of the CRS Northeastern Region and Steve Thom of the Western Region. Each person undertook to write one section, and we agreed to circulate drafts within the month as the final text was due by February 20. A spirit of selfless collaboration marked the project from the start. When we compared texts, we found that the individual sections fitted together surprisingly well. With little disagreement and plenty of flexibility all round, we hit our copy deadline.

Dr. David Campt, a tall, lanky African American, often propped against a wall or sprawled in a chair, kept a watchful eye on us, and would intervene occasionally with penetrating comments or probing questions. Campt had been hired by the White House as an expert on racial dialogue. At our final meeting, Paige Chargois suggested that each of us share a personal reflection on our work together. Contrasting it with his experience at the White

House, Campt commented, "I have never worked with a group of people where there was so little ego."

The *One America Dialogue Guide* begins by drawing a distinction between dialogue and debate. While debate tends to focus on bringing others into alignment with one's own position or beliefs, dialogue "invites discovery . . . it expects that participants will grow in understanding . . . [and] question and reevaluate their assumptions." Effective dialogues, it states:

- Move towards solutions rather than continue to express or analyze the problem. An emphasis on personal responsibility moves the discussion away from finger-pointing or naming enemies and towards constructive common action.

- Reach beyond the usual boundaries. When fully developed, dialogue can involve the entire community, offering opportunities for new, unexpected partnerships. New partnerships can develop when participants listen carefully and respectfully to each other. A search for solutions focuses on the common good as participants are encouraged to broaden their horizons and build relationships outside their comfort zone.

- Unite divided communities through a respectful, informed sharing of local racial history and its consequences for different people in today's society. The experiences of "walking through history" together can lead to healing.

- Aim for a change of heart, not just a change of mind. Dialogues go beyond sharing and understanding to transforming participants. While the process begins with the individual, it eventually involves groups and institutions. Ultimately dialogues can affect how policies are made.[4]

The guide outlines key steps in planning a dialogue, recruiting participants, and managing the process. It offers a simple four-phase conversation structure and sample questions and tips for facilitators.

Unfortunately, the document never received the public attention it deserved. During our second work session, January 22–23, 1998, the media were erupting with the news of Clinton's alleged affair with Monica Lewinsky. There was gloom in the room and groans of, "There goes all our work down the tubes." No question, the initiative as a whole suffered from this distraction.

The guide, when published, was given minimal publicity by the White House, but it remains one of the most useful documents to emerge from the initiative. In a concise form, it contains the best thinking of the major organizations engaged in racial dialogue in the United States.

### Preaching to the Choir?

In a conversation soon after the launch of the initiative, Mike Wenger—who had originally proposed the idea in a paper to William Winter—outlined three areas of priority: to identify and nurture leaders at all levels; to highlight promising practices in the most accessible way; and to find ways to go beyond "preaching to the choir"—to engage people of more conservative views who might not naturally feel at home in conversations about race. Without a doubt, the initiative did much—largely through Wenger's dedicated efforts—to connect activist groups across the country, and the publishing of a directory of promising practices provided a valuable source of information.

In the third area, however, the initiative was less successful, and it did not appear to ease polarization at the national level. Perhaps if the seven-person advisory board had more deliberately and publicly demonstrated bipartisan leadership, the response might have been less predictable. The appointment as cochair of someone with whom conservative Americans could readily identify might have drawn unexpected participants into the conversation. But impressions formed early. Leaving a meeting with Wenger, a colleague and I encountered a prominent journalist of conservative views who expressed forcefully his opinion that the initiative was "all about blame and bashing whites." Our best efforts to assure him that this was not the intention left him unconvinced. The White House was never able to shake this perception in some sections of the population.

After a year of meetings and discussions across the country, the advisory board members concluded: "Although many Americans want honest and constructive racial dialogue, it is difficult to achieve. Most people are uncomfortable talking about race, or are ill-equipped with the knowledge and understanding of the issue, or are tired of constantly talking about race without seeing concrete results that reduce disparities."

The report noted that race and ethnicity continued to be "salient predictors of well-being in American society." It urged a substantial increase in the civil rights enforcement budget and efforts to increase early childhood learning and to strengthen other areas of education, and called for exploration of ways to reduce income disparities through job training and supplement for small businesses.

Educating America about race proved the most challenging aspect of the initiative. Conscious and subconscious attitudes persist "because we are still affected by the myths, stereotypes and superstitions that are associated with our long history of race relations." The board admitted that one year was insufficient to achieve the initiative's goal. It called for a multimedia campaign to inform Americans about racial diversity; a call to action to national and community leaders to guide state and local efforts to bridge divides; and a continued focus on youth as the country's greatest hope for realizing the goal of an America that values diversity and embraces common values. It also suggested the creation of a permanent "Council for One America" structure to continue the work of the initiative.[5]

Reflecting on the initiative, David Campt says: "For a while it made it difficult for public figures to say that race relations don't matter. Since the civil rights era, the white establishment and media had pushed the theme of 'getting past' the issue. With Rodney King and O. J. Simpson, the line was, 'Race should not matter any more.' Because the president put it on the public agenda, it gave some legitimacy to the work of the racial activist population which had been pretty much on the fringe. It bolstered the anti-racist movement, and even pushed foundations to make some grants to support it."

In Campt's view, the initiative "never created good television." Of the thirty-five staff hired to run the project, only one (Campt) knew anything about racial dialogue. A town meeting in Akron, Ohio, that was supposed to provide a big splash as a public dialogue is one of his "top-ten regrets." Campt had the task of "making the dialogue happen," although he says this was never formally recognized and he was never given the necessary authority or respect:

> We had a selected group of about fifty of the general public. Then we had a few experts, a moderator, and, of course, the president. I had to push to get diversity (i.e., conservatives) into the group. I had set up a process to interview people so that I knew their views. But the moderator did not know. Just before we started, he asked whether he should wear an earpiece so that I could give him some di-

rection on who might have different views. A woman on the staff shot down the
idea. The result was that the dialogue never got beyond platitudes. It's very easy
when you have the president there to fall into this—you don't want to disagree
publicly; it's hard to show racial conservatism. We were never able to sell the
initiative to a broad audience; it did not catch fire.

The original plan was for Clinton to produce a book setting out his vision in response to the advisory board's report. Although much work was
done on this (including by Campt himself), it never saw the light of day.
Campt says that some members of Clinton's staff were never enthusiastic
about the initiative: "People who controlled access to the president thought
it was a big political risk. The hallmark of a presidency is a perpetual campaign. There's always a tension between the public relations aspect and engaging the American public around difficult issues that it disagrees about.
If the president believes in certain notions of social or racial justice, can
you simultaneously invite or give a platform to people who have a different
view?"

None of the advisory board's proposals made much headway, and the in-
coming Republican administration quietly withdrew institutional support
for any continuing public outreach.

The Clinton initiative prompted many newsrooms to launch informa-
tive and often constructive explorations of racial progress and challenges.
Typical was the *Dallas Morning News*, which ran three front-page stories
on efforts in different cities, including Richmond, to build interracial partnerships. The *St. Louis Post-Dispatch* headlined a front-page investigative
report on Richmond: "Old Confederate capital checks its racial pulse". Reporters for the *New York Times* carried out a yearlong exploration resulting
in a series of fifteen articles on how Americans in many sectors of work experienced racial issues in their daily lives, and the Sunday *New York Times
Magazine* for July 16, 2000, was titled "Talking about Race."

Liberals and conservatives battled it out on the airwaves and in the press.
Books by Derrick Bell, Henry Louis Gates, Cornell West, Glenn Loury,
Shelby Steele, bell hooks, Andrew Hacker, Chris Rice, Spencer Perkins,
and many other thoughtful writers contributed to the national dialogue.
It seemed that everyone had something to say about race. Affirmative action, welfare reform, and police-community relations often sparked heated
debates that changed few minds.

## Apology and Reparations

Few things provoke more emotional reactions than the question of a national apology for slavery. Until 2008, proposals for an apology by the federal government garnered little support from Republicans or Democrats (even under Carter). Every year since 1989, Representative John Conyers, a Democrat from Michigan, has introduced a bill that would "acknowledge the fundamental injustice, cruelty, brutality and inhumanity of slavery in the United States." But appeals to justice (the country grew and prospered through the "free" labor of black Americans,[6] and taxes on cotton picked by slaves added hugely to the U.S treasury) and historical precedent (in 1993, Congress apologized to Japanese Americans for their internment during World War II; also in 1993, Congress offered a formal apology to native Hawaiians for the role the United States played in overthrowing the Kingdom of Hawaii in the previous century) failed to move politicians to action. Not even the documented confirmation that the Capitol itself—the "house of liberty"—was built by slave labor provoked a formal statement from the nation's leaders.[7]

Congressman Tony Hall's unsuccessful efforts (launched separately from Conyers's bill) in 1997 and again in 2000 to secure a congressional apology highlighted the political and cultural divide over racial issues. In 2000, of the Ohio representative's fifteen original cosponsors, all but one were Democrats, and ten were from northern states. Some commentators regarded an apology as merely symbolic or as avoidance of tackling the real problems; but many Americans feared that behind the call for apology lurked the threat of a demand for reparations.

The strongest intervention on the subject by a national newspaper came from the *Philadelphia Inquirer,* with two full-page editorials supporting Conyers's bill as "an excellent starting point" and calling for a national conversation on reparations. Rather than a "festival of finger pointing," the editors called for a three-step process of "acknowledgment, atonement and reconciliation." Such a process, they claimed, would help America address a long-delayed moral task and would be spiritually satisfying. The responsibility for atonement lay with the federal government, which, acting for white people, had allowed slavery for seventy-six years. A reparations commission would educate Americans and allow them to "see history through each other's eyes." The newspaper suggested a $500 billion reparations fund devoted to addressing the shortfall in academic resources, and to building and renovating schools in the nation's neediest areas.[8]

The *Inquirer* editorials picked up Randall Robinson's passionate call for reparations in *The Debt: What America Owes to Blacks*, in which he dismissed the political correctness of affirmative action programs as palliatives and called for "a virtual Marshall plan of federal resources."[9] Slavery, he wrote, has produced "victims *ad infinitum*, through institutional discrimination long after the active stage of the crime has ended."[10]

At the other end of the political spectrum, another eminent African American thinker and writer, Shelby Steele, claimed that liberalism in America was more the result of a need to expiate white guilt than a commitment to develop true equality between the races. Universities avidly court blacks to increase their diversity, yet black students have the highest drop-out rate and lowest grade-point average of any student group. "If black equality were really the goal, wouldn't policy focus on educational development before college?" he asked.[11] Steele condemned reform that "demands no principles from its beneficiaries and no sacrifices from its supporters—the fruit of liberalism with little moral authority but much moral vanity."[12]

The public debate excluded any meaningful conversation about how a process of racial reconciliation might "provide a framework for discussing black reparations in a way that both benefits all Americans and carries the potential for material change in race relations."[13] The United States, in stark contrast with South Africa, has never formally adopted reconciliation as its national policy, nor have its political leaders been willing to engage in the difficult but necessary conversations about our history, the economic, social, and psychological legacies of slavery, and the century of legalized apartheid that followed Emancipation.

Bill Bradley highlighted the urgency of addressing the chasm of racial thinking and its impact on America's ability to address poverty as a matter of survival. "Unless we can save the poorest, most disconnected among us, we will not save ourselves," he wrote in his memoirs in 1996. He noted that only by ending racial thinking can America sharply reduce poverty. "Racial thinking obstructs America from seeing how to reduce poverty, because many in the white majority view blacks as undeserving or unwilling to work. But to refuse more resources to fight poverty because you don't want to help blacks actually hurts more whites than blacks because poor white people outnumber poor blacks by thirteen million."[14]

Finally, on July 29, 2008, the House of Representatives passed by voice vote (with no nays) an eloquently worded formal apology for slavery and the years of Jim Crow segregation, introduced by Representative Steve Cohen of Memphis and sponsored by 120 fellow legislators. Spurred by a similar action by the Virginia state government the previous year, it called apology "an important and necessary first step in the process of reconciliation" and expressed "commitment to rectify the lingering consequences of centuries" of brutal dehumanization and injustice. The Senate followed suit in 2009.

But the resolutions received little media attention and lacked the nationwide emotional impact seen in Australia in 2008, when Prime Minister Kevin Rudd's heartfelt words of apology to the Aboriginal people as the first act of the new parliament received massive live television coverage.[15]

Obama's remarkable speech on race in Philadelphia on March 18, 2008, was a breakthrough moment. Perhaps his presidency will enable America finally to come to terms with its racial history and take substantive steps to remedy the structural inequities resulting from it.

**Faith and Politics**

Largely missing among the many books, papers, and speeches on race relations and racial equity in recent decades has been conversation between those approaching change from a faith-based/spiritual perspective and those addressing it from a perspective of education; or between those who believe in the primacy of relationship building and those whose first priority is dismantling structural racism. The identification of religious or moral values with the political Right often resulted in an allergic reaction to any overt linkage of spirituality to social change efforts by left-leaning activists. Until recently there was little recognition among those in the secular racial justice movement of the significant rethinking occurring within Christian evangelical churches. Equally, those in the faith-based movement tended to remain within their own circle of belief. Generally, there appeared to be little safe meeting ground between secular activists working for systems change and faith-driven advocates for community transformation. Jim Wallis of Sojourners was an exceptional voice, encouraging the Left to recognize the contribution of faith to American life, and urging evangelicals to embrace social justice issues.

Just as Hope in the Cities was unusual in its determination to engage leaders across the political spectrum, it also was one of the few networks that maintained strong ties with both faith-based and nonreligious efforts for racial change.

Many of those working for racial reconciliation from a spiritual motivation might feel constrained to express their belief lest they be identified with a conservative political camp. One person wrote:

> As I read [your letter] I found myself longing to be part of such a surge of spiritual energy and courage. . . . Somehow it is difficult for many people to acknowledge the interface of spiritual beliefs and racial reconciliation. So many people claim spirituality, particularly in the context of organized religion and particularly among Christians, to be a private, "personal" issue that is not to be shared publicly lest we become affiliated with the oppressive "religious right."
>
> I have spent the last 17 years working in the field of racial justice and reconciliation because I believe that God has called me to this work. . . . Although I have never spoken to you directly about it, I sense that you, too, are in this work for spiritual reasons. Is this true? If I am overstepping my boundaries here, please forgive me. . . . I have taken the risk of speaking my heart in this little e-mail epistle; somehow I felt it was safe to do so. If I have taken too much risk, please accept my apology.

Important shifts were occurring within some sectors of the white Christian community, where evangelicals were "digging out of a deep hole to earn the trust of the black Church."[16] Billy Graham, who had hesitated to support Martin Luther King Jr.'s more direct approach to the race issue in the 1960s, wrote in *Christianity Today*, "Racial and ethnic hostility is the foremost social problem facing our world today." William Parnell, in the same issue, observed: "We're going to have to take some rather courageous and extraordinary steps to avoid a race war. The first step is the sincere repentance of racism by white evangelicals."[17]

In a 1999 survey of evangelical literature, Chris Rice found thirty-five titles dealing with race, ethnicity, and reconciliation published in the 1990s alone, more than double the number of the previous twenty years. In seeking to account for this "unprecedented decade-long trend of progress," he pointed to the Rodney King episode and the 1992 uprising in Los Angeles as well as the 1995 O. J. Simpson trial and verdict, which raised the visibility of racial polarization to a level not seen since the assassination of Martin Luther King.

But another important factor was the growing strength of a few highly committed and influential faith-based activists such as John Perkins, who founded the Christian Community Development Association. Now active in one hundred cities, more than five hundred community development corporations, schools, colleges, businesses, and foundations approach economic development and racial reconciliation from a faith perspective. Perkins's philosophy, summarized in his "three R's—Relocation, Redistribution, and Reconciliation"—encourages Christians to move into high-poverty areas, build relationship-based partnerships, and recover neighborhoods block by block. In the words of one activist, "Your problems become my problems, and we work together for justice." John Perkins often found a warmer embrace from white Christians than from black churches, whose members perhaps felt threatened by his message. Whites, on the other hand, might embrace his message of reconciliation but be slower to hear the claims of economic justice.

Chris Rice and Perkins's eldest son, Spencer, led an interracial ministry in Mississippi until Spencer's tragically early death at the age of forty-six. Today Rice directs a reconciliation center at Duke Divinity School.[18]

One of the few organizations to successfully bridge political and cultural divides among national leaders is the Faith and Politics Institute. Launched in 1991 to create a community of conscience across partisan, ideological, racial, and religious lines, the institute engages members of Congress from both parties in dialogue and reflection groups on moral and spiritual issues. Pilgrimages to civil rights sites and a visit to South Africa have exposed more than one hundred members to new experiences and perspectives, and enabled them to get to know each other in new and different ways.

The institute began with the collaboration of Doug Tanner, an ordained Methodist minister; Joe Aldridge, another Methodist minister and lawyer; and Anne Bartley, who had directed Clinton's Washington, D.C., office when he was governor of Arkansas. Illinois congressman Glenn Poshard hosted the first reflection group in his office. Much of the focus has been on racial issues.

Terri LaVelle, who served as program director for seven years, sees tangible results: "The members have articulated a greater sense of awareness around issues, particularly race, they thought were resolved, and in some cases the way they vote has changed and working relationships have developed across party lines." She mentions former Senator George Allen (R-VA), who in 2005 cosponsored with Senator Mary Landrieu (D-LA) a Senate resolution apologizing for the government's failure to enact antilynching legislation decades earlier. This was the first time the body had apologized for America's treatment of African Americans. LaVelle says Allen acknowledged the influence of the civil rights pilgrimage on his willingness to take this action.

The institute's first cochairs were John Lewis (D-GA) and Amo Houghton (R-NY). According to Houghton, the institute "honors our differences while leading the charge for conscience in politics, civility and respect in dialogue, and the quest for healing."[19]

### Promoting Inclusive Communities

Local elected officials were also taking constructive action. Spurred by the leadership of Mayor Bob Knight of Wichita, Kansas, a Republican, cities in forty-eight states joined the National League of Cities Campaign for Racial Justice.

Jim Hunt is a city councilor from Clarksburg, a small town in West Virginia and the birthplace of the famed Confederate general Stonewall Jackson. West Virginia is one of the least diverse states in the country, and Clarksburg is 95 percent white. When Rev. David Kates became its first African American mayor, the Ku Klux Klan threatened disruption. Hunt and Kates worked to unite the town in a positive response and launched an ongoing initiative to build bridges across racial and ethnic divides.[20]

As president of the National League of Cities (NLC) in 2005–6, Hunt led a program to promote inclusive communities, drawing on the Clarksburg experience. By the end of Hunt's term, one hundred city governments had joined the inclusive communities program. "What has really impressed me is that it's not just a courtesy," he said. "The opposite occurred. People started to think deeply about it before passing the resolution. The key thing has been to motivate the governments and to involve them in different ways to what you assume. It's fine to get churches and other agencies involved but if the government doesn't commit you've got problems."

....

Operating from its Richmond base, Hope in the Cities continued to build collaborative partnerships. Its advisory board represented the racial, religious, and economic diversity of the Richmond region, and an informal network of leaders in other states provided national perspective. These collaborators included Jim Hunt at the National League of Cities, Martha McCoy of Everyday Democracy, Doug Tanner of the Faith and Politics Institute, John and Spencer Perkins, Chris Rice, and other instigators of the Christian Community Development Association, Reid Carpenter of the Pittsburgh Leadership Foundation, Ray Bakke of International Urban Associates, Laura Chasen of the Public Conversations Project, Liz Salett of the National MultiCultural Institute, and many others.

In the spring of 1998, the W. K. Kellogg Foundation made a grant to Hope in the Cities to "expand its successful model of open conversations leading to constructive action on themes of race, reconciliation and responsibility" in other U.S. cities. That summer, I received a letter from David Campt, who had heard that we were seeking a consultant to strengthen our team. He wrote, "The truth is the position sounds very much like what I thought my responsibilities would be with the Initiative." Campt had come by an unusual route to his work with the White House. An adopted child from Detroit, he won a scholarship to Princeton to study computer science and completed a doctorate in city and regional planning at Berkeley. He had worked in the Bay Area as a facilitator, evaluator, and consultant on cultural competency, diversity, and team building. He combines a sharp analytical mind and an imposing presence with a refreshing lack of self-importance and a disarming sense of humor.

Campt's participation as a lead trainer and facilitator increased Hope in the Cities' capacity immeasurably and made possible an outreach to cities hundreds of miles away from Richmond, both geographically and culturally.

# 9

## Reaching Out

### Natchez

A call from Frances Trosclair, the city clerk of Natchez, Mississippi, informed us that Mayor Larry "Butch" Brown was eager to engage the resources of Hope in the Cities. Perched on a bluff overlooking the river, Natchez is the oldest settlement on the Mississippi. The city is famous for its superb antebellum mansions built by rich cotton planters whose wealth derived from an agricultural economy dependent upon slave labor. Thousands made the arduous journey, often on foot, from slave markets in Richmond, Virginia, to the Forks of the Road in Natchez, one of the Lower South's busiest slave markets. For decades, Natchez promoted itself as a city "where the Old South still lives." Until recently, the presentation of Natchez history, complete with southern belles, mint juleps, and gracious southern hospitality completely ignored the plight of those African Americans who made this lifestyle possible.

The Spring Pilgrimage, which draws thousands to Natchez, started during the Depression as a way to save the city financially. The original idea was to show the beautiful gardens surrounding the antebellum mansions, but freezing weather destroyed the gardens so tourists were shown inside the homes instead. The role of African Americans, however, was totally unacknowledged. The Confederate Pageant is another source of controversy. In its early years, blacks were included as cotton pickers or singing spirituals. African Americans felt degraded and discontinued performing. Most of the proceeds of these events have gone to the white community. Moves to lift up a more truthful and inclusive picture of Natchez history raised the specter of lost tourist dollars with the consequent economic impact on the community as a whole.

Yet nineteenth-century Natchez was also home to several distinguished and wealthy free African Americans. In 1879, Hiram Rhodes Revels, a barber and pastor of the AME Church, became the first African American to serve in the U.S. Senate. A former slave, John Lynch, served as speaker of the Mississippi House of Representatives and won election to Congress during the postwar Reconstruction period. Elizabeth Taylor Greenfield, the "Black Swan," was America's first African American concert singer. Born into slavery in Natchez, she sang before Queen Victoria in London in 1853.

African Americans and European Americans are present in equal numbers in a population of twenty-six thousand residents. In 1995, the Natchez–Adams County Chamber of Commerce initiated a thirty-one-member Unification Committee in response to the fact that the Chamber did not reflect the diversity of the Natchez community. Although the committee was designed in part to improve race relations, it was having difficulty getting full participation from African Americans.

Tee Turner and I flew to Jackson, picked up a rental car, and drove south on the Natchez Trace, the parkway commemorating the ancient trail connecting southern portions of the Mississippi River, through Alabama, to salt licks in today's central Tennessee. The Cherokee, Choctaw, and Chickasaw nations first blazed the path, which was later expanded by European settlers.

Frances Trosclair and Alma Fletcher, the African American cochair of the Unification Committee, had turned out practically the entire city leadership of Natchez—including the chairman of the Chamber of Commerce, the police chief, the school superintendent, a senior banker, a city alderman, and heads of grassroots organizations—for a workshop on the reconciliation process employed in Richmond. A survey of the forty-four participants revealed that even African Americans in leadership positions "did not feel a full sense of ownership in the key areas of decision making." Most European Americans said that African Americans "see racism where it does not exist." However, nearly all respondents of both races agreed that "a white child in Natchez has a much better chance of achieving economic success in his or her lifetime than a black child."[1]

During this and other public workshops, and in subsequent strategy sessions and small-group dialogues that took place over the following three years, key areas of concern emerged. Topping the list were the social separation of blacks and whites in churches and in schools (the high school had separate proms for blacks and whites); the quality of public education; and economic development and equity in job opportunities. Also among the priorities was the desire for greater recognition of the role of African Americans in the portrayal of local history and the promotion of histori-

cal research, including documentation of oral history. Many participants
stressed the need for reconciliation and healing between the races.

As a community known for gentility—at least in public—Natchez faced
difficulties in moving to open dialogue. (As early as the mid-1980s, Frances
Trosclair and a few others had stirred debate by proposing to establish a
small biracial committee to act as a community listening post and to ad-
vise the city and county governments on issues involving race.) Some in the
Unification Committee urged less emphasis on small-group explorations of
honest feelings about race; they wished to concentrate on action to promote
more equal opportunities in the community and to improve the school system. Others wanted a communitywide activity around acknowledging local
history. But several spoke in favor of exploring racial divisions at a more personal level within the group, with a view to "owning this history and expel-
ling its demons with forgiveness and reconciliation." Alma Fletcher called
for a parallel approach: a communitywide call to action and a continued
effort by the focus group to work to know and understand each other.[2]

A dozen Natchez leaders—businesspeople, clergy, grassroots organizers, and government officials—took part in facilitation training and a six-
part dialogue. The president of the Chamber of Commerce, who had earlier
questioned the value of dialogues on race, joined a training session led by
Cricket White and Tee Turner. "I've learned something from each one of
you here," he said. "Those are things I won't forget for the rest of my life."
In her evaluation, Trosclair declared it the best and deepest experience of
interracial dialogue to occur in Natchez.[3]

But the effort was hard to sustain. Trosclair and Fletcher, two remarkable women with a passion for racial reconciliation and high credibility in
the community, were able to convene "movers and shakers" and keep them
at the table. They demonstrated interracial partnership based on honesty
and respect. But community organizing for racial dialogue is hugely time-
consuming and emotionally demanding. Fletcher was embroiled in labor
disputes at work, and Trosclair was also overextended. In time, others took
over the leadership of the project. They, too, found it difficult to maintain
focus and momentum. One wrote to Hope in the Cities: "There are many
wonderful people here, their hearts and minds are in the right places, but
are unable to come together to confront the issues you stand for. . . . There
are several of us from the original committee who will continue to work
towards the goals in a very quiet and useful way."[4]

Local sensitivities also appeared to be a factor. Some of the impetus for change was championed by newcomers. The president of the Chamber of Commerce had moved from Los Angeles five years earlier; and the new co-chairs of the Unification Committee were also non-Natchezians. Several of the original committee members withdrew from active participation. Frances Trosclair says that racial separation in churches and schools "continues with very little improvement." There had been "a minimal effort" to encourage African American participation in the Spring Pilgrimage.

But whatever its shortcomings, the Trosclair-Fletcher initiative came at an opportune moment and gave timely support to a movement for change that is still emerging. The dialogues coincided with such important new developments as the inauguration of African American history tours and the relocation of a Museum of African American History and Culture at a prominent site.[5] Many Natchezians believe it is time to come together to embrace their shared history and create models of partnership and interracial relationships built on mutual respect and caring. They are committed to building a community that honors the stories of all its citizens and where opportunity is open to everyone regardless of race.

In 2004 the city elected its second African American mayor in its long history.[6] The new mayor, Philip West, stressed themes of unity and jobs; but he also made a priority of asking the owners of the city's antebellum mansions to present a balanced picture of plantation life, telling a reporter, "It's been a kind of a love-hate thing, but now I think the hate would be subsiding . . . because all of us recognize that we must embrace the real truth about who we are . . . in order to be able to move forward for the future."[7]

In April 2008, after thirteen years of community advocacy, the unveiling and dedication of interpretive signs at Forks of the Road, the former site of the slave trading market, signaled another step in the region's readiness to confront its history and open the way to healing and reconciliation.

### Oregon Uniting

It would be hard to find a community more different from Natchez than Portland, Oregon. This city in America's Northwest was founded in the 1840s while Natchez traces its history to 1716. Portland's population of over 550,000 is twenty times that of the Mississippi city. Oregon is known for its liberal values while Mississippi is steeped in a conservative southern culture. Whereas the Natchez population is evenly divided between African Americans and European Americans, the Portland metropolitan region's minority population stands at about 17 percent, with about 2.5 percent black, 5.2 percent Asian, and 9.3 percent Hispanic.[8] The state of Oregon itself is overwhelmingly white. African Americans and Asians account for just 2 and 3.4 percent respectively. The rapidly growing Hispanic population stands at 10 percent of the population, an increase of about 150 percent in the past decade. The public schools were 20 percent Hispanic in 2007. There is a small but significant Native American population.

Despite their differences, Portland and Natchez share at least one thing in common: the need to talk about racial inclusion and justice. The author Michael Henderson notes, "Oregon's whiteness is not altogether accidental."[9] In 1849, the Territorial Legislature passed a resolution banning "Negroes and mulattos" from living in Oregon for fear that by intermingling with the Native American population they might instill "feelings of hostility against the white race."[10] The legislation was repealed in 1926. Although never fully enforced, it promoted a spirit of exclusion that, according to many minority groups, continues to this day. An editorial in the *Salem Statesman Journal* said that the act "provided the justification for other discriminatory laws that were enforced for nearly 100 years and helped shape racist attitudes that persist today."[11] And as Henderson observes, "It was not a question of 'Come and visit but don't stay,' as one Oregon governor famously told tourists, but 'Don't come at all.'"[12] Indeed, one black Hope in the Cities coworker says that the only time she was subjected to public verbal racial abuse was in Portland. Despite its liberal reputation, minorities have often remarked on Oregon's hard racial attitudes.

All the more surprising, therefore, was the action by elected leaders on April 22, 1999. Prompted by a Portland-based coalition, Oregon formally acknowledged its discriminatory racial history at a "Day of Acknowledgment" at the State Capitol. A resolution passed by the state legislature, and signed by the president of the Senate and the Speaker of the House, stated that Oregon's history had been "marred by racial discrimination, exclusion, bigotry, and great injustice towards people of color," including Native Americans, African Americans, Latinos, Chinese Americans, Japanese Americans, and Pacific Islanders. In particular, the resolution noted the 150th anniversary of the notorious Exclusionary Act of 1849. The Senate passed the resolution unanimously, but in the House seven members abstained. In the debate, which was videotaped, one dissenter said, "I don't believe we serve ourselves well by recalling a painful past." Another remarked, "What really counts is what we do today, and in the future, not to engage in symbolism but in substance."[13]

In introducing the resolution, its author, Rep. Anitra Rasmussen, had said: "We as Americans have a particularly shallow connection to our history. . . . It is easy for us to deny any connection to the actions of people long dead, for it is part of our culture to believe that we can always start fresh, to start over without obligation to the past." The less pleasant aspect of Oregon's racial history was not taught in schools, Rasmussen noted; "but mark my words, it is remembered, and it lies close to the surface waiting to be told."[14] Importantly, the resolution not only called on Oregonians to acknowledge the wrongs of their state's past but to celebrate its heroes who stood up for justice. It concluded by urging "constructive dialogues and actions as we work towards a future of equality."[15]

Nearly eight hundred members of the public packed the House Chamber at the invitation of the Speaker. Former U.S. senator Mark Hatfield, who in 1953 had sponsored the country's first public accommodations act, and Myrlie Evers-Williams, a former NAACP leader and widow of the slain Mississippi civil rights leader Medgar Evers, served as cochairs. Notwithstanding some controversy over the House votes, a widely published AP account reported: "There were no words of anger or blame at the ceremony, when Oregonians, of all colors and religions, packed a House chamber. Buffalo soldiers dressed in traditional navy-blue uniforms and Native Americans with feathered head-dresses posted the flags. The House swelled with song as former Rep. Margaret Carter led the crowd in a rendition of 'The Battle Hymn of the Republic.'"[16]

The governor said it was not easy for some people to come to an event that spoke to Oregon's racist past, but "Oregon will not be a good place to live unless it is a good place for all of us to live."[17]

Anitra Rasmussen, whose conviction ensured passage of the resolution, had been stirred to action by a visit to South Africa. Fresh from this experience, she joined a group in Portland that was already in the initial stages of planning a strategy to persuade legislators to publicly express sorrow for the 1849 law and to commit to a new future of respect and equality.[18]

The organizing group, later called Oregon Uniting (OU), began as a grassroots coalition of individuals and organizations committed to advancing racial reconciliation and justice in Oregon. It was founded in 1997 in response to Hope in the Cities' call for honest conversation. In November 1997, Hope in the Cities' parent organization, Initiatives of Change, sponsored a conference at Portland State University on healing the wounds of history and interracial dialogue, in association with the Urban League, the Ecumenical Ministries of Oregon, the Institute of Judaic Studies, and the city's Office of Neighborhood Associations. Its purpose was to establish ongoing dialogues among diverse ethnic, racial, and religious communities. Two hundred people attended, including some of Oregon Uniting's founding members. After the conference, some attendees wanted to build on the relationships they had established and to create a vision of a racially just and unified Oregon. From this shared ideal, Oregon Uniting was born.

For Rasmussen, the challenge was: "How do you deal with unconscious racism? How do you transform it, make it visible? And how do you deal with the fact that your home state, your birthplace, the land where the roots of the mighty Douglas fir reach as deep into your soul as it reaches into the soil—how do you deal with the fact that your state has such a racist history?" She said Richmond's walk through history and pioneering work in racial dialogue "showed us that there is something we can do further to heal not only the wound of the past but to forge a new future."[19]

Niki Toussaint, who served as OU executive director, describes the organizing strategy: "To get the state's political leadership to sign a resolution, we got the community involved. We asked educators, social change agents, religious organizations, city and county officials, and social service agencies across the state to sign similar resolutions to demonstrate citizen support. Our team identified two of the most well-known and respected Oregonians to carry our message of reconciliation [Mark Hatfield and Myrlie Evers-Williams]. To draw them in, we offered opportunities for each opinion leader to help OU define the project. Their support helped us gain entry to the House of Representatives and the Senate. When the state's political leadership came on board, our project became newsworthy."

Toussaint says OU was able to get bipartisan support because the event was framed in a way that was not perceived as divisive: "We chose to steer away from blame and focus instead on the efforts of all people of all races who had worked to overturn unjust legislation and make our state more inclusive. This conciliatory yet honest approach had wide appeal."

Following the Day of Acknowledgment and initial training by Hope in the Cities, Oregon Uniting rapidly expanded its program of dialogues in Portland, Eugene, and other parts of the state. To advance an oral history project on the unpublished history of early Oregon civil rights leaders, OU partnered with the Oregon Historical Society, which offered pro bono training for OU volunteers. In turn, OU agreed to archive the ethnographic audiotapes at the institution.

Working with educational leaders, OU began to institutionalize dialogues on race in some schools and universities. OU facilitators led students in several schools through eight to twelve hours of dialogue as part of their course work. At Portland State University, facilitators led freshmen through eight weeks of dialogue as part of some course requirements.

Oregon Uniting's "reconciliation team" was called on to help resolve race-related issues involving the Portland Public School Board. In the first case, the board needed to pursue intragroup healing after an African American board member made a public anti-Semitic statement about a colleague. OU also facilitated a dialogue for board members, the school superintendent, and minority students, after two hundred high school students signed a petition demanding cultural sensitivity training for teachers.

In 2003, OU members presented an eighth-grade curriculum to a regional educational conference. The curriculum contained previously unavailable research on a century of legislation that denied fundamental rights to minorities. It discussed the contemporary consequences of white preferential treatment, as well as the contribution to the state by Oregonians of color. OU developed the curriculum in response to two bills passed in the legislature following the Day of Acknowledgment. The lawmakers required the Department of Education to provide multicultural curricula to all Oregon schools. The bill had been repeatedly presented but pushed aside every session since 1993. Another measure passed required instruction in Oregon history and government in the state's schools, with stipulations that the courses include "all our stories."[20] Yet the state failed to authorize funding, and it had not been implemented. OU took up the challenge to make it happen.

In OU's Education Committee, OU volunteers worked alongside teachers and administrators from Portland Public Schools (including Title IX Indian Education), two other area school systems, and a private school. The Oregon Historical Society's education director worked on the committee, as did the directors of the Multicultural Resource Center and NCCJ. With funding provided by the Spirit Mountain Community Foundation, OU hired a curriculum development specialist from the Northwest Regional Education Laboratory to ensure the curriculum met state standards. OU also trained social science teachers to deliver the curriculum in a sensitive manner and to deal with controversies that might arise. In 2008, Portland Public Schools was the first school district to recommend *Beyond the Oregon Trail: Oregon's Untold History* as a textbook for eighth-grade social studies.

Other OU activities included the introduction of a corporate dialogue and a collaboration with an organization called Innovation Partners on a civic leadership project to get historically underrepresented groups onto boards and commissions.

Despite early success, Oregon Uniting leaders encountered great difficulty in sustaining the project. The mostly unplanned, rapid growth created the need to raise money to support the large cadre of volunteers and maintain OU's alliance infrastructure. Few of the leaders possessed skill in fund-raising. Added to this were the common difficulties encountered by social change initiatives, which, as Toussaint observes, are usually launched by "innovative self-starters who like changes, are willing to take risks, work long hours, and make short-term sacrifices for long-term success." Toussaint herself worked without salary for a period.

Organizational development requires structure and the recruitment of good managers. The transition can be difficult, and tension may arise between the original visionaries and managers. Despite heroic efforts, OU was unable to make this transition. When funding did not materialize, feelings of incompetence and/or self-disappointment were projected onto teammates. All Asian American and Latino leaders and several whites pulled out, leaving a mostly African American board. Conflict intensified as financial pressures increased. "By the time new board members were recruited, the core leadership was already emotionally torn up," says Toussaint. New board members tended to avoid honest dialogue, focusing instead on fiscal management and mergers.

In some cases, personality conflicts and resistance to embracing the "personal change" aspect central to the Hope in the Cities process added to the stress. Although lack of fund-raising know-how was the major challenge, Toussaint acknowledges that a more intentional focus on spirituality and team building would have helped.

In the end, OU chose to merge with another leading diversity organization with a similar mission, the Understanding Racism Foundation, several of whose board had also been founders of OU. The new organization, Uniting to Understand Racism, continues to promote honest conversation and education toward the goal of reconciliation and justice.[21]

## Dayton Dialogues

Dayton, Ohio, is a gritty, hardworking community in the Miami Valley, fifty miles north of Cincinnati. In 2003, the city proudly celebrated the achievement of its most famous native sons, the Wright brothers, who ran a bicycle shop on West Third Street. On December 17, 1903, they flew the first powered aircraft in controlled flight at Kitty Hawk, North Carolina, earning the city its reputation as the "birthplace of aviation." Over the years, Dayton made a name for itself as a home of inventions: parachutes, cash registers, movie projectors, motorized wheelchairs, and microfiche are all products of creative Dayton minds. During World War II, the Wright-Patterson Air Force Base became a hive of activity, and is still one of the region's largest employers.

Dayton's history of race relations, like the rest of Ohio, is complex. In the mid-eighteenth century, French trappers and Scots-Irish settlers arriving in the Miami Valley encountered the Miami and Shawnee Indians. A long period of uneasy relations, frequently punctuated by violence, ensued between natives and newcomers.

By the middle of the nineteenth century, Irish and Germans were arriving in large numbers. The German influence was so strong that instruction in public schools was given in German, and bilingual teaching continued until early in the twentieth century. The black population grew slowly, discouraged by Ohio's notorious "Black Laws." One year after joining the Union in 1803, Ohio passed legislation requiring blacks entering the state to present certificates of freedom. No white person could employ a black person without such certification. Anyone breaking this rule, or harboring an escaped slave, was subject to fines. In 1807, the law was toughened still further: blacks now had to provide a bond of five hundred dollars signed by two white men within twenty days of entering Ohio.

Dayton experienced its first race riot in 1841. But the region was also notable for its Underground Railroad stations, which gave refuge to escap-

ing slaves on their way to freedom in Canada. Montgomery County sup-
plied six thousand soldiers to the Union army, more than half of them from
Dayton.

As Dayton's industry grew, stimulated by World War I, large numbers
of African Americans migrated from the Deep South. They encountered
whites from Appalachia who were also looking for jobs. In many ways, the
groups were similar: both knew poverty and poor schools. They had large
families and no experience of living in the city. Many brought with them a
deep religious faith—and also their prejudices.[22]

In recent decades, Dayton has faced challenges familiar to many American metropolitan areas. Racial violence in the 1960s and school integration
in the 1970s speeded white flight to the suburbs; changing economic patterns led to a decline in the center city. Its population dipped below 150,000
within a sprawling metropolitan region of just under 950,000. Whites make
up about 53 percent of the population and blacks 43 percent; there is a small
Spanish-speaking population.

Dayton is polarized by class as well as race. It has a history of strong
union presence, and what one city official called "an unbridgeable chasm of
distrust between labor and management." Some unions have resisted inclusion of African Americans.

On a wet Tuesday in March 2006, the downtown streets were largely
deserted. Vacant stores and boarded-up buildings greeted the visitor. But
appearances were deceptive. Beneath the urban blight, a determined team
was weaving the fabric of new community relations.

Seated around an oval board table, hosted by Walter Ohlmann, the CEO
of a Dayton advertising association, members of the executive committee
of the Dayton Dialogue on Race Relations (DDRR) reflected on a remarkable ongoing story. The group included a federal judge, the recently retired
publisher of the *Dayton Daily News*, an African American pastor, a community activist, the head of the local mediation center, the director of the
city's Department of Recreation and Parks, and the executive director of
the Human Relations Council.

Since its first organizational meeting in 1999, DDRR has organized dialogues using the Hope in the Cities curriculum throughout the region, involving more than three thousand participants. According to a report to
the Dayton Foundation, in 2001 and 2002 alone, some 1,200 people took
part in eighty interracial dialogues.

"Understanding through Reconciliation and Action is an exciting initiative . . . by people who represent the community, religious, business, legal,
civil rights, governmental, education, media and community organizations
and who believe that our diversity is our greatest strength," the DDRR
Web site announced. The original Steering Committee of more than sixty
prominent community leaders of different racial and social backgrounds,
including the president of Wright State University, the Montgomery County sheriff, and an official from Dayton Firefighters Local 136. Leaders of the
Dayton public schools, nonprofit organizations, area banks and businesses,
the Jewish Federation, and the Catholic Archdiocese also lent support.

"We hope you believe, as we do, that we must honestly acknowledge our
racial history and that everyone who has a stake in the process must come
to the table," say the organizers. "If you want to do more than talk but you
want to act then we invite you to . . . learn how you can take personal responsibility to be involved in the process of transformation that will help
create the kind of communities that are fair and just and that we and our
families deserve."

DDRR emphasizes that "true racial healing requires teams of committed individuals who are prepared to work together over a longer period and are willing to model the kind of change they are calling for in the
community."

To a visitor's question, "What is the glue that has kept you together?"
Robert "Yogi" Hamilton, of 27 Good Black Men, responded: "You can have
all the best organization and commitment, but unless you have a hunger in
the community for what you have to offer, it won't go far. Dayton has a hunger for what the dialogues offer. We've had so many volunteers we've had to
cut it off. Sometimes, the problems seem so large. The dialogues give people
an opportunity to make a difference."

Brad Tillson agreed: "Dayton is receptive in ways that other communities are not." Tillson's parents were involved in the civil rights movement,
were personal friends of Stokely Carmichael, and participated in the voting
rights marches of 1965 in Selma, Alabama. Tillson arrived in Dayton in 1971
as a young reporter to work for the *Dayton Daily News.* He became CEO
and publisher in 1996. In 2003, he received the Citizen Legion of Honor
Award as the region's outstanding community leader.

Jerald Steed, who directs the Human Relations Commission, reported:
"We did a gut check a couple of years ago. And we found that most people

were still wedded to the project. This is not pretty work. It's not something people do unless they have a passion." Indeed, it is striking that many of the original leadership team are still active. In a field notorious for burn-out, the Dayton effort demonstrates remarkable stamina.

"Of course," added Steed, "it did not hurt to have a judge who has a passion, and who is willing to show up at any time with nothing to gain." The judge in question is Walter W. Rice, who has served on the U.S. District Court for Southern Ohio since 1980 and has been with DDRR since its inception. Known as "the moral conscience of the community" for his willingness to take on tough issues such as school desegregation, Rice told the press at the launch of the Dayton Dialogue, "This may be one of the most important initiatives in which I have ever been involved."[23] He cochairs DDRR with another highly regarded judge, Adele M. Riley, an African American, thus modeling the interracial partnership at the heart of the initiative.

Walter Rice offers two other clues to DDRR's sustainability. Noting the racial violence that rocked a larger neighboring city in 2001, he says: "Cincinnati went to the brink and fell off. We have pledged not to do the same." An exhausting day of travel the day before the interview and a painful back condition have not dampened Rice's enthusiasm. Born in 1937 into a Jewish family in Pittsburgh, he explains: "My parents always taught me that differences of race didn't matter a hill of beans. But I've never felt it in my guts as I have in these dialogues, never at the emotional level. The dialogues reinforced what I always knew in my head but am increasingly feeling in my heart."

Cathy Shanklin grew up poor in an Alabama community dominated by the KKK. She did much of the initial organizing of the dialogue project, as assistant director of the Human Relations Commission: "We took three years to develop the model. We had strong parents with Hope in the Cities, but we created our own identity. By taking that time, which was sometimes grueling, we came up with something that hits at the very core of the community. We have had the tenacity to hold fast to the foundation and the focus has not become blurred."

Although the first dialogues were general, community-based events, many subsequently took place within organizations including local banks and other businesses, churches, and colleges. One hundred Montgomery County employees took part. Such dialogues are easier to organize and offer more potential for sustaining relationships. Often the groups adopt action plans such as working on Habitat for Humanity projects, taking part in the annual Martin Luther King Jr. march, neighborhood cleanup projects, or monthly luncheon meetings. DDRR also responded to requests for help from the public schools. When violence broke out in one school, "We found the problem was not so much the students but the teachers who are mostly white, and who are functioning in a majority black environment," said one facilitator.

The Dayton Dialogue keeps in the public eye with a monthly television program on the local government access channel and events that allow larger numbers of people to experience "a taste of dialogue."

However, Shanklin emphasizes the power of "in-home" dialogues—conversations that take place in private homes in different parts of the city. It has proved much harder to organize and sustain these in-home dialogues, but "that is where you get to the root of the problem. That's where you get the word of mouth, that's where the segregation is. That's where people make decisions about where to send their kids to school."

Audrey Norman-Turner, the indefatigable dialogue coordinator until her death in 2006, had similar experiences: "Anyone who has engaged in the dialogue has to say that it is life-changing. This causes people to remain at the table. The in-home dialogue was my initial experience. There is a very special relationship that I formed because the husband of the host is challenged with cancer, as I am, and so we call each other. Without the in-home dialogue, our paths would never have crossed."

DDRR trained seventy facilitators who work in interracial pairs. They meet regularly to plan, share experiences, and encourage each other. One evening, a group of twenty gathered for a box dinner. After introductions, the visitor asked, "How has the experience of being a facilitator changed you?" At first the group was hesitant. "I've never asked myself that question before," said one. Then the stories began to flow.

"During the last three to four weeks I have become increasingly aware of my unconscious racism. And how costly and psychologically dangerous is the ground we are inviting people onto," said a white male in his forties. "I've been a racist for thirty years. All the people I've done work with are white. I work with white contractors, and I sell to white people. It's a challenge to walk away from solid relationships and build relationships with people I don't know. When a lot of people take the lid off that box, it's really scary. It's a real deep hole I'm looking down. When I hand the keys to someone's house to a subcontractor I've known, I feel I can trust him. But when I hand the keys to someone I don't know, I'm taking a risk."

An African American woman said: "I went to Gettysburg, and for the first time I saw the total picture. Not North or South, but I thought of mothers and sons. I would never have thought of that before. My prayers were very segregated. I've made a conscious effort to be inclusive in my prayers."

Under the leadership of President Kim Goldenberg, Wright State University adopted the Hope in the Cities dialogue curriculum for use on the campus. It began with two dialogues in the homes of the president and the provost, with senior staff and heads of student government. Jacqueline McMillan, who served as executive assistant to Goldenberg, recalls an exchange between two staff members, black and white women who had both grown up in segregated Mississippi: "We were riveted, just seeing the two of them make connections."

Faculty and students take part in their own dialogues and train as facilitators. The university pays a modest stipend to faculty facilitators; it pays students by the hour and offers them credit. The university wants to create "learning communities" whose members take classes together and live in the same dorms. Dialogue is part of building these learning communities. "Students who form relationships early are more likely to finish," says McMillan. She adds that actions resulting from the dialogues are often very simple. "We can't change the world tomorrow, but we can decide to have grits in the cafeteria. It's the low-hanging fruit. People say if we can do this, we can do more."

By 2006, DDRR could look back on seven years of public engagement. In reviewing the Dayton story, I examined factors that enabled the project to sustain itself when so many similar efforts fragment. Much of its success is due to the commitment of the city's leaders. Valerie Lemmie, who served as Dayton's city manager before going on to lead the administration in Cincinnati, knew and appreciated the work of Hope in the Cities from her tenure as chief executive of Petersburg, twenty-five miles south of Richmond. In the spring of 1998, we began conversations about the feasibility of a Dayton dialogue, and that June I visited Dayton at the invitation of Rev. Robert Jones, a leading African American pastor, along with former *Cincinnati Enquirer* editorial writer Bob Webb. Jones had been inspired by the documentary film on Richmond's "honest conversation" and believed something similar was needed in Dayton.

Lemmie welcomed us at city hall for an exploratory meeting. She introduced City Commissioner Dean Lovelace; Jennie Roer, the regional director of the National Conference (now NCCJ); Sarah Harris, a former Montgomery County commissioner; and Cathy Shanklin, then assistant director
of the Human Relations Commission.

The University of Dayton had recently conducted the first comprehensive
survey of racial attitudes in the Dayton area for NCCJ, which was hosting a
series of single-event dialogues based on the survey results. Jennie Roer explained that the level of denial in Dayton among the white population was
such that they needed to be presented with the findings of the survey as a
first step in the dialogue process before issues of healing and reconciliation
could be addressed. Lemmie led the discussion, encouraging a collaborative effort with a Hope in the Cities initiative, and pledging the full support
of her office. She also backed up Rev. Jones's desire for a long-term initiative
commitment and a process that "moved from the head to the heart."

Commissioner Lovelace rapidly emerged as the champion and conven-
er of the dialogue project, providing crucial political backing to Lemmie's
conviction. He was to remain a steady but unobtrusive presence, lending a
strong and credible public voice.

Sarah Harris facilitated the start-up phase, which included an inventory
of all efforts for community building and racial justice and reconciliation in
the region: "We gathered all who are interested in race relations in Dayton.
We had people who were suspicious; they wanted to know if it was confrontational. We had people who were weary, tired, who said, 'We are going to
give you one more chance.' So we decided to build a strong infrastructure
that would sustain the effort. We've used a process that would bind folks
together for the long haul.

"We've not only gone to every civil rights organization like the Urban
League, NAACP, and the SCLC, but also to those who don't agree. People will say, 'I wasn't at the table,' so they don't buy in. But some of those
who do come don't want to be with others they find there! We started by
asking people, what does community mean to you personally? It was an
eye-opener."[24]

My colleague Geoffrey Pugh attended an early organizational meeting of
representatives of neighborhood groups, nonprofit organizations, and city
agencies on April 30, 1999. At the request of the local congressman, the
slavery-apology campaigner Tony Hall, Pugh wrote an account of the occa-

sion, noting that a few days earlier Bishop Herbert Thompson had described Dayton as "the most stratified city in the diocese, perhaps in the state." The conversation, reported Pugh, produced "a surprising level of honesty, with some emotion and much laughter." In the space of one hour, all sixteen leaders spoke, "with reality and not for effect," standing shoulder to shoulder with each other in spirit.[25]

Jerald Steed says the city's institutional support gave the group "time to test the water." The decision to invest two years in careful preparation, and the willingness of the leaders to engage in extensive "honest conversation" among themselves before going public, meant that the project was "building on rock, not on sand." Dayton leaders came to Richmond for intensive training in Hope in the Cities methods that fall, and Hope in the Cities also provided on-site facilitation training.

Commitment to "modeling the change" meant interracial leadership from the start. As the first cochairs, Walter Rice and Sarah Harris provided a white-black, male-female partnership of equals that spoke volumes.

A further contributing factor in Dayton's sustainability was faithfulness to the process. Facilitators emphasize that they trust the curriculum. "The more we do the dialogue, the more convinced I am of the model," says Rice. DDRR remains focused on its mission to "eradicate racism in the Miami Valley by building a community that values racial, religious, cultural interdependence and differences among all residents."

Finally, and perhaps most important, is a willingness to work out issues. "Sometimes organizations can implode from within," Steed observes. "It's hard for strong-willed people to work together. People have stayed the course—and there are no shrinking violets here! People are committed to the issues more than personalities."

The death of Audrey Norman-Turner was a severe loss to the network. But Cathy Shanklin became executive director in 2009. To some extent, DDRR is a victim of its own success. Some facilitators would like to have more flexibility in using the curriculum, but because it has worked so well in the past, the project leaders are reluctant to allow improvisation. There is also the challenge of funding, most of which has come from city or county government. In addition, Walter Rice believes DDRR is not doing well enough in reaching those who fled the city: "We've got to show that this is everyone's problem."

Dayton remains a deeply divided city. Loss of jobs, a residential exodus, and an influx of immigrants add to the stress. In May 2007, an education levy to raise $15.17 million for the Dayton public schools failed dramatically, with the voting falling largely along racial lines: West Dayton voted in favor and East Dayton voted against. But Rice and other leaders believe the issue goes beyond race to a lack of understanding and a breakdown of trust.

Relations between the black community and the police force, still more than 90 percent white, are strained. In 2006, controversy erupted over a speaker at a Black History Month event. Twenty years earlier, a sixteen-year-old black youth was convicted for his role in the fatal shooting of a police officer. In prison, experiencing remorse, he decided to turn his life around and earned a law degree. But police officers and their families protested bitterly that he should not be held up as a role model; they took the matter to city hall.

"It hurts me personally that this is still going on. We all fall into the trap of not hearing each other," says facilitator Tom Wahlrab, who coordinates the Dayton Mediation Center. "It's a dangerous place that we paddle around in. This dialogue is not the answer to everything. But it would be different if we did not have the dialogue. We need a process that brings people together to connect with each other, not just commissions where people pontificate."

I put it to Tillson, as a pragmatic journalist, "If someone were to ask you how Dayton is different as a result of the dialogue, what would you point to?" Tillson responded: "I'd be careful not to claim any final successes because I don't believe there are any in this area. That said, I think DDRR has given 'talk' a good name in Dayton. There is a sense in the community that talking can be an important element of dealing with this issue. It's not a substitute for action and change, but it is not wasted energy. This strikes me as very important because, when the going gets tough, the first opportunity for conciliation is talk and if the community is receptive to that it can make a difference."

**Lessons**

The examples of Portland, Natchez, and Dayton highlight the possibilities and the challenges facing local organizations dedicated to working for honest conversation across race and class divisions. From 1998 to 2000, in addition to the three cities already mentioned, Hope in the Cities trained community facilitators in Camden, New Jersey; Baltimore, Maryland; Hartford, Connecticut; Selma, Alabama; and Norfolk, Virginia. The project included training weekends in Richmond for fifty representatives of these partner communities.

In their assessment, Hope in the Cities leaders outlined several lessons and challenges:

1. IT QUICKLY BECAME CLEAR THAT IN SOME COMMUNITIES FOR-MAL DIALOGUES WERE ACTUALLY SECONDARY TO FORMING AN IN-TERRACIAL CORE GROUP WILLING TO WORK TOGETHER ON ITS OWN RELATIONSHIPS AS WELL AS ON ISSUES WITHIN THE COMMUNITY. In every case, the process of building a viable team in a locality was long and difficult, and in some cases ultimately unsuccessful. But it was impor-tant to be satisfied with small steps and for the local community organizers to know that Hope in the Cities was committed to them for the long term as people, not just as "project participants."

Success does not mean a specific number of dialogues or public events. The work has to be seen in a larger perspective of improved communication and partnership across traditional divides in the community as a whole.

Selma, Alabama, is known throughout the world for pictures of police with clubs, dogs, and water cannons assaulting voting rights marchers in 1965. One Selmian said, "We are dealing here with the last vestiges of slavery."

Although it was difficult to sustain formal dialogues in Selma, local lead-ers said that the trust and relationships formed between people of different races generated a united community spirit that encouraged economic de-velopment initiatives, including a twenty-one-house "blitz-build" by Habi-tat for Humanity, with the involvement of the Department of Housing and Urban Development, and the support of the Enterprise Foundation in cre-ating a Community Development Corporation. Councilman Yusuf Abdus-Salaam, who first brought Hope in the Cities to Selma, said, "Much of what is being done now was made possible by Hope in the Cities' work of building bridges across racial lines."[26]

On March 7, 1999, black and white Selmians walked side by side behind a Hope in the Cities banner on the thirty-fourth anniversary of the Selma to Montgomery march. Previously most whites had avoided the anniversary marches because of the intense feelings they aroused. Two months later, 250 people gathered at the historic St. James Hotel for a banquet celebrating

"Hope for Unity in Selma" and featuring the former governor of Mississippi, William Winter, who had served on Clinton's race initiative.

Yusuf Abdus-Salaam, now serving as a state representative, says, "The key to Selma's future is that you have large numbers of whites willing to take an open stand on issues that only the most courageous progressive would take in private in the sixties."[27]

One of the Selma Hope in the Cities organizers, Lawrence Wofford, founded the Democracy Project, a summer leadership institute for fourteen-year-old black youths, culminating in a three-day journey to civil rights memorials. Wofford said he wanted the boys to "learn the need to sacrifice something to make change for the greater good of the society."

2. THE NEED TO CREATE A SOLID INSTITUTIONAL BASE CANNOT BE OVEREMPHASIZED. Busy people often find it difficult to commit themselves to a series of dialogues spread over several weeks. One of the biggest challenges is creating a process that is "doable" for a group of volunteers. The amount of time needed to organize and maintain networks places a significant burden on local organizers, most of whom are already heavily committed to other work in the community. Dayton was successful because the city government was prepared to fund a staff position and provide some infrastructure. But the work of building a sustainable movement is not purely an organizational function. It requires individuals who are able to think beyond the usual structures and procedures and have an intuitive sense of how to work within an organic process that is constantly evolving. Frequently, the most significant aspect of the work is seen in the strategic engagement of individuals outside of a formal dialogue structure or other program activity.

3. INHERENT IN THE DIALOGUE PROCESS IS THE TENSION BE-TWEEN TALK AND ACTION. As Paige Chargois puts it: "We need these same folks to get back to where they live and make that difference, so that the clerks behind the counter can be different, so that the preachers in the pulpit will be different, so that the car salesman won't give a different price to a black person than a white person. . . . [W]here you need to take this learning and this experience is back into your own home." But without some sense of common strategy and support, individuals easily slip back into the comfort of old ways or become disheartened and disillusioned. Every group needs to maintain a balance between contemplative and active

work. Different people require different levels of each, and it is important to be aware of the needs of individuals to avoid frustration.

4. OFTEN THERE IS A NEED FOR HONEST DIALOGUE AND/OR REC-ONCILIATION WITHIN RACIAL/ETHNIC GROUPS AS WELL AS BE-TWEEN GROUPS. In one city, there was division between two factions in the African American community that were both supposedly working for racial justice. In some contexts it may be essential to enable dialogue participants to talk within affinity groups.

5. PARTNERS IN DIFFERENT CITIES RESPONDED DIFFERENTLY TO THE EMOTIONAL AND SPIRITUAL DIMENSIONS OF RACIAL HEALING. In southern cities like Natchez and Selma, where social values of graciousness and hospitality are revered, individuals of different races interact more often and more intimately. The Natchez dialogues are notable for the fact that each one took place in a different home. But there are exceedingly strong pressures not to "rock the boat" past the level of graciousness, and there is often a lack of sophistication around the concept of "white privilege." However, prayer is a strong underlying current in the South, and blacks and whites could come together around the concept of spiritual centeredness. For many African Americans, especially in the South, the concept of reconciliation is rooted in spiritual, if not religious, experience. Activists in northern cites like Portland or Hartford might have a much greater sophistication and comfort level with racial concepts, but they are often intractably segregated emotionally, psychologically, and physically. Their personal relationships with people of other races are often professionally, organizationally, or intellectually based. The unifying belief in prayer and spirituality as a basis for common life is often missing, if not actually eschewed.

6. THE INVOLVEMENT OF POLITICAL LEADERS AT THE BEGINNING OF THE PROCESS MAY JEOPARDIZE ACCEPTANCE OF THE PROCESS FOR SOME PARTICIPANTS BECAUSE OF CYNICISM ABOUT GOVERN-MENT. HOWEVER, WITHOUT THE APPROVAL OR SANCTION OF LO-CAL POLITICAL LEADERS, THE PROJECT MAY BE SEEN AS DOOMED FROM THE START. In some cases, considerable time and effort is needed to overcome a history of mistrust resulting from failed initiatives, as well as

exploitation of communities for political purposes by organizations carrying out "studies" to fulfill project objectives and grant requirements.

....

Groups from cities that had initiated Hope in the Cities dialogues gathered at a national forum at Howard University in June 2001. The forum led to the creation of the National Coalition for Dialogue and Deliberation. Sandy Heierbacher, who coordinates NCDD, says several workshop participants began talking about the need to provide opportunities for dialogue and deliberation practitioners to experience each other's models, share strategies, and get to know their colleagues in the field. Cricket White of Hope in the Cities drew in other conference participants who had taken the lead in various dialogue and deliberation efforts.[28] "Her enthusiasm was infectious," says Heierbacher, whose organization now involves seven hundred organizations and individuals.

After a burst of activity in the late 1990s, several major foundations that had funded racial dialogue projects lost their enthusiasm for supporting efforts to resolve such seemingly intractable issues and moved to safer ground. The election of George Bush and the events of September 11, 2001, closed the door on any serious public discussion at the national level about race. It took Katrina to shock Americans (though sadly not their national leaders) into acknowledging the extreme social divides in the country, while the massive demonstrations by Hispanics in 2006 underscored the need for just and comprehensive immigration reform.

But despite the inability of national political leaders to take responsibility for racial issues, and the lack of funding for sustained work, local efforts continued and in some cases flourished. The Richmond journalist Michael Paul Williams wrote: "Race has become far too politically polarizing to be debated with much effect among heavy hitters on the national stage. The true hope may lie in the numerous local conversations springing up in cities such as Boston, Philadelphia, and yes, Richmond."[29]

Hope in the Cities concluded that its model of honest conversation was relevant to many localities, but that an ongoing investment would be needed to produce lasting change: "There can be little doubt that *given the necessary resources and willingness to sustain the effort* many more communities could be enabled to heal historic wounds and to build constructive partnerships."[30]

# Family Choices

Engaging
or Withdrawing?

In 2004, Andrew, our youngest son, graduated from high school. The end of our twenty-year involvement with Richmond's public schools coincided with the fiftieth anniversary of the historic Supreme Court ruling on segregation. But in the 2003–4 school year, twenty-one Richmond schools— nearly half of all elementary, middle, and high schools—had fewer than ten whites in their student bodies, and eight had none at all.[1]

Later that summer, I joined a forum of scholars and practitioners at the University of Denver to consider intergroup relations fifty years after *Brown v. Board of Education.* Tom Pettigrew, a leading social psychologist and researcher, said in his keynote address, "Integration has not failed; America has failed integration." According to Pettigrew, a 1974 Supreme Court ruling allowing suburban schools in Detroit, Michigan, to be protected from a metropolitan desegregation plan set the pattern for a national trend that allowed local jurisdictions to act as "racial Berlin walls."[2] Since then, he said, we have seen a "persistent use of non-racial reasons for anti-black attitudes and behavior." Pettigrew, who teaches at the University of California, Santa Cruz, is a native Richmonder and served as an expert witness for the Richmond School Board in the plan to consolidate the region's schools that was rejected by the Supreme Court.

In its July 28, 2007, ruling, the U.S. Supreme Court effectively buried *Brown* by outlawing even voluntary schemes to create racial balance, as practiced by Seattle and Louisville. In his dissent, Justice Breyer likened the inequality in the nation's schools to "a caste system rooted in the institution of slavery and 50 years of legalized subordination." Forty years after the assassination of Dr. Martin Luther King Jr., we had lost almost all the progress made in the decades after his death, say Gary Orfield and Chungmei Lee in their August 2007 report for the UCLA Civil Rights Project in which they note "accelerating isolation" and "profound inequality" of poor and minority students.[3]

In 2004–5, the four school systems of metropolitan Richmond (Chesterfield, Hanover, Henrico, and Richmond) served 146,500 students. Overall, 54 percent of students were white and 46 percent were black; 36 percent were from low-income families and entitled to free or reduced lunch (the indicator used to estimate the level of poverty in the student body).[4] Given these demographics, one might consider schools with a 60/40 racial mix to be reasonably well integrated racially, and schools with a total of 20 to 40 percent disadvantaged students to be quite well integrated economically. Yet by these measures, only 12 percent of the region's schools could be described as racially integrated. There were just 1,886 white students in the city schools in 2004. Of these, 662 were concentrated in two popular elementary schools and 121 in one high school. In addition, the city's public schools are losing students. In 2004, the total student enrollment of 12,814 at the elementary level stood in stark contrast to the 5,848 in high school. And while there were 2,091 students in ninth grade, the number plunged to 1,110 at the senior year, an alarming loss.[5]

Separation by race and class is closely linked. Only 24 percent of the region's schools are economically integrated (i.e., 20 to 40 percent of students receiving free or reduced lunch). In the schools that are mostly or entirely black, more than 65 percent of children live in homes with very low income. According to Housing Opportunities Made Equal, poverty is concentrated in thirty-one neighborhoods, which are home to 10 percent of the region's population, but 40 percent of its poor, 28 percent of whom are children. In 2003, only 39 percent of schools serving this population achieved full state accreditation, compared with 77 percent in the region as a whole. Thanks to determined efforts by dedicated teachers and mentors, this statistic had changed dramatically for the better by 2007, as we shall see in the next chapter.

Issues of economic disparity are not confined to the city schools. Significant differences exist within county jurisdictions as well. Some schools in eastern Henrico County are 80 percent black and low-income, while others in the more affluent neighborhoods in the west are 85 percent white, with no students on free or reduced lunch. In the metropolitan region as a whole, 57 percent of schools underperformed the State Standard of Learning average in 2004–5.[6]

Few things arouse such deep emotion and provoke such polarizing debate as the education of our children. Nowhere—except in our churches—are the racial divisions so glaring. When Susan and I came to live in Richmond, we knew that our commitment to racial reconciliation meant investing our family fully in the community. Deciding to place our three boys in public schools was part of that commitment. But the truth is, we never debated it very much. Coming from Europe, where nearly every child goes to state schools, it seemed the natural thing to do. In any case, we could not have afforded private education.

We chose to live in an integrated neighborhood less than a mile from John B. Cary Elementary School, a highly regarded "model" school focusing on experimental and innovative enrichment programs. A citywide lottery, weighted to achieve a balance of race and gender, determined selection. Anxious parents would crowd city hall to witness the drawing of names.

The students regarded the principal, Dr. Cooley, with awe and affection. He would greet them every morning on the steps of the school, a slim cigar between his lips. At graduation he appeared, to wild applause, in a spotless white suit. Cooley was an excellent administrator who ruled the school with a firm but restrained hand, and allowed his gifted team of teachers to work without interference. Cary's test scores always surpassed other city schools; this was not surprising, given the excellence of the staff and the commitment of the parents, who were mostly well educated and middle-class.

Later, when selection by lottery ended and Cary became a neighborhood school, the number of minority students from lower-income families increased. At a heated meeting of the Parent Teacher Association, a pony-tailed, white baby boomer rose to protest the trend: "We are proud of our diversity in this school, but we don't want to have too much diversity!"

Participating in an urban school system is hard work requiring constant vigilance. A friend described it as an emotional roller coaster. We all want safe, nurturing, and intellectually stimulating environments for our children. Competition for college places grows ever fiercer. Should we risk our child's education for the sake of a utopian dream of community harmony? Corey Nicholson, a successful young African American attorney, says: "I discussed with my friends about putting our kids into public schools. From the reaction, you would have thought I had molested their child!"

Yet researchers conclude that a diverse student body promotes learning outcomes[7] and better prepares students for an increasingly diverse workforce and society. But schools that are highly segregated by income or race deny children the opportunity to learn from those who are different, thus diminishing the quality of education. Scott E. Paige, in *The Difference: How the Power of Diversity Creates Better Groups, Firms, Schools, and Societies*, reports that scientific models prove that diverse groups of problem solvers can outperform groups of individuals with the highest IQs, who tend to think in the same way.[8] In his landmark 2001 study, Richard Kahlenberg highlights the particular benefits of economic integration.[9]

So why have we not integrated our schools? Do we not think it is important? "Young people don't believe we are committed to this issue," says Dr. J. Austin Brown, who served as principal of Richmond's Huguenot High School. Students are paying the price of inaction by adults. "They have waited long enough. We have failed them."

Brown himself did not wait. After a confrontation between Hispanic and African Americans in his school, he asked student leaders to produce a plan to build better relations in the school community. They wanted to hold a forum, but said their own school was not diverse enough for real dialogue, so they asked Brown for permission to arrange a partnership with James River High School in neighboring Chesterfield County.

The contrast between the two schools illustrates the racial and socioeconomic divisions typical of many metropolitan regions. In 2004, Huguenot's student population was close to 90 percent black, 7 percent white, with a small but growing number of Hispanics and Asians. Just three miles to the west, James River was more than 70 percent white, about 15 percent black, with a significant Hispanic and Asian population. Both schools were fortunate in their dynamic, innovative, and dedicated principals, and both schools were doing well academically, but students at Huguenot felt keenly their lack of opportunity to experience diversity.

Brown contacted John Titus, his counterpart at James River, and gave the go-ahead for the forum. The students planned the agenda and chose their own moderator. They told Brown, "We want you to be there but not to lead it." The forum was a huge success as 250 students shared stories and viewpoints with one another. "It was what they desperately wanted," says Brown. "My one regret is that we did not follow up. The kids wanted to do a follow-up project, but we let them down."

Brown is clear where the responsibility for change lies. "The dialogue must involve those who can make things happen." He cites the need for area principals to come together and talk about these tough questions, something that rarely happens now. "But we meet together about our football programs because we think it's important!"

Clara Silverstein was part of the first wave of integration in the early 1970s, a decade before our eldest son began school. She and thousands of other Richmond students were "bused" across the city in an effort to achieve a better balance. Silverstein attended some of the same schools as our sons and encountered indifference, disdain, and hostility. Now an editor at the *Boston Globe*, she recalls her experiences: "I see myself creeping around linoleum corridors, hunched over, afraid someone is going to trip me as I walk." Former black friends ignored her; she was pushed and stared at. The attitude was, "Shut up and put up. No one wants you to complain. No one wants you here at all."[10]

Children can be cruel, but what struck me most about Silverstein's story was the complete lack of adult support for the white children who were bused: "My voice is usually lost in the historical account of busing. Because I am white, nobody threw rocks at me. No police escorted me to my classroom. I graduated and can still enjoy the privileges of being white. But if I learned nothing else, I did come to understand the scourge of racism."

"There was no group like the NAACP to prepare white kids for our new school assignments. . . . Nobody addressed the day-to-day realities of what it might feel like to be a white child in the racial minority." African American children were supported by their peers, but whites received no support. Few adults encouraged them to stay in the system. Instead, there was disapproval. "When I explained that I was in a public school, and yes I would be bused, some looked surprised, while others actually gaped in horror. I was left to duck my head, mumble and wonder if there was something wrong with me."[11]

By the time our boys came along, overt racial hostility had lessened, although they say that they can fully identify with Silverstein's experience. Adults had learned that it was no longer politically correct to voice disapproval of integration. However, in some social settings, conversation would dry up when we mentioned our children went to the city's public schools.

Whites had been preparing to abandon the public schools in Richmond since the late 1950s. In 1956, Governor Harry Byrd announced a campaign of "Massive Resistance" to integration, and the Virginia General Assembly enacted legislation designed to obstruct compliance with the Supreme

Court ruling. The Assembly established the Pupil Placement Board to determine which students would be assigned to which schools. Theoretically, students could apply to any school, but in 1958, when six black pupils applied to join two all-white Richmond schools, all were turned down. (Neighboring Prince Edward County went as far as to close its schools from 1959 to 1964 to avoid integration. The State of Virginia then provided vouchers for the white students to attend private schools [see chap. 18].)

By 1963, out of 26,000 blacks in the Richmond schools, only 312 were enrolled in twelve white schools. In 1966, the Freedom of Choice plan allowed parents to choose any school—if space was available. Of course, it seldom was.

Finally, in 1970, Judge Robert Merhige ordered Richmond to come up with a plan to eliminate racially identifiable schools. At the start of that school year, 13,000 students out of a total of 50,000 were reassigned and "bused" to different schools. Governor Linwood Holton made national headlines when he personally escorted his daughter to John F. Kennedy High School, where she was the only white child in her class. But the spirit of resistance was still strong, and on the first day of school some five thousand white students were missing.[12]

The following year, frustrated by the slow progress, Merhige ordered mass busing of students, and on January 10, 1972, he approved a plan to merge the Richmond and Henrico County school systems. According to press reports, county residents drove to Washington in a convoy of 3,261 vehicles to express their outrage. Within four months, the Fourth Circuit Court of Appeals had overturned the merger, and in May 1973 the Supreme Court upheld the circuit court's decision by just one vote. But by then white flight had taken hold. Within a few years, only a handful of white students remained in the city, and the vast majority of African American professionals had joined the exodus to the suburbs.

As Richmond city schools struggled to meet the challenge of educating an increasing percentage of disadvantaged children, attention began to focus on what some regarded as an unfair distribution of state resources. The Virginia state formula for funding takes into consideration the wealth factor of the city, which is inaccurately inflated by its corporate structure. Consequently, Richmond is considered wealthier than Chesterfield, Hanover, and Henrico, and receives less money. In 1984, the Richmond School Board filed a lawsuit seeking $48 million from the state for an extensive remedial program to eliminate lingering vestiges of past state-mandated racial segregation. Ironically, it was Judge Merhige who dismissed the suit, ruling that problems in the city schools could not be blamed on the state's past segregation policies and that the city schools already received a large share of state education funds. In 1986, Merhige approved a neighborhood school plan to end busing.

Silverstein writes: "I hated Judge Merhige for not making his son go to the public schools. His father had ordered me to go to a school where I was tripped in the halls and spat on in the cafeteria, but had spared his own son that kind of treatment."[13] Silverstein notes that even the parents who started experimental public schools ended up sending their own kids to private schools: "Like many liberals, their political beliefs could not override their concerns about the success of their own children."[14]

History looks different depending on where you stand. Merhige endured extraordinary personal and public attacks. "The *News Leader* wrote such vitriolic things about Judge Merhige in 1971–72 that my wife and I considered settling elsewhere," said Judge Robert Payne, "but Judge Merhige faced with courage every day the people who spat on him, who killed his dog and threatened his children."[15]

### Our Sons Look Back

Susan and I entered the school system with naïve optimism. But over the years we had to confront the fears, insecurities, and pressures that inevitably arose. Our daily times of reflection were indispensable opportunities to examine our anxieties honestly, to maintain our inner equilibrium, and to find clarity about a particular course of action. These moments anchored us and confirmed our conviction that if we cared for the city, our children would also be cared for. This conviction was often tested.

"We did not realize how alone we would be," says Susan. And at first we weren't. Several white friends—including some neighbors—as well as black friends had kids of the same age in the same schools. "I think we all felt that we were in this together and that we were part of building something new in the schools," Susan recalls. "But as we progressed through the system, the number of whites steadily dwindled. Each year another friend would transfer to a county or private school."

In 1992, the national press reported that two Richmond elementary schools, in an attempt to encourage white participation, were "clustering" white children rather than distributing them evenly throughout all classes.[16] Parents who wanted to be involved in the public schools, but felt their children needed emotional support, suddenly found themselves depicted as racists. Rumors of segregation ran wild. Even though the administrators implementing the policy were black, the national media referenced a "Civil War mentality." Faced with public outcry, the school board was forced to review the policy. One board member, whose child attended one of the schools in question, found the experience so distressing that she left the city.

When Andrew was in fourth grade, a new principal caused great discontent among the staff with her authoritarian ways. Several of the best teachers indicated that they would seek a transfer. Repeated appeals for intervention from the PTA to the school administration went unanswered. Some parents decided to move their children. As we thought about what to do, we both agreed that Andrew was doing well and he was happy; there was no need to move. During the course of the summer, a new principal arrived, and none of the key staff left. However, by the time school started in September many parents had transferred to Mary Munford, an elementary school adjacent to the Windsor Farms neighborhood. Meanwhile, Andrew finished at Cary as the one white male in his class.

Despite its location in the heart of one of the wealthiest sections of the city, Munford was 97 percent black in 1976. In the late 1980s, white parents "rediscovered" the school, and by 2006, 68 percent of the children were white.[17] The story of Munford is a striking example of the "swings" that occur as middle-class parents, with the option of mobility, seek the best options for their children.[18]

A sense of abandonment sometimes weighed heavily, probably more on us as parents than on our three boys. "Most dispiriting was the impression that overall, the schools were no better at the end of our twenty years in the system than they were at the start," says Susan. "Our boys were fortunate in their teachers, but I always felt that the waters closed just behind Andrew."

All three boys went on to successful college careers. But compared with the available resources in county and private schools, it seemed like city kids were getting by on the second-best. "When in your senior high school year, there is no money for a yearbook and no soccer coach, it feels like

nobody cares," says Andrew, who graduated from American University in
2008. Saturdays would highlight the reality of Richmond's two worlds as we
dashed between city soccer league games played on a bumpy field, wedged
between Twenty-eighth and Twenty-ninth streets on Richmond's Southside, and the acres of immaculate, weed-free turf of the Richmond Strikers
soccer club at the rapidly growing far-west suburb of Short Pump.

In the course of writing this book, I asked Neil, Mark, and Andrew about
their experiences in the public schools: "Did we make the right choice in
putting you in the public schools? Do you feel that you were part of a social
experiment? Did you ever feel abandoned?"

"No," says Mark, who graduated cum laude from George Washington
University, "I felt very supported. But I do think that it's very hard for someone to do well in the city schools without support at home. Every one of my
friends who is going in the right direction had good family support."

Each of our sons states categorically that their experience prepared them
for the real world. They worry that so many of their contemporaries grow
up in culturally isolated environments. Mark says: "I was the only white
person I knew at college who could say, 'I know what it's like to be a minority.' Many of my black friends didn't know either. They went from practically all-black high schools to somewhere like Howard, so it wasn't until
after they graduated that they found out."

Andrew says: "I started at kindergarten, so being a minority was all I
knew. It was normal. At middle school there was some feeling of isolation
and loneliness. Becoming friends quickly with Vaughn and Corey helped;
they were very much into the black culture in school. They were my best
friends all the way to college. Through our church I also became good
friends with students at a local private school. Meeting their friends was often uncomfortable because they said things I thought to be very offensive.
I was even asked how I managed to go to school with so many black kids. It
was a weird feeling to feel almost like an outsider in your own race. But on
the other hand, I don't have many fears now about being in an uncomfortable setting or getting on with people. I feel like I'm a more independent
person."

As a freshman, Andrew secured an internship with our congressman,
Bobby Scott, an African American. He wrote home: "I am starting to real-
ize how ignorant some people are of other races. Everyone is shocked when
I tell them I'm from a 'black' school, or even that I'm working for a black

congressman. I don't think they are racist, just that they've never been exposed. . . . It's a different world. I'm trying to educate, but it's hard."

All three boys were late developers physically, and in their first years at Binford Middle School, they were dwarfed by some of their classmates. "As a small white male it felt like we went from a loving place at elementary school to what seemed like a youth detention center," Mark told me. "We had kids there who should have been in jail, kids dealing in drugs, stealing cars; there were fights. It was extremely racially divided. Most white kids and a few blacks were in honors classes, and then there were the rest. It was like two schools. It seemed like everyone was so angry in middle school. Of course it was partly the age." Neil agrees about the atmosphere but adds, "I could crush people at touch football because I was fast, even though small, so I got respect."

Although Binford held a reputation as the best middle school, its forbidding appearance did little to create a sense of comfort. "On the blacktop in one corner were all the black kids, and in the other all the white skateboard kids," says Andrew. "I had no problem hanging out with black people; but you had to be accepted, had to be cool, know how to act, and what to emphasize about yourself. You start in your comfort zone and move out. I would not have moved out but for Vaughn and Corey. In other settings, nobody ever guessed I was from a nearly all-black school."

On one occasion, Mark felt he was the victim of discrimination by a black female teacher who gave him an F for a paper and awarded consistently higher grades to African American girls for inferior work. The teacher was known to have a difficult personality, but Mark was a talker, and he had gotten on the wrong side of her early on. We discussed how he might make a friend of the teacher. Maybe she had experienced discrimination herself? In any case, we said, knowing what discrimination feels like is a valuable lesson in life. The important thing for Mark was to concentrate on passing the class. To his credit, he did his very best to build a positive relationship, and he passed the class with a C, which was a small victory.

Our boys grew up amidst a constant flow of people of different backgrounds and cultures who came to our home for meetings, meals, and often to spend the night. We wanted them to know that this was not just a home for them but a place to build a spirit of community. Although we sometimes talked about our world perspective and the things that were important to us, we rarely discussed our faith with them. We always said that we hoped

they would become people who cared about others and would make a positive difference in the world. None of them is religious in a formal sense. But
children observe their parents' attitudes and choices as they establish their
own values.

One day, when Neil was in seventh grade, he came home from school
to report a disturbing incident. The students had stepped off the bus that
morning to find racist graffiti, "F— the niggers," and a swastika painted on
the outside of the building. Immediately the students divided in two groups:
an angry African American group and a smaller scared white group. The
graffiti had been done by outsiders, but during the day fear and anger swept
through the school, and several white students were roughed up. One was
thrown down a staircase. The first boy to be assaulted cried out, "I'm Jewish—why would I put up a swastika?" Fortunately, no one was seriously
hurt, but the school had no public address system, and for a while things felt
out of control. Most white students called their parents. "My friend Chris
Brumfield and I were the only white kids who did not go home," said Neil.
"And most white students left the school at the end of that year."

As Neil described the frightening day he had lived through, he said,
"During the first period I really prayed at my desk and I know that is the
reason that nothing more serious happened." And then he said that a boy
in his class, an African American whom he didn't consider a close friend,
came to him and said, "I will walk with you today between classes to make
sure that nothing happens to you." So out of what was a difficult situation,
Neil learned two lessons: one in faith and one in friendship.

At fourteen, Neil's life took an unexpected turn when Phillips Exeter
Academy, a prestigious prep school in New Hampshire, offered him a full
scholarship. And so he made the move from an impoverished urban school
to an elite private school with the largest endowment in the country.

"Arriving at Exeter was like landing on the moon," he says. "It was the
most diverse school I had seen, with about 20 percent Asian and 10 percent black students. I got into an argument with my roommate because I
thought that the population of the U.S. was 50 percent African American!"

Mark and Andrew went on to Richmond Community High School,
founded in 1977 as the nation's first full-time, four-year, public high school
for academically talented students primarily from minority and low-income
families. Businessman-philanthropist Andrew J. Asch Jr., who provided the
initial funding, believed that bright students from less privileged families

should have the cultural and educational opportunities his own children had enjoyed. In 2005, the two hundred students of this school, with minimal facilities, achieved a 100 percent in reading and language arts and 98 percent in math in the state's Standard of Learning tests (SOLs). Typically, every graduating senior goes on to higher education. Mark's class of fifty accumulated offers of $5 million in scholarships and financial aid.

Mark says: "At Community High we were all friends. Race played no part. Everyone was expected to go to college. Most of my friends were black. Nobody felt uncomfortable; it was a safe space." Andrew won election as "mayor" in a predominantly African American school.

How have their experiences influenced their thinking today, and what are their views on education?

"Affirmative action? Not a solution," says Andrew. "It's a Band-aid on a giant cut. The real problem is that there is no program to fix education at the lower level." Andrew has two suggestions: combine high schools across jurisdictions and provide free choice. "People don't think about how to bring a really bad school up, they only worry about pulling a fantastic school down."

Mark contrasted his experiences at his university, where he was in "a $40 million building with multiple projectors and reclining chairs," with those at Richmond Community High School, "where sometimes we didn't even have textbooks. Our history book ended with Vietnam. We did not read the great classics. We only had three or four electives.

"I don't have any regrets. We all ended up in first-class universities. Sure, we had to work our butts off when we first got there. But the public schools did set us up socially by teaching us the thing that is fundamental in life: being with people who are different."

In Mark's view, private schools skim off the cream: "My friend A. J. went to Exeter and then to Yale, but he would have succeeded anywhere. Education all starts in the home. Kids pick up values very early in life. No matter how much money you pour in, if kids are not prepared, it's all for nothing."

Neil, who graduated from law school in 2008, says: "It's obvious from the system that nobody cares about the kids. So why would you expect them to act any differently? Fear of failure is stronger than desire for success." He recommends a year of college prep for all high school graduates.

He says: "A lot of who we are now has to do with the neighborhood and our childhood. We learned to manage conflicts, to deal with issues. When

Corey invited Andrew to sleep over it was a big deal. The big thing for me is when you hang out you talk the same with everyone; you don't use two different voices. If you can't speak the same, it means you are discriminating."

Susan concludes: "I guess I hoped that if our boys were in the public schools, some African American kid would have the experience of knowing at least one white person who was an OK guy, and it would help to break down some of the stereotypes. Equally, for our boys, if the black guy sitting next to them was better than them at math, or won the science prize, they are less likely to have negative images of African Americans."

I have included this family narrative because it is easy to talk in theory about racial integration in schools but hard to make choices when your own children are involved. The following chapter describes efforts to address the public policy issues involved in creating healthy, integrated public schools. But in the end, no policies will work without the support and participation of parents of all backgrounds who are willing to come together and talk honestly about their personal hopes and fears.

# If Every Child Were My Child

Race, Economics,
and Jurisdiction

Every Monday morning, Don Cowles drives the five miles from his home in Richmond's exclusive Windsor Farms to Woodville Elementary School. One hundred percent of the students are African Americans, and more than 90 percent come from low-income families.[1] Don works as a volunteer teacher's assistant and tutor. "Mentoring happens, but the fundamental thing is building relationships of equality across race and class," he says.

Cowles grew up as an "army brat," constantly on the move. He attended five high schools before going to Princeton. He says he saw this simply as "my family making a gift in support of public service." His father completed active duty with the U.S. Army in 1975 as deputy chief of staff for operations and plans, following service in World War II, in West Germany during the Berlin crisis, and in Vietnam, from which he helped to direct the withdrawal of U.S. forces.

Don met his wife, Jane, as a fellow congressional intern in Washington during their freshman year in college. They started married life with Don in law school, then moved to Manhattan, he with a law firm and Jane as a hospital administrator. Nine years later, seeking a different environment in which to raise a family, they got in their car and drove south. It was a choice between Charlotte and Richmond, and when a job opportunity came up for Don in Richmond, they took it. Jane chose to devote herself to the young family and to numerous school and community activities. They raised two daughters; their son, born prematurely, survived just a few days.

In 2001, after a successful business career during which he became a senior vice president with Reynolds Metals Company, Cowles felt a compelling urge to refocus his life. This personal turning point coincided with the acquisition of the company by Alcoa and a restructuring that offered the possibility of financial independence. "Assume everything you have done is

137

preparing you for the next step," was his guiding thought. In typically thorough fashion, Cowles shared his reflections in a six-page letter to his family. Looking back over fifty years, he saw that all his life—as an itinerant youth, lawyer, and businessman—he had been working to reconcile competing interests. Because of his transient childhood, and "having experienced both rejection and hospitality," Cowles says he "felt called to do something about building community." Early in 2002, he called me at the Hope in the Cities office. Over lunch a few days later, he asked me to accompany him in discerning, as he put it, "what I should do with the rest of my life." Within a few months, he had joined the Hope in the Cities board as Audrey Burton's cochair.

Cowles was already deeply committed to building new relationships across race and class through a promising new venture at St. Paul's Episcopal Church. Situated next to the Virginia State Capitol, St. Paul's blends conservative Richmond tradition with highly visible activism. In 1998, the vestry appointed a task force to identify a single project to which the congregation could devote its energies and resources, to "dream a dream that would change the world." Ruby Martin, a prominent member of the African American community who had served as secretary of administration in Governor Douglas Wilder's cabinet, led the task force, along with Buford Scott, a European American business leader. When Martin died in 2003, Scott continued their work. Ben Campbell facilitated the crucial early meetings. The vision that emerged challenged church members to "change their own pattern of thinking about themselves and the role and work of the church" and anticipated an "inside" and "outside" impact, "affecting and changing St. Paul's, its members and the city and counties that surround the Church." St. Paul's called this vision the Micah Initiative.[2]

At a series of public hearings, the city's school superintendent, the chairman of the school board, a school principal, juvenile and domestic judges, community activists, and leaders of nonprofit organizations shared their perspectives. These hearings highlighted the plight of at-risk children in the schools. It was evident that the public school system wanted to partner with churches and other groups that might augment what the schools themselves were able to do. Parents and caretakers of at-risk children needed skills training and support. Panelists urged St. Paul's to be prepared to stick with one project for a long time, not to "reinvent the wheel" but to

be bold and creative. Above all, they said, remember that "personal relationships are crucial."

The task force defined specific core values and criteria for the initiative:
spiritual transformation and racial reconciliation; a community-based process with opportunities for parishioners to serve, grow, and learn; inclusiveness as regards race, religion, gender, and age. It recommended Woodville
Elementary School, located near a public housing project in the city's East
End, as the site of the Micah Initiative. Don Cowles joined Betsy Carr, a
member of the task force, in leading the next stage of implementation. The
initiative started with just six volunteers. They recognized early on the importance of approaching the enterprise in a spirit of offering support rather
than with suggestions of how to "fix things." Relationships must be based
on equality, mutual respect, and learning, not paternalism. Building a solid
volunteer base preceded allocating large amounts of money. The head of the
Woodville PTA stressed that the school community needed to see regularity and consistency by white volunteers. The first years were not easy, but
over time trust formed.[3]

Betsy Carr became St. Paul's outreach coordinator. When she ran for
the school board a few years later, Woodville's principal called her "a true
advocate for children," adding: "She has no hidden agenda. She's like the
flywheel that provides energy for the whole project."

By 2007, one hundred volunteers were entering Woodville every week.
Good Shepherd Baptist Church, an African American congregation, and
UPS Freight (formerly Overnite Transportation Corporation) joined St.
Paul's in the Micah Initiative to support the school. Volunteers offer one-
on-one mentoring, classroom or reading assistance, and act as "room parents." They help staff the office and library and organize camping trips, visits
to the beach, and cultural experiences. A partnership with Communities in
Schools, which identifies resources and coordinates nonacademic services
in schools, allows teachers to concentrate on teaching. Micah volunteers
serve on the school's planning and management team and the citizens' advisory group.

Parent involvement in parent-teacher conferences increased from 20
percent participation in 1999 to 80 percent in 2001. Six hundred and fifty
family members joined the holiday dinner in comparison to 150 the previous year. The Micah community began to come together in shared worship,

and several black families joined the St. Paul's congregation. Academic results are impressive. Overall Standards of Learning scores rose from the 30s to the 80s and 90s.

By 2009, the Micah Initiative had inspired a citywide movement of eighty-one faith communities (including Muslim, Jewish, and Hindu organizations) with seven hundred volunteers in partnership with twenty-five elementary schools.

Even affluent Fairfax County in northern Virginia, which boasts one of the finest school systems in the state, took note. A story in the *Washington Post* explained that in Fairfax strong scores by students at one end of the spectrum overshadowed weaker scores at the other. Although many white students excelled, minority students performed less well than their counterparts in Richmond. The article focused on Woodville, where commitment to excellence and achievement is the norm.

Due in part to the success of Micah, the valiant efforts of teachers, and a focus on reading and math skills, by 2008, forty-two of Richmond's forty-seven public schools enjoyed full state accreditation, based on the state's Standards of Learning (SOLs).

True to the vision of the task force, Micah is changing the "pattern of thinking" within St. Paul's. The partnership impacts mentors as deeply as their mentees. Often with moist eyes, volunteers describe the affection and friendship offered by Woodville students and the richness it brings to their lives.

Woodville is indeed a small miracle. It is changing the world for hundreds of youngsters. But is it enough? What will happen to these young students when they move on from Micah's caring environment? Mentors confess heartache that those they have nurtured so carefully—and who often struggle against huge disadvantages at home—will not receive the necessary attention and support, and may succumb to the prevalent culture of failure. National studies show that gains made in the early grades are often lost in the middle grades. It is in these years that African American boys in particular lose the drive to succeed if they are not surrounded by a culture of high expectations. An inner-city high school teacher told me that when she mentioned reprimanding a student for sleeping in class, a colleague responded, "At least he's not causing trouble."

Test scores tell but part of the story. At one of the nation's leading private schools, every student is expected to "learn how to think, discuss, question, and analyze." Is this our dream for every child in every public school? Will they appreciate great art or develop new talents? Will they learn to appreciate the richness of diversity? Or is our highest goal for children in poor neighborhoods to keep them from dealing drugs on street corners or becoming teenage mothers? Even if they stay in school, how will poor children without parental presence or encouragement compete for places in elite high schools or colleges with students from middle-class homes where summer reading, tutoring, advanced placement courses, camps, theater, museums, travel, and other enrichment activities are the norm? In 2008, Richmond's highly competitive Governor's School, which draws from eleven localities, launched a review of admission policies after studies showed that in the previous seven years black students accounted for between 21 and 30 percent of applications but only between 4 percent and 14 percent were admitted.[4]

Competency in reading and math—the focus of so much of the testing in the No Child Left Behind (NCLB) program—is the meager minimum, according to recommendations by the bipartisan New Commission on the Skills of the American Workforce, in 2006. It emphasizes twenty-first-century skills: knowing more about the world; thinking outside the box; becoming smarter about new sources of information; and learning to work with people of diverse backgrounds.[5]

We will know we have truly succeeded when mentors are willing to entrust their own children to schools with students of different racial and economic backgrounds. If a school is not good enough for my own child, why should I consider it adequate for others?

Above all, we must go beyond remedial action to address the roots of socioeconomic segregation. Don Cowles writes: "Across Metropolitan Richmond, inspired individuals, schools, businesses, civic organizations, and faith communities are striving heroically. . . . Thousands of citizens have mobilized through hundreds of initiatives and have invested tens of millions of dollars each year to mitigate the damage caused by our segregated society. These heroic efforts are making a difference, but they are inadequate. A new way is required—individually and collectively. . . . What would we do differently if every child were my child?"[6]

## Taking Dialogue to a New Level

While Micah was taking its first steps, the need for systemic change prompted Hope in the Cites to focus "honest conversation" on issues underlying specific public policy choices. Thousands of Richmonders had taken part in small-group dialogues and history walks, and attended public forums. Hundreds more had joined "visioning" projects organized by the Greater Richmond Chamber of Commerce, Leadership Metro Richmond, and other organizations. The new perspectives, genuine friendships, and collaborative activities generated by these projects were quietly but steadily changing old mind-sets and breaking down stereotypes.

None of these developments, however, addressed the underlying structural and institutional barriers rooted in race and economics that ensured the isolation of the city and separated people from opportunity. A 1986 study of forty-three mid-size cities with populations between 150,000 and 450,000 had revealed that Richmond's West End contained by far the richest neighborhoods, while the city's poorest neighborhoods were exceeded only by Atlanta's. And a Brookings Institution study of ninety-one regions showed Richmond with the greatest disparity in job growth between city and counties. While the suburbs built since 1970 netted over twenty-seven thousand new jobs in the years 1994–97, the city gained only about two thousand.[7]

Older suburbs were also losing population and wealth. Many African Americans moved to these suburbs, which, like the city itself several years earlier, were experiencing white flight. In new high-growth areas, subdivisions, office parks, big-box retailing, restaurants, and entertainment complexes clustered together. These areas needed more schools, more infrastructure, and additional revenue. New political dynamics emerged as some residents challenged proposed increases in property tax rates and others questioned unbridled development with consequent loss of open space and traffic congestion. Each jurisdiction functioned autonomously from its neighbors, and regional agreements were entered into only when it served the self-interest of the locality. One observer likened these agreements to treaties among independent states. Any serious efforts to address issues related to metropolitan governance appeared as threats to local sovereignty.[8]

In 1999, Hope in the Cities and Richmond Hill decided to take the "honest conversation" to the next level by examining "the interconnected issues of race, economics, and political jurisdiction." Ben Campbell said, "Just getting people to like each other better didn't change the structures that continue to keep us apart." He asked, "How can we build on the positive energy of recent years to encourage real changes in the region's priorities?" A year of preparation by an informal "Committee of Concern," funding from local foundations, and partnership with twenty local organizations positioned Hope in the Cities and Richmond Hill to launch a series of ten residential dialogues. The dialogues were designed to develop an understanding of "intractable" issues that had hitherto proven impossible to address, and that present both challenges and opportunities for the future; and to name and map the root causes of the problem—the underlying relationships and history of distrust. The organizers invited participants to "explore the advantages of accepting Metropolitan Richmond as a single vibrant community."

In a welcome to participants, I wrote: "The Metropolitan Richmond Dialogue is neither an exercise in racial sensitivity nor simply an attempt to create new visions. We hope that each person will leave the dialogue empowered with the knowledge to take effective action . . . and having built a deeper level of trust to enable us to move into the more risky areas of social change.

"What underlying issue, if addressed directly and persistently, would ultimately impact all important relationships in the area? And would cause a realignment of regional priorities in such a way that we truly make this a place of opportunity for everyone? How do we create conditions of true statesmanship in Richmond? What would political courage look like?"

I noted that after World War II, the Schumann Plan integrated the coal and steel industries of France and Germany, thereby ensuring that the two countries could no longer wage war: "Is there a first 'domino' in the Richmond region that we could identify? How can we together generate an unstoppable movement for change that will transform the way we do things? What steps can we take today that will make possible tomorrow what seemed impossible yesterday?"

We drew on the expertise of Harold Saunders, who had helped broker the first Camp David Accords as Jimmy Carter's assistant secretary of state. Later, as head of international programs for the Kettering Foundation, he led a multiyear dialogue with a group in Tajikistan that helped establish a democratic basis for the country as it emerged from the Soviet era and a civil war. This unofficial group comprised respected individuals from different sectors who "had the ear of leaders." Saunders described it as "a mind at work in the midst of a nation rebuilding itself." The image captured our imagination. We hoped that out of these dialogues would grow "a nucleus of people committed to becoming a mind at work in the midst of a Richmond metropolitan community healing and re-imagining itself."

To achieve this, Hope in the Cities combined a detailed fact-based analysis by John Moeser of Virginia Commonwealth University with a dialogue environment that built trust and deepened relationships. The facilitation team, all with national and international experience, included David Campt, Brenda Exum of Norfolk State University, and Lisa Schirch and Barry Hart of Eastern Mennonite University's Conflict Transformation Program. Over a twelve-month period, the project involved 183 people, 88 from community-based organizations and 95 from corporations, in ten carefully balanced groups. Each group gathered at the Richmond Hill retreat center on a Friday evening to begin forty-eight hours of dialogue.

The program began with a detailed statistical analysis of the region. This provided a common knowledge base of demographic trends and inequities in housing, education, and employment.

Following this, participants shared personal "core values" as a means to build a sense of connection with each other. Those core values were then posed against the realities of the region. Participants shared expectations and personal experiences that validated the statistics.

An "environmental scan" listed past and present sources of pride and complaints, as well as fears and aspirations for the future; and a historic timeline enabled participants to walk through their groups' cultural experiences in the context of political and social changes. Often the groups would examine both the intent and the actual impact of specific actions and policies.

The participants divided into affinity (same-race) groups to discuss, "What do we, in this group, need to hear from the other group in order to build trust?" A second, more challenging question was, "What are we, in our group, doing that in some way is perpetuating the problem?"

Finally, the participants came together to look at the interlocking jurisdictional and economic systems to explore how change in one area might impact another. The dialogues closed with personal commitments and action plans.

Marty Jewell, a "notoriously skeptical" community activist (now a city councilman) entered with "the least imaginable expectations."[9] At the end, he marveled: "This is cutting-edge. Regular folks, black and white, haven't been together to talk like this in Richmond, ever."[10] Leaders of the Greater Richmond Chamber of Commence took part, also with some misgivings. The mood was: "We've done this before. If we are going to sit around and hold hands we're out of here." Afterward, one participant spoke for many when he said, "This is the best facilitation we have seen—and we are not unsophisticated about these things." John Sherman, president of the Greater Richmond Chamber of Commerce, said, "Everybody in the region should do this."[11]

Issues of inequities in housing and education surfaced repeatedly in the dialogues. Some of Moeser's statistics shocked the dialogue participants: 30 percent of children in the city live in poverty. Disparity is growing throughout the region, with poverty in successful Henrico County growing by 36 percent during the 1990s. An antiquated funding calculation resulted in the state paying 45 percent of Chesterfield County's school budget compared to 29 percent of the city's budget.

Cricket White, who managed the project, believes the combining of conversation about race, economics, and jurisdiction allowed the groups to penetrate deeply the racial issues by avoiding two common obstacles: "Blacks did not experience the usual frustration of feeling that the 'other half' of the conversation was not taking place. Equally, by including the racial and jurisdictional issues, whites were able to examine race honestly without feeling they were in a 1970s-style encounter group. We also saw that no matter how sophisticated the participants, there is a profound hunger to connect honestly." It was vital that institutional leaders be invited into the process without predetermining the outcome: "People can talk about the elephant in the room and discover that the elephant can be their friend."

For Robert Bolling, a senior program manager with the Richmond Chamber of Commerce, the greatest challenge of taking part was "the fear of exposing personal beliefs" without this openness being reciprocated by non–African Americans: "On the flip side, there was intrigue in exploring my beliefs about race and economics in my birth city with a group of persons willing to do the same."

Bolling said the pivotal moment for him came after a session in which participants divided into racial groups for discussion: "During a break after the groups had shared, a white male approached me and told me that the whites had not been truthful in what they had shared for fear of offending the blacks. After a short discussion, we agreed that he would reconvene the white group to discuss the matter. In the end, the white group not only shared its issues, but also its reservations about saying those things." Although the conversation was "heated and caused much anger, discomfort and resentment," said Bolling, "it enabled participants to get through to each other on a much deeper level."[12]

Ellen Robertson, who started a nonprofit housing corporation in the city's impoverished Highland Park district and served as the first African American female chair of the city's planning commission, said she would always remember the dialogue with the Chamber of Commerce: "It helped me to realize that people don't know themselves. It's hard to accept who you really are." She said she learned that "all hurting people need to be treated with kindness and gentleness. No one heals by pouring salt in the wounds." Even though she might disagree with their stance, "I left feeling true love for people I had no reason to love, and wanting the best for them. . . . There was healing in places I did not know I needed to be healed."

The Metropolitan Richmond Dialogue addresses a common weakness of dialogues where participants don't have specific knowledge on issues such as housing, education, and health care so the conversation is not sharply defined. At the same time, it emphasizes personal relationships and individual responsibility as a basis for common action. In a survey for the Aspen Institute of leading organizations engaged in racial equity and inclusion projects, Ilana Shapiro describes Hope in the Cities' Metropolitan Richmond Dialogue as a "unique dialogue model" that "unites participants in a healing agenda and that relinquishes blame and focuses on constructive social change," adding: "The focus on historical racial injustices, processes of acknowledgment and forgiveness, and current racial and political issues merges the spiritual and psychological aspects of racial reconciliation with grounding in community issues and structures."[13]

But despite the innovative nature of the dialogue, Hope in the Cities' own evaluation highlighted significant unmet challenges. Although the groups were balanced racially and socially, only one-third of the participants came from suburban jurisdictions, an indication of the lack of urgency still felt in the counties. And most of the "action groups" sparked by the dialogues proved impossible to sustain. Hope in the Cities did not have sufficient staff to support them, and in some cases action groups duplicated existing efforts. Moreover, short-term action plans tended to divert attention from the intended focus on systemic issues.

Recognizing these weaknesses, Hope in the Cities decided to identify a specific long-term project that would engage the energies of the farthest counties as well as the city. In two off-the-record discussions with fifteen state and local elected officials and business leaders, facilitated by Hope in the Cities, conversation centered on issues of leadership and political courage. Comments and questions included:

- Why is it that certain public individuals can close down certain conversations?

- There is a leadership style that says, "If I can keep people separate, then I keep my power."

- I have never seen a place where so many powerful people acknowledge that certain things need to change but also say, "That will never happen."

- Local officials go to church, go grocery shopping, and exercise with their constituents. They get immediate feedback from them and have to be ready to take risks.

- We don't have a large enough constituency to support courageous decision making.

As the group considered what steps might justify risking "power, position, and pride," many responses centered on children:

- Of all the folks I have talked to, what motivates them is their children.

- When we grew up we wanted to be doctors or teachers or nurses. The answer I get today when I ask six- or eight-year-olds is, 'I want to live to be sixteen or eighteen.' The sense of hopelessness is overwhelming. Third-grade reading levels are used as predictors for future prison construction. If that seven-year-old actually lives to eighteen, he doesn't need to worry. We'll have a bed for him.

- We need to think about restructuring our entire school system.

**Framing the Moral Question**

The fiftieth anniversary of the 1954 *Brown v. Board of Education* Supreme
Court ruling on school desegregation galvanized Hope in the Cities to ask,
"Why have we not moved closer to the vision laid out by *Brown?*"

John Moeser arrived at one meeting visibly shaken: "I've just been listening to a radio interview on education with senior African American leaders,
and their feeling was, 'We've given up on *Brown*. We would be happy just to
get to *Plessey*.'"[14]

Hope in the Cities board members shared different life experiences with
each other. "I had an introverted four-year-old. I just could not put her on
the bus," said one white woman. Another said: "I put my children in the
neighborhood elementary school. Then I saw the chaos that was going on.
My priority was to get them into college. So we moved to the West End. But
our children did not thrive. They both felt squelched. One is an artist, the
other a musician."

"I did not have the option," responded an African American. "The black
community did not pick houses according to schools. Proximity was not
the issue because we always had walked by schools we could not attend."

"Parents need to take the risk," said a Chesterfield County resident.
"Typically, they will move away from the problem. They are not interested
in changing the system. That takes time. Their focus is on getting their own
kid through high school. We had some poor kids in my district, and when
we wanted to move some of them into a new school, there was strong resistance from middle-class parents." Reflecting on his own experience, he
added: "My son got seventeen college credits at his high school. He was
with about fifteen kids who were taking high academic classes. It was like a
separate school."

Moeser confessed to initial doubts about the wisdom of focusing on education, noting Hope in the Cities' lack of expertise in the area. But as he told
a gathering of Richmond leaders: "We are an organization vitally concerned
about issues relative to race, class and political jurisdiction. And what factor is a bigger determinant in where families with school-age children live
and where businesses choose to locate than schools? And what more determines the composition of our schools than the neighborhoods where we
live? And what more clearly defines our neighborhoods than social class

and race? Nothing touches more lives, more directly, with greater intensity than the neighborhoods where we live and go to schools."[15]

Driven by the conviction of Don Cowles, in partnership with Audrey Burton, Hope in the Cities launched a three-year project in 2004 by asking the community, If every child were my child ... what might I do differently? Hope in the Cities had confirmed through its research that "world-class" schools are in fact "healthy, integrated schools." Several U.S. school districts are working to create such schools. They include Boston, Louisville, Milwaukee, Minneapolis, Rochester, and St. Louis. Because Raleigh/Wake County is similar to Richmond in terms of size and demographics, we studied its record as described by Bill McNeil, the 2004 national superintendent of the year. McNeil told us that his district looks at ten characteristics, which include high academic achievement, good facilities and adequate resources, community and parental support, good leadership, as well as a trained staff and a diverse student body. The district tracks individual school performance using seventy-nine measures, and allocates human and financial resources to overcome shortcomings.

Raleigh/Wake County began more than thirty years ago by merging its school districts. With the support of the business community, it created strong magnet schools to attract students across the region; then it implemented student-assignment policies with targets that promoted integration in a strategic move that shifted the focus to *economic* rather than *racial* integration.

Research documented by Richard Kahlenberg in *All Together Now: Creating Middle-Class Schools through Public School Choice* shows that a school crosses the tipping point when more than half its students come from poor families. Its environment becomes so stressed that overall student performance declines precipitously. This has nothing to do with the innate abilities of the students. It is attributable to difference in school environment: differences in the peer culture of achievement, in parents' capacity to support the school, and in teacher qualifications. Vitally, Kahlenberg also demonstrates that both lower-wealth and higher-wealth students perform better in economically integrated schools.[16]

Raleigh/Wake County bases its student assignment on three targets: no school will have more than 40 percent of its students on free or reduced lunch; no more than 25 percent of students will perform below grade level;

facilities should operate at from 85 to 115 percent capacity. The goal is an effective and safe learning environment for everyone. In 2004, 85 percent of schools were within these guidelines and the others were close to reaching the target. In contrast, across metropolitan Richmond, 36 percent of schools were at the "tipping point," and nearly 60 percent underperformed state Standards of Learning averages.

### A New Form of Advocacy

In launching the project, Hope in the Cities was concerned that an advocacy role would jeopardize its ability to facilitate between different viewpoints. After many hours of debate, the board concluded that its role was to "advocate for honest conversation" by ensuring that the community as a whole could understand the issues.

Ben Campbell says: "People ask why we don't do traditional advocacy. I say it's because we intend to be effective. You have to respect the things that people have to do for themselves and their institutions. Otherwise you won't get the change you want. The cheapest way is to take a quick position. It has no impact on those who disagree with you, and you spend a lot of your capital. If you take education we say, 'We won't tolerate anything less than significant improvement in education for all our children.' Everyone agrees with that. Then you hold up the data." In his view, the proper role of advocacy is to "bring people up to the glass and get them to look at possible solutions." Advocacy is about "not letting people duck the issue." "This is deliberate prophetic action that forces people to be accountable."

"If Every Child Were My Child" raises a discomforting moral question for the region, and it invites everyone to participate in moving toward solutions. It recognizes that action is needed on many levels and that every voice must be heard.

In 2007, the initiative completed a third year of promoting conversations about creating "healthy, integrated public schools." These conversations involved administrators, principals, teachers, parents, and students. Business leaders also became actively engaged in the public debate for the first time. At one public forum, former school board chairman Melvin Law said that he was happy to hear the dialogue, noting that the community had "tried to have this discussion in 1972 but not in this spirit."

Across the nation those who care about education are looking urgently for new ways to address old problems. The 2007 Supreme Court ruling left the door open for selection along economic lines. Some observers point out that Thurgood Marshall, the lead lawyer for the NAACP Legal Defense Fund on the *Brown* case, believed that integration was necessary because if black children had the right to be in school with white children, then (white) school board officials would have no choice but to equalize spending to protect the interests of their children.

We are unlikely to create healthy, integrated schools without addressing the poverty and systemic inequality at the root of student underachievement. Too often, interventions take the form of placing blame on hardworking teachers or beleaguered school boards, pointing to incompetence or waste, while refusing to address the underlying systemic causes. One parent who put four children through Richmond's public schools wrote: "It has been difficult for me to listen to the perennial attacks on the system . . . often coming from people who have no personal experiences with the [public] schools, do not send their own children to the schools, and do not wish to share responsibility."[17]

What will we do to end the shame of what Jonathan Kozol calls America's educational apartheid?[18] Sheryll Cashin of Georgetown University Law School writes: "I think the possibility for integration could be much enhanced if more white people and more middle- and upper-middle-class people could become comfortable with not always being overwhelmingly dominant in numbers. This does not mean that their interests would necessarily be subordinated. It does mean that they would have to share power, resources, or influence. This is what it means to be part of a larger community."[19]

When today's students become adults, America will be a multiracial society with no majority group, where all groups will have to learn to live and work successfully together. "It is a simple statement of fact to say that the country's survival depends on finding ways to prepare groups of students who have traditionally fared badly in American schools to perform at much higher levels and to prepare all young Americans to live and work in a society vastly more diverse than ever in our past," write Orfield and Lee in *Historic Reversals, Accelerating Resegregation, and the Need for New Integration Strategies.*[20]

In recent years, white families have begun to move back into center cities, and an increasing number are placing their children in elementary schools that are predominantly African American. Some school communities experience new tensions based on different cultural approaches as well as desire for control on all sides. One black principal said it felt like "a hostile takeover." But inclusion cuts both ways. When our son Neil was selected as his school's "scholastic standout," we were invited to a presentation luncheon for all the city's schools at a downtown hotel. As the children stood clutching their awards, a black photographer went down the line taking pictures of every child except the two or three white students. On another occasion, when a school cookout was announced, the African American mothers produced a wonderful meal, but never thought to invite Susan or other white parents to contribute.

How will we create genuinely inclusive school communities? As a senior administrator says, if efforts to attract middle-class families back into the urban schools are successful, these challenges will arise more frequently.

Don Cowles writes: "Certainly, building inclusive school communities is challenging work. It is personal work. It can't be assigned to governments and school administrators. It is the work of each student, parent and educator—forming new relationships with people who may be different.

"Also, the process may necessitate healing historical wounds. Trust may have been broken, recently or long ago. Difficult apologies may be in order. However, hope can be restored in new relationships. We may need to reaffirm our shared values, such as respect, responsibility, honesty, and accountability. Accepting a few fundamental principles might free us to celebrate our diversity."[21]

## Muslims and Christians

Strong Faith
Does Not Mean
a Closed Mind

The methods of honest conversation designed to address racial and economic divisions in Richmond proved highly relevant to building trust between faith groups in the aftermath of the events of September 11, 2001. In Richmond, as in many parts of the United States, concerns about terrorism and civil rights stimulated a desire for better understanding.

Richmond is fortunate that relationships between the faith groups have stood the test of the pressure of global events. During the conflict in Lebanon in the summer of 2006, Imad Damaj of the Muslim Coalition of Virginia says that his solidarity with Christian and Jewish colleagues actually increased. "Of course," he adds, "you have to have the relationship in place before the crisis."

Rev. Canon J. Fletcher Lowe Jr., a former director of the Virginia Interfaith Center for Public Policy, makes a similar point. When he took up his post in 1997, he was immediately drawn to two members of the board, Muhammad Sahli, a Palestinian-born Muslim, and Leivy Smolar, a rabbi.

"When the center embarked on an endowment campaign, we became the principal visitors to potential donors," says Lowe. "Most of the significant pledges came from our visits, with me giving some background on the center, Muhammad speaking to its interfaith dimension, and the rabbi, from his experience as a college president, 'closing the deal,' in terms of requesting a pledge. I don't know whether any of the donors were impressed, but I sure was, going around raising money for an interfaith organization with a Muslim, a Jew, and a Christian."

In the wake of September 11, the three men were in daily contact. "By Monday, September 17, we felt there needed to be a communitywide expression of solidarity and unity. We decided to ask the rabbi of the largest synagogue in town if he would host an interfaith service on Sunday, September 23. He agreed. With minimal publicity, the service was held, filling the 900-plus synagogue."

In Richmond, Christians, Muslims, and Jews have worked together to build houses in some of the city's neediest areas. It is not unusual for Christians, Buddhists, and Muslims to join Jews at a Seder table for a Passover meal, hosted by a conservative synagogue. Richmond's Muslim community regularly welcomes religious, political, and nonprofit leaders to Iftar meals during the month of Ramadan. In many American communities, such gestures of inclusion are common. But the bridges between Muslims and evangelical Christians have been harder to cross.

The first steps toward much-needed dialogue between these groups in Richmond were set in motion by a couple in their eighties. Ben and Virginia Brinton live in a retirement home in Richmond's far West End. They have been part of the Initiatives of Change team since its early days in Richmond and are strong supporters of Hope in the Cities. Their energies are limited, but their commitment to bridge building is undiminished. Shortly after September 11, they joined the Interfaith Council of Greater Richmond. "Neither my husband nor I knew any Muslims in Richmond personally," says Virginia. But at their first council dinner, they met Malik and Annette Khan. Annette is a Caucasian who grew up in Wisconsin. Malik is a chemical engineer who had come from Pakistan twenty-five years earlier. At the time, he was the president of the Islamic Center of Virginia. Over the meal, the two couples quickly discovered mutual connections and concerns. "From then on we just kept talking, and our hearts were open to each other," says Virginia. A month later, the Brintons welcomed the Khans to their home for dinner, and a friendship was born.

Soon after the Brintons' intervention, Muhammad Sahli, who served on the board of Hope in the Cities, invited me and a few colleagues to a consultation with Malik Khan and other Muslim leaders at the Islamic Center. They told us: "Since September 11 we have been invited to speak in dozens of churches, but this is not the same as dialogue. Also, these are mostly churches already sympathetic to us. The people we really need to talk with are conservative and evangelical Christians, and we have no contact with them. Can you help us with this?"

I called Ben Trotter, a Baptist friend of conservative views whose son had just returned from Afghanistan. Trotter and I met with Malik Khan to explore the possibility of a dialogue. He suggested we meet a young Iranian-born American, Hadi Yazdanpanah. Hadi was enthusiastic at the idea.

We agreed to invite Muslims and Christians for face-to-face, honest, and sustained conversation about concerns and perceptions, and to consider ways in which the two communities, which share the Abrahamic faith, might move beyond accusation and their isolated circles to take constructive action together. We went on to hammer out the purpose of the dialogue as follows:

- Enable understanding of different faith traditions

- Affirm values held in common

- Encourage critical self-assessments and acceptance of individual responsibility

- Appreciate the role of history in shaping attitudes and fostering divisions

- Begin to build bridges of trust

- Discover opportunities to work together to build a healthy, inclusive, and hopeful Richmond metropolitan community

- Explore how future dialogues might include others in the region and beyond

With the advice of Andrew Fuller, who is engaged in international evangelism, we set out to contact other Christians. Muslims, seeing their civil rights threatened and their religion maligned, were eager to engage. But some Christians were hesitant, and it took months of one-on-one conversations to convene a group. We stressed that the Muslims were looking to meet Christians who were firm in their faith. Everyone would be encouraged to express his or her belief without reservation. Often the statement that the primary purpose was to build relationships proved to be the clincher. Even so, one of the Christians who had agreed to participate (provided he could be assured of confidentiality) withdrew at the last minute, saying that he would not be comfortable. Ironically, he had told me that he had come to Richmond partly in reaction to old racial attitudes in Kentucky; yet he could not bring himself to meet with Muslims.

## Finding Common Ground

The task of identifying participants and preparing for the dialogue took a year of careful work. Finally, one Saturday morning, the president of the Islamic Center of Virginia and a prominent evangelical Christian sat side by side for six hours to begin an honest conversation. Six other Muslim leaders and five Christians joined the dialogue. The Muslims represented diverse backgrounds, including Pakistan, Iran, and Lebanon, as well as native-born black and white Americans. The Christians were generally conservative and evangelical.

As we began the introductions and discussed the purpose of the dialogue, Cricket White, my cofacilitator, and I could sense the tension in the room. The ice was soon broken in an unexpected way. Fritz Kling, an evangelical Christian, described how his grandparents had been missionaries in Brazil, losing one child to disease and contending with thirty-foot pythons in their garden. "Admittedly, some things [done by missionaries] were not done right. But as a Christian I'm not going to beat myself up, because a lot of schools and hospitals would never be there but for the sacrificial work of those missionaries."[1]

To our surprise there was no argument from the Muslims. Instead, Malik Khan turned to Kling and said: "That's true. I went to a Catholic school and received a first-class education." Immediately several other Muslims shared similar experiences. Somehow this simple affirmation helped everyone relax as people said to themselves, "It's going to be okay—we're not going to get ambushed."

After introductions and agreement on ground rules, we asked the group to break into pairs and to engage in some simple storytelling in response to a question:

*We are living in a world of great change and mobility. The cultural context in which your parents or grandparents practiced their faith may be very different from your experience today. Would you please share a personal story or experience from your family that illustrates a value that is important to your faith tradition?*

This proved a very effective way to find common ground. As the pairs reported back, many of the values mentioned were valid for both Christians and Muslims. Our second question was:

*Are there things in your everyday experience of American life and culture that you feel support or run counter to the values of your faith tradition?* Both groups expressed concern at a secularism that "excludes faith from public places" and imposes values contrary to faith traditions. Muslims and Christians found common ground in their views toward abortion and sexual purity. But, while deeply concerned at the impact of the moral laxity of popular culture on their families, Muslims also said they were amazed and challenged by American Christians' engagement on issues of social justice.

The dialogue was marked by surprising openness. Differences were acknowledged. "If I did not believe Islam was the best religion I would not be a Muslim," said one participant. Christians voiced similar sentiments from their own faith perspective. At one point, someone said, "In the spirit of free enterprise, let the best win!" Everyone was comfortable with this. Yet both groups were pleasantly surprised to discover that the other group was not monolithic in its views. "This is my first time sitting with evangelicals who don't all believe Jerry Falwell speaks for them!" said a Muslim. The dialogue surfaced the complexities and fissures not readily apparent in both groups.

"Can interfaith dialogue, without compromising core principles, really lead to a world that works?" asked one participant. "How can we show that a faith-filled community is not necessarily a constrained community?" asked another. "Strong faith does not mean a closed mind."

One evangelical participant commented later that liberal Christians befriend Muslims because they value inclusion above all, and don't put theology or dogma over tolerance: "Evangelicals value theology and doctrine so highly that they will enter into dialogues and relationships only if we don't have to 'give away the store' theologically, intellectually, or morally. We fear being compromised. I know that is something many Muslims can relate to. In this way evangelical Christians are much more similar to observant Muslims who are used to no-compromise strictures of their own."

**Tough Questions**

The next phase of the dialogue explored the personal, family, and community impact of September 11. *What stereotypes had emerged? What did the participants think was in the mind of the other group?* Again they broke into pairs to talk about personal experiences with a person of another faith that ran counter to the stereotypes.

The Muslims' fear of government repression through the Patriot Act and other measures surfaced early and often. A young woman said: "We Muslims find ourselves in a very strange situation. After September 11, the liberals embraced us and supported our civil rights, and for that we are grateful. But they did not embrace our values and that concerns us." Turning to the Christians, she went on: "On the other hand, we share your values and we would like to be embraced by you, but you are the ones trampling on our civil rights and locking us up. In the coming election, we are being forced to choose between values and our security." Another Muslim said, "If there is another September 11–like event, I fear the evangelicals will be the first to turn on Muslims."

The group shared a simple meal together. Later that day, a breakthrough moment occurred when Muslims and Christians met separately to consider two further questions:

*Both Islam and Christianity have great traditions of peace building. What have we in our group done, currently or historically, that undermines this tradition? What do we need to hear from the other group in order to begin to build bridges of trust?*

On reconvening, the Christians began by acknowledging the negative legacy of the Crusades and colonialism. They also admitted their complete failure to recognize that Islam could be an ally in fighting social and moral ills, and expressed regret that they had never built any personal relationships with Muslims. They asked Muslims to be unequivocal in denouncing acts of violence and anti-Jewish statements. They admitted a slowness to stand up against public expressions of Islamaphobia, or to challenge their peer groups, and they offered to help with media, which, they conceded, does not always cover positive statements by Muslims.

For their part, Muslims said they realized that they were too isolated, that they had secluded themselves from involvement with the concerns of the wider community and had not been vocal enough on human rights violations. From the Christians they wanted to hear a "commitment without reservation" to the principle of religious pluralism, rights, and privileges. They also urged them to learn about Islam from reputable sources.

Conversations ranged over religious schools, freedom of the media, treatment of women, and insensitive use of language. The participants pledged to support each other in speaking out against stereotyping and acts of violence.

That afternoon, as the group adjourned, everyone insisted that the conversation continue the following month. Five years later, the group was still in dialogue. The group generally meets on a Saturday morning once a month, although busy schedules sometimes hamper regularity. After the first few dialogues that took place at the Hope in the Cities office, the group unanimously accepted the offer of Dr. Charles Beckett, who directs the Center for Christian Understanding of Islam, to host the dialogues at his center. Beckett had spent many years as a missionary in Bangladesh. His scholarly knowledge of both religions is deeply respected and valued by all participants.

During the first summer, Fritz Kling and Malik Khan met over coffee for more personal conversation. Later Kling told the group: "I have begun to be an advocate for what I know from one Muslim friend. We've built a level of trust." Malik Khan responded: "When Fritz called it was a pleasant surprise. His genuine effort was touching." Their honest sharing provided a focus for a rich exchange on several critical issues.

For the Christians, the issue of violence remained an overriding concern. "I think someone is a nice guy, but what does he say at home, or at the mosque?" said one.

"What are you afraid of?" a Muslim asked.

"Before September 11, 2001, when I thought of the term 'Muslim'—if I ever did—it was pretty benign: carpets and shoes with pointy turned-up toes. Ignorant, yes, but benign," the Christian replied. "But after September 11, we are afraid of terrorism, suicide bombings, and the killing of innocent people. . . . Terrorists expressly state that Americans and Christians are their enemies. It's difficult not to take that personally." Another added: "And we have been taught that Islam is the fastest-growing religion in the world, that it will overtake all of our churches. We have been taught much of our fear."

The Muslims were unequivocal in their condemnation of atrocities from a personal and a religious standpoint. "We can say from a human and civil behavior standpoint, regardless of politics, this is wrong," said one.

"But how often do we need to apologize for acts of Muslim terrorists?" asked a student. "Muslims in the West have to answer for Muslims everywhere, but Christians are not expected to apologize for slavery or the Crusades."

"Yes," responded a friend, "it is unfair, but we cannot hold onto the past any more. At this point in time, we need to take the position that we stand with the truth whether it is with Muslims or against Muslims."

Muslims and Christians pressed each other to clarify their beliefs. "It seems that evangelicals have a high regard for Jews. Muslims have a high regard for Jews and Christians. So why don't evangelicals have a high regard for Muslims?" asked a Muslim. "We acknowledge that there is truth in both the Christian and Jewish theology. Why is it that you don't acknowledge that sometimes we have a part of the truth, too?" he continued. Someone observed that fundamentalism in all religions is usually a reaction to loss, threat, or humiliation. The negativity that Muslims experience in America is sometimes more a reaction of Christian conservatives to liberal secularism than an attack on Islam.

Charles Beckett challenged the group to "look beyond the discussion of *what we believe* about each other, and to instead look at *how we live,* and at the eternal nature of God/Allah as we understand him and how that informs and guides our behavior."

As the dialogue progressed to more sensitive areas, the group talked about personal risk and the need to support each other in speaking out against "fringe" individuals who do not represent the large center of either religion. Muslims also looked for affirmation that all human life is equally valuable. Sometimes it did not appear that Christians believed this, for example in their attitude to the Palestinian people.

A Christian cautioned against asking others to "take risks that we ourselves are not prepared to take": "It is very hard for groups who have been oppressed or who feel threatened to be honest about their own internal issues. Therefore we need to think about what risks we ourselves are prepared to take that will give moral support to our Muslim colleagues."

"Muslims showed great courage today in being very open," said a Christian at the conclusion of one dialogue. "No one will go out the door the same as they were when they came in. I wish that my congressman could have been here!"

## New Insights

Six months after the dialogues began, a leading evangelical participant e-mailed the group from Indonesia, where he had met with the head of one of the world's largest Muslim organizations: "I told him that American Christians have much to learn about living in a society of religious pluralism, and Indonesia has a long history of that. He was an extremely impressive man. For their part, I heard from every quarter that that fragile balance is now being tested. I also had the opportunity to visit a Muslim school. It was all very enlightening, and I was received much more warmly than I could have expected. I met with all of them in a desire to learn more about Islam worldwide, and it was extremely helpful."

Two years later, I asked the participants to reflect on their experiences.

Charles Beckett told me, "I was surprised that my statement of personal faith was accepted without hesitation by the Muslims, and that I did not feel I needed to apologize for my convictions."

For Farouk Ali, who served as the student body president at Virginia Commonwealth University, the greatest fear was that the dialogue would be "a gigantic waste of time." His Muslim friends at college asked: "What's the point of dialogue? It seems we have to compromise every time." "But," said Ali, "my expectation of all talk and no action has changed. I am trying to interact more with Christian groups on the campus." Ali is now a policy analyst at the Virginia Interfaith Center for Public Policy.

Fritz Kling said: "I was concerned that Muslims might perceive me as the mission-focused evangelical out to colonize the world. It was helpful, during the dialogue, when Muslims and Christians recognized that both groups proselytize, and should not fault the other for that."

Malik Kahn concluded: "We need a revival within the Muslim world. Our scholars must teach the true message of Islam. More importantly, the *spirit of the message* needs to be imparted, which is much more peaceful than it has been made out to be. We condemn violence. I will always do that. The press must be responsible and not promote hatred or schisms. I also want Muslims in the West to understand that they are living in an open, free society. We need freedom with personal responsibility and accountability."

## Ten Agreements

In the third year of dialogue, the participants agreed on the following ten points:

1. We all value hospitality and graciousness, and want the greater Richmond area to be a region that welcomes, accepts, and affirms people of different backgrounds.

2. We all feel blessed to live in the United States, a country for which we feel love and to whose Constitution and founding principles, especially religious freedom and separation of church and state, we express loyalty.

3. We all strive to maintain very high standards for moral behavior in our personal lives, families, and communities.

4. Our faiths call us to be agents of morality, compassion, and justice in our community. We value opportunities to pursue all these aspirations together jointly in public and private ways.

5. We welcome and protect the privilege of propagation of our faiths (evangelizing and da'wa) as essential religious duties in both Christianity and Islam.

6. We treasure relationships based on who we know each other to be, and not on how others of your faith act or speak.

7. We will, based on our personal relationship with each other, feel free to dialogue on religious issues, here and around the world, which cause us concern.

8. We will openly attest, among others of our own faith, to the positive relationships and respect we have for each other.

9. We pray that God's wishes and direction in our lives will find expression in our continuing relationships.

10. We recognize and affirm our humanity as a gift from God. We will honor all of the above "agreed-upons" and, if we still don't see eye-to-eye, we will agree to disagree while holding hope for future positive discussions and eventual affirmation.

The group is considering how to expand its outreach through roundtable discussions with different congregations.

## A Global View I

South Africa
and the Power
of Story

The Richmond experience of honest conversation has informed reconciliation and community building efforts in many parts of the world. During a sabbatical in 2005, Susan and I visited colleagues associated with the Hope in the Cities network in South Africa, Britain, and France. We met with leaders at all levels, conducted workshops, and reflected with those we met on common challenges. The following chapters draw on these encounters.

We had first visited South Africa in 1977, during some of the darkest days of apartheid. Married just three months, we found ourselves leading an international group of twenty-five young people from Europe and the United States. Accompanying us were several young black and white South Africans. They were discovering their own country, together, for the first time. We spoke in high schools and in churches, met with senior politicians, and discussed with community organizers. Encounters with black students in a still-smoldering Soweto following the 1976 uprising and with white students at the ultraconservative Pochestroom University are etched in our memory.

We recalled these experiences with our former traveling companions who are now seeking to make reconciliation a reality in the new South Africa. In Tshwane/Pretoria, we spent two weeks with Pieter and Meryl Horn. Pieter is an Afrikaner whose grandfather narrowly escaped execution by the British during the Anglo-Boer War. In Cape Town, Samuel and Virginia Pono welcomed us to their home in a newly integrated neighborhood. Pono is a Xhosa elder and jazz musician from Queenstown in the Eastern Cape. As a young man, his love of music was matched by his hatred for whites. Yet his decision thirty years ago to work with Horn in honest partnership provided an early model for South Africa.

We accompanied Pono on a visit to Robben Island, where political prisoners had spent years toiling under the fierce sun and cold rain. Former inmates now conduct the tours. Most of the visitors were South Africans who are discovering their own history for the first time. Our guide had been incarcerated for seventeen years. He told us that until 1978 the men slept on the hard stone floor. Common-law prisoners were trusted more than political prisoners and sometimes were used to carry out torture. We saw the cells where Nelson Mandela and other leaders spent years in solitary confinement, and the small cave in the lime quarry where the prisoners organized their own school during breaks.

Our guide told the story without elaboration, accusation, or bitterness, and he ended by expressing his hope that the experience of visiting the prison would help South Africans build a new, reconciled country. On the boat, Pono hailed a friend from Queenstown who had spent seven years on the island as a prisoner and now runs the ferry and has made his home on the island. "It's so peaceful," he said.

On many levels, the transformation in South Africa is miraculous. In bustling shopping malls, people of all races stroll as equals. The energy of young entrepreneurs and the vigor of the public debate in the media impressed us. Many schools appeared to be doing a better job of integration than the United States, and enrollment by black African students doubled in the decade after 1994. But a 2007 study by the South African Institute of Race Relations showed that the quality of education had shown "scant improvement" since the end of apartheid. The institute also reported that absolute poverty had doubled since the ANC took power and that the gap between the "haves" and "have-nots" is glaring and growing.[1]

Cape Town, with its stunning waterfront and mansions perched below Table Mountain, is surrounded by vast "informal settlements." Nearly fifty thousand people migrate to the city each year seeking employment. In Cape Town, Johannesburg, Durban, and other urban centers, the new black elite is disconnected from the grassroots communities; in some cases young people can no longer speak the vernacular of their grandparents. Fear of crime is overwhelming. Houses hide behind high walls and electric fences, and many people live in new "security villages." Of course, the AIDS crisis touches almost everyone in the country.

It is apparent that there has as yet been little opportunity for real conversation between ordinary South Africans of different backgrounds. The emotional catharsis of the Truth and Reconciliation Commission may have obscured the need for simple honesty among the vast majority of South Africans who were not involved in the criminal acts of the old regime, but who were participants in a racialized system. A senior retired judge, John Trengove, told us, "There are hundreds of thousands of white people who have never understood what the policy of apartheid meant to the people who experienced it."

Trengove made this remark in conversation with an interracial group of friends in the home of Peter and Shirley Gordon in Somerset West, an idyllic community east of Cape Town. The Gordons are part of the "colored" community which blends the cultures of Asia, Europe, and Africa. As the setting sun turned the mountains gold behind what Peter Gordon proudly calls the most beautiful street in Somerset West, Shirley reminded us that on our first visit they had been battling for the right to remain in their home after the neighborhood was declared "white" under the Group Areas Act.

Trengove told us of his encounters decades earlier with Dr. William Nkomo, an early pioneer of new race relations in South Africa. Nkomo had been expelled from the African National Congress because of his militant views and had won election as the first chairman of the ANC National Youth League, formed in reaction to the ANC's more passive approach. Later he became an advocate for nonviolent change and became the president of the South African Institute of Race Relations.

"Nkomo was the first black person I met where there was not a master-servant relationship," said Trengove. "I come from a very traditional background. We accepted the fact that there were two classes: the privileged and the hewers of wood and carriers of water. Nkomo challenged me to start living the faith I professed."

As we were leaving the Gordons' home, Trengove turned to us and added: "We have a problem I am very concerned about. The Dutch Reformed Church has apologized at the national level for its support of apartheid. But whenever the subject comes up at the local level in our churches people say, 'Why do we still need to talk about this?'"

In April of that same year, the premier of the Cape Province caused a stir with his call to "open up the debate on racism." Dr. Fanie du Toit, a program manager at the Institute for Justice and Reconciliation, responded in a commentary in the *Cape Times:* "Reconciliation is approaching a turning point. We have crossed, or are in the process of crossing the bridges of coexistence and cooperation. We decided not to kill one another (coexistence) and to some extent we are learning to work together (cooperation). For some, these achievements seem sufficient. But a further need remains. It is to build trust across divides that defined our past. If we fail to do this as a basis for shaping a new future, apartheid may yet have the last laugh."[2]

Many whites feel they have no future in the new South Africa; from some we heard resentment, disappointment, and fear of rejection. For black South Africans, of course, change cannot come quickly enough.

In this context, we shared experiences from America's ongoing struggle with racial division and the approaches that have proved effective in Richmond. Civil servants, community activists, representatives of NGOs, and clergy joined us for a day of dialogue and skills building in Pretoria. The politeness between people of different racial backgrounds reminded us of Richmond, but one person said, "It feels like we are walking on eggshells."

As we broke for lunch, Susan and I asked the participants to seek out someone they did not know. Their task was simply to tell each other about the neighborhood in which their parents and grandparents had grown up and how the neighborhood they themselves lived in today was similar or different. At first they were awkward and hesitant; they clumped together in larger groups. But when we reconvened after lunch, they said, "Can we please have another half hour and try this again?"

This time, once started, they were unable to stop. It was as if the floodgates had opened. Thirty minutes became an hour. When we finally regrouped, it seemed the conversations could have lasted all afternoon. The atmosphere had changed markedly. As they reported back, participants were energized and sometimes emotional. A white African woman had been listening to the story of a black African about her childhood in Soweto, with no electricity, no lights, and an outside toilet. The woman wept as she said, "I just could not get out of my head the image of this young child having to go out in the middle of the night in the dark and how frightening that must have been." One simple story had illuminated an experience shared by millions.

In Cape Town, we again witnessed the power of personal stories. Vilma Maritz, a white Afrikaner, recalled an occasion in the late 1970s when she offered to drive a friend back to her home in Soweto, the vast black township southwest of Johannesburg. Because of the high level of violence, all outside visitors had to report to a police checkpoint. Despite Vilma's protests, a very large officer with a rifle clambered into the back seat of her very small car. Having delivered her friend, Vilma returned to the checkpoint and dropped off the police officer. Heading out of Soweto, she lost a hub cap. "I had not been driving for very long," said Vilma, "and I stopped because I did not know whether the car could run without it." A young boy ran to pick it up and brought it over, and within minutes a crowd had gathered to help. Then they sent Vilma on her way, telling her with great concern, "It is very dangerous for you to be here alone—you must be very careful." Vilma said, "I was so touched by their care, I have never been afraid of a black person since."

Samuel and Virginia Pono introduced us to their friend Police Inspector Kevin Williams, who is responsible for Kensington, one of Cape Town's traditionally colored areas. The colored community makes up more than half the population of the city. In a 2005 poll, 66 percent said they believe that the black-dominated government does not care about them. They saw job preference and housing priorities going to black Africans. As in the days of apartheid, the community feels itself trapped in the middle. A commonly heard phrase is, "First we were not white enough, now we are not black enough."

Inspector Williams, who is an evangelical preacher as well as a police officer, convened thirty-five community leaders to meet with us. After some initial conversation, we asked them to divide into groups of four or five and to "identify a key issue in the community that needs honest conversation." Gangs, drugs, family values, and relations with squatter camp residents were top concerns. But as participants became more comfortable with open dialogue, a young man said, "As a colored community we don't know who we are, and if we don't know who we are, we can't make our real contribution to South Africa." Embarrassed, some of his colleagues tried to brush it aside by saying, "Oh, it's not so bad." But he insisted, "No, this is the real problem that we must talk about."

Later, Kevin Williams remarked that the Ponos were the first black African family that he and his wife have known at a personal level.

### Right-Wing Towns Set the Pace

Some communities are finding ways to build partnerships and meet pressing economic needs. Middelburg and Witbank are twin cities set in the heart of South Africa's coal country. Enormous power stations dot the landscape. Mpumalanga Province has the largest municipal dam in the Southern Hemisphere. It is known as a very conservative area that strongly resisted change during the transition from apartheid. Yet, Middelburg has won national awards as the best-run municipality in South Africa, with a 95 percent payment rate of local taxes—an astonishing achievement in a country where nonpayment is often the norm. Andre Brandmuller, a former chairman of the Chamber of Commerce, attributes this success to a high level of communication, even among those who disagree.

In the run up to the 1994 elections, explosive tensions forced the pace of change. "We went through two-and-a-half years of chaos," said Fiona Martin, a white Rhodesian-born South African who helped set up an interracial Peace Committee for the province. "I was personally labeled a traitor, my phone was tapped, rocks were thrown on my roof, and a car followed me around."

Working with her in these efforts were Sydney Choma and Ben Mokoena. Both had been exiles during the struggle against apartheid. Their leadership helped to calm tensions during the transition to a nonracial municipality. Mokoena became mayor of Middelburg with Choma as chair of the Executive Committee. Fiona Martin was elected mayor of Witbank.

Andre Brandmuller's father, Peter, had chaired the provincial Peace Committee. As a lawyer, he handles many property sales. We were struck by the great improvement in housing since a visit six years earlier. Solid houses have replaced many of the township's shacks. The old workers' hostels are now subdivided into private residences, many with carefully tended gardens. Peter relishes the smile on his clients' faces when he hands them the property deed for their home. Property values are rising, even in integrated areas. The general sense seems to be, "We're going to make this work."

The relationship with Richmond began in 1995 when the premier of Mpumalanga Province brought a delegation to the United States on a study tour. Fascinated by the Richmond story, he said, "Eighty percent of what you are telling me is also true for South Africa." Fiona Martin was part of the group. She drew ideas from the Richmond model to launch "Opening the Window to Change," a series of workshops for people in the public sector, especially government, education, and police.

Through Fiona Martin we established a continuing exchange with community leaders, including Sydney Choma, who had spent ten years on Robben Island. In 1999, at a consultation with other mayors from the region, including some representing very conservative districts, he spoke of the experiences on Robben Island that convinced him and his fellow prisoners that reconciliation was possible. Many of the white prison officers came from humble backgrounds with little formal education. As the detainees helped their jailers with their educational needs, the two groups had discovered the humanity in each other: "The experience convinced us that reconciliation is possible."

On this visit, Andre Brandmuller invited us to the Rotary Club over which he now presides. At lunch, an Afrikaner named Anton Meerkotter said how hard it had been to move through all the changes in Middelburg, but there was quiet pride in having been part of a remarkable process. The Rotary is small, with only sixteen members, but highly active, raising millions of rand for a care village for orphans and other charitable enterprises. Meerkotter told us that his son has married a black South African, "something we could never have imagined, but we love her." Now his daughter is dating a Jewish boy in California.

In South Africa, racial categories become increasingly confusing and nonsensical. We were overwhelmed by the extraordinary richness of diversity and mix of cultures. What does it mean to be a South African? It's one thing to break down the walls of apartheid. It's another to build bridges. With the ending of legal separation, people are searching for a new sense of identity. "How can we move from talking about *my history* or *your history* to talking about *our history*?" asked one dialogue participant. Understanding and honoring their different stories and embracing a shared history may be a vital step for South Africans in building new relationships based on trust.

## A Global View II

From Rhetoric
to Reality
in France

France, like the United States, is a nation characterized by lofty ideals. The revolutionary vision of "liberté, égalité, fraternité" has inspired millions around the world. "All men are created equal" was the bold claim of America's founding fathers.

But America's history of slavery and racial discrimination is evidence of our difficulty in matching rhetoric with reality. The social and economic divisions in our cities today are direct consequences. France faces similar, though different, challenges.

The death of two young blacks in October 2005 as they ran from police sparked a wave of car burnings and violent protests that began in suburban Paris (*la banlieue*) and quickly spread to cities across the country. It was not a "civil war," as some media voices suggested; and it would be a mistake to equate France's crisis with America's deep-seated pathology of racial division and poverty. A generous social safety net ensures that most of the unemployed and poor in France are fed, housed, and educated. And even in the most desolate suburbs, there is nothing approaching the catastrophic level of violence in America's poorest neighborhoods. France's brilliant national soccer squad is composed largely of players of African descent, in stark contrast to practically every other European team. I received an e-mail from one Parisian friend who emphasized the tremendous achievements of many North Africans: "The vast majority of them are well integrated, have good jobs, and have every reason to feel proud. Not all French people are racists and stubborn, and most are getting along very well together!"

True, but during a visit to Paris in June 2005, Susan and I found an urgent desire for honest conversation about the gap between great ideals and daily reality as it is experienced by ordinary citizens—particularly those who have come from other continents and who represent different cultures. The protests could not have come as a surprise to many observers. But as one businessman of African origin told us, "In France, everyone has a place and everyone must keep in his place. . . . We have a caste system based on race and class." Until recently, the word "race" was virtually taboo, in line with the belief that if one embraced French values and culture, the color of one's skin should not matter. The reality is different.

There are virtually no black or Arab TV presenters. All but one of the 555 members of the National Assembly representing continental France are white. President Sarkozy put three women from immigrant backgrounds into his government, and Rama Yade is the Senegalese-born junior minister for European affairs and human rights. But there is just a handful of mayors from immigrant backgrounds out of about 36,000. Although the percentage of blacks in France who hold degrees is higher than for the general population, racial discrimination in job opportunities is well documented.

None of this should give the rest of Europe any cause for complacency. In fact, the French approach of offering full citizenship to immigrants was laudable and stands in stark contrast to that of countries like Germany, which adopted a "guest worker" policy and only recently—and grudgingly—began to move beyond its traditional concept of national identity based on bloodlines. Perhaps because the expectation in France was so high, the disappointment has been so deep. The youth—most of them second-generation citizens—who are burning cars are not seeking to be recognized as minorities: they are demanding to be acknowledged as the full French citizens that they are.

Issues of dignity and respect are often as important as economic opportunity. According to Alain Touraine, an expert on integration, the problem is not poverty. He calls for public debate to break down stereotypes.

**Initiative Dialogue**

While good public debate is essential, personal encounters and off-the-record dialogues are usually more effective in moving people beyond posturing to honest conversation. Fortunately some dialogues have already begun. In Paris, a group known as "Initiative Dialogue" has been meeting since 1999. French Muslims from different backgrounds and representatives of the majority population engage in forthright but respectful exchanges. The dialogues started informally, discussing how to build relationships based on trust. They began with family issues. One Muslim woman said that she wanted to help young Muslims feel part of French society.

At one dialogue we attended, there were about twenty people, including several Tunisian French, two Syrians, and a Lebanese. I briefly described the Richmond experience and invited discussion. "In the U.S. you have black and white people who at least believe that they are part of the same [national] community. People here are not even recognized as being part of the same community," observed one Muslim. "Leaders give the impression they have nothing to learn from others. The attitude is: 'We agree to speak with you as long as you don't show us our weaknesses,'" said another. "In the political system there is a deliberate will to exclude and to find excuses to justify that."

Several objected to the fact that many Muslims felt compelled to hide their identity. In their view, the issue was not about headscarves but whether France was ready to accept Islam as a full part of the national culture. "People say the issue is about immigration but the real issue is French identity."

During most of the discussion, Muslims had done the talking while the majority group listened sympathetically. However, as the afternoon wore on, a Muslim turned to them and said, "We really need to hear from you."

An essential ingredient of any dialogue is full participation by people from the majority community. In dialogues between black and white Americans, the tendency is for black participants to play the role of "educators." They recount their painful stories while white participants murmur their sympathies or perhaps ask: "Are you really sure it was racism? Perhaps you were just interpreting it that way?" Black participants can become emotionally exhausted by reliving the same traumas time and time again, while whites—many of whom have never fully explored their own identity—avoid the hard work of digging deeply into their own feelings and experiences.

Many French from the dominant culture are fearful and resentful. If dialogue is to be truly honest, their voices must be heard, just as strongly as young North Africans who feel excluded.

Frédéric Chavanne says the dialogue has four objectives: "to talk about the things of everyday life that preoccupy us; to talk about subjects that cause anger or offense; to ask ourselves what in us contributes to the problem; and to carry the future of society together."

Chavanne, whose parents were farmers in Morocco, says, "Events of re-cent years such as terrorist attacks and laws on the headscarf, which might have led to distancing or even to rupture, have been on the contrary the occasion of strengthening a common will to work towards a reinforcement of social cohesion." Shared meals in homes and celebration of each other's religious festivals lead to deeper friendship and understanding.

But honest conversation can be uncomfortable, even among friends. "At one dialogue Béchir Labidi, a Tunisian political refugee, asked, 'Is democ-racy a universal value?'" Chavanne recalls. "Without reflecting, I answered, 'Yes, certainly.' My answer did not satisfy him at all. 'Then why do you sup-port regimes that don't practice it?' We felt him ready to explode."

"We must dare to be frank without pointing our fingers at the mistakes of others," says Chavanne. "The unconscious collective memory of the West carries a negative prejudice toward Islam. One must recognize it if one wishes to free oneself from it. It carries the memory of a colonial era which ended badly, fear of the young people in the suburbs, of a militant Islam perceived as aggressive and used for political ends, fear of integration." The majority population for its part, he says, needs to understand the grievanc-es of French Muslims stemming from discrimination, the divisive legacy of colonization, the impact of the Israeli-Palestinian conflict, and "the feeling that the Muslim world is put on a black list." In addition, the sense of being overwhelmed by Western culture weighs heavily. One Senegalese confided that political or economic domination affected him little, but he found the cultural domination unbearable.

Chavanne reflects on his own background as the son and grandson of a French colonialist: "I am proud of what my grandfather accomplished in the course of his life. I remain convinced that he contributed to the construct-ing and enriching of the country, but I also ask myself about the trauma of a foreign occupation and the consequences for today that we have not finished measuring.

"I spent my childhood in a bubble, ignoring the feelings of the Moroccan families among whom we were living. We considered the inhabitants of the countries we conquered as second-class citizens. We claimed that everyone was French, but it was not true. Everyone was not French in the same way. This denial of dignity led to violent confrontation. Even after years of work-ing on this relationship I feel that condescension can rapidly come to the surface again. Our mentality needs to be decolonized."[1]

In France, many look to government and to authority figures for solutions in building better relationships between groups. But members of Initiative Dialogue are taking the initiative by reaching out to their neighbors and building bridges of friendship. "There is a belief that if you create a law you are helping integration," said one participant. "It's not true; you have to do it at the grassroots."

Jamila Labidi says that thanks to Initiative Dialogue she sat around a table with "Français de souche" (indigenous French) for the first time. She discovered another face of France through people who welcomed her, took an interest in her, included her, and extended a hand to work together: "I discovered a culture and an ethic which neither the media nor even my personal studies had offered me. With time, this culture became a bit of my own. So last year, after nearly fifteen years in France, my family was able to share in the joy and significance of the Christmas festival." She and her husband, Béchir, lead a dialogue circle in the north of Paris, near an area where rioting took place.

Frédéric Chavanne's wife, Nathalie, tells a story that illustrates the power of personal relationships to break down stereotypes. "I had often wished that my teenage daughter would wear a skirt just once in a while, but nothing I bought her ever seemed to please her," she says. She confided her problem to a Muslim friend in the dialogue group. "Come with me—I know exactly what your daughter wants," responded the woman. Walking into a high-fashion boutique, she immediately selected a denim skirt. Imagine Nathalie's surprise and delight when her daughter exclaimed, "Now that is a skirt!" Nathalie laughs in amazement, "Who would have thought that this Tunisian woman in traditional Muslim dress would know just what style my teenage daughter would like?"

## The Risks of Honest Dialogue

Nathalie Chavanne's friend Samia Driss says, "As someone who wears the headscarf, I encounter prejudice by people who assume I am oppressed. Even my neighbor, who I thought was a good friend, said, 'Samia, you know you are an oppressed woman.'"

Driss, who has a degree in accounting, went to a city office for a job interview. "The woman only offered me a job as a cleaner or in child care. I was very uncomfortable but I did not react to her. But I cried in the car.

Then I decided to go back and meet with her again. The woman said, 'Well, which job do you want?' I said 'I have not come to accept a job but to say that you really upset me. You can't offer me that kind of job.' The woman asked, 'Why did you not say anything?' I replied, 'I was so shocked that I could not speak.' She did not offer me another job, but I felt liberated because I had spoken to her about it. It's better to be honest even if it upsets other people."[2]

Nathalie also discovered that honesty can be challenging. At a recent dialogue, the question of the veil provoked some heated exchanges: "In a moment of openness I talked about my fear of an all-powerful Islam. My remarks deeply hurt one of the Muslim participants in the dialogue who was surprised that after all these years I still held these fears. He wondered whether we had been wasting our time."

This incident demonstrates how hard it is to have really honest dialogue and why it is so important to create places of safety for all participants. We should not be shocked when fears, hurt, or even anger are voiced in a dialogue. If people feel that they cannot express their true feelings without risk of attack, the dialogue will remain on a superficial level. For this reason, smaller dialogue groups generally create safer space. In larger groups there is a danger of moving from dialogue to debate.

Not surprisingly, some Muslims are impatient for action, according to Alain Tate: "They say, 'We have discussed enough. What are we going to do concretely to change the situation?'" Alain, a quiet-spoken, immaculately dressed Frenchman in his late seventies, has provided sensitive support for the group with his wife, Anne-Marie.

In February 2006, the group hosted its first public event in a majority Muslim area of Paris. "Until now, we have often had more Muslims than indigenous French, but this time more French came," says Tate.

As a result of such public events, new dialogue circles are emerging in different neighborhoods in participants' homes. Leading one circle are the Smiths, a white couple who chose to live in an area with more than seventy nationalities, where some friends are fearful of visiting. But Michel Smith says the dialogues create a space where "real people" can meet and "discover how close we are in desires, values, problems."

The conversations often begin with each person describing childhood memories, sharing a subject they care about, and expressing appreciation for each other's culture. "We discover that we are similar in our emotions, pleasures and sorrows," reports one participant. As confidence builds, the dialogues can approach more difficult issues. "Over the course of our meetings, the way we see each other has changed," says Chavanne. "It requires long-term commitment and a willingness to approach others and talk about oneself. It is simple and anyone can do it."[3]

As the Initiative Dialogue team continues to work on its own relationships, it hopes to multiply the dialogue circles throughout France, building on what members have learned experientially. "Our vision is that long-lasting relationships be established in all the cities of France where different cultural groups live together, and that this will permit us to identify the fears and frustrations and seek to answer them," says Frédéric Chavanne. "I don't see any other means to bringing about a lasting solution to the tensions which now prevail at the heart of French society."

**Educating for Peace**

Our visit to Paris was organized by Laurence Le Moing, the young information officer for Initiatives of Change, France. She arranged a dawn-to-dusk week of interviews with senior politicians and civil servants, people in business and academia, and even a controversial comedian. We met Laurent Klein, a Jewish school principal, and Mehrézia Labidi-Maïza, the Muslim head of the school's parent-teacher association. Over lunch in a crowded restaurant in the Nineteenth Arrondissement—an area known as "Little Stalingrad"—they told us of their work to build relationships. Their book, *Wake up Abraham, They Have All Gone Crazy*, gained national attention.[4]

Laurence told us about an "education for peace" project that she was piloting with a diverse team in two Paris schools. She said she wanted to sensitize the pupils to the importance of personal responsibility in solving conflicts. "We want to give them tools so they don't fall into violence when they face a difficult situation," explained Laurence. "For that, they first have to acknowledge the different forms of violence; understand that each of us can be either an actor or victim of violence; and discover that dialogue, listening, respect, and individual change are the basis of a peace culture."

The two schools could not be more different. One is a Muslim academy located in one of the suburbs involved in the disturbances. The other is a state school with an almost entirely white student body. Many of the parents are in the military or police force.

The Muslim school draws from a wide geographical area. Parents want their children to go there to avoid getting caught up in violence on the streets. It provides a framework where they learn Arabic and about their culture. "Lots of parents think that the state schools are not giving values," said Laurence. "There is a generation of parents who abandoned their culture, and wanted to integrate. The younger generations want to reclaim their cultural roots. They say, 'We are French, we feel French but we are told we are not French.'"

One focus of conversation is the question of victimization. Many young French Muslims experience discrimination daily. When they go to a shopping center, they are stopped and searched before they are permitted to enter. It's difficult to be an individual; peer pressure is very strong.

The state school actually presented the bigger challenge for Laurence and her team. "When we started, the students were completely unengaged and uninterested," she told us. Coming from mostly middle-class backgrounds, they said: "Why are you talking to us about violence? We are not part of the violence. It is people in La Corneuve who are violent." They could not understand that verbal insults, discrimination, and ignoring people are also forms of violence. In fact, these students are not immune to physical violence. A few months earlier, boys from more privileged backgrounds beat a girl and posted a video of the assault on the Internet as a joke.

Both of Laurence's parents are teachers. "I used to get fed up hearing their stories. Now I see what they are living every day," she smiled. "With teenagers you have to be authentic. This was a way for me to test my conviction and theories. The practice is not so easy!"

A typical workshop begins by students exploring the meaning of violence (physical, verbal, and emotional) and its causes—in society and in themselves. They learn how to express deep feelings as a way of avoiding violence. They come to understand that we all have prejudices and can all be victims and perpetrators of violence. The workshops emphasize listening and putting oneself in the shoes of another person. Students examine the role of personal responsibility in demonstrating nonviolence as modeled by Gandhi and King and how personal change can lead to reconciliation.

The team uses two facilitators: one provides continuity and the other alternates according to the subject. "Of course we need skilled facilitators, but we also need people who can share their own personal experience with the teenagers," Laurence says. The Education for Peace Team includes a French Muslim of Tunisian descent, a French citizen who was born in the Congo, the grandson of a French colonialist farmer in Morocco, people of strong faith, and others of no religious background. When we talked in January 2006, Laurence and her colleagues had just completed four sessions. There had been something of a breakthrough in the state school. "The hardest thing at first was getting students to overcome peer pressure and talk openly." One workshop in the Muslim school was tense, following the publication of cartoons depicting the prophet Mohammed. One girl was so upset that she had to leave the room, but later she called one of the facilitators and was able to express what was in her heart.

Education for Peace has expanded to other schools and continues to develop its curriculum to include such topics as the problem of water and how it relates to peace. Students work to identify ways to protect and conserve water.

I asked Laurence whether she knew of other groups doing similar work in schools. "We did a survey of other NGOs, and we think what we are doing is rather unique because we are interested in the roots of violence, not just the symptoms," she said. "The other NGOs want to give immediate solutions to issues of violence. They are not so interested in why people turn to violence. We are not only interested in physical violence. It's not just a nonviolent approach but a proactive peace approach. We work at the level of individual responsibility: each of us has the possibility to change and to do something."

What has the experience meant to her personally? "I knew that France was not a very welcoming country, but I am facing the question of discrimination in a very concrete way," she replied. "It has made me think about my culture, and the question of equality.

"One woman, who wears a headscarf, thought she had a good relationship with her neighbor. But when she met her on the street with a friend, the neighbor ignored her. Another young woman works at a child care center. When a white three-year-old called her 'auntie' the father got totally mad.

"It's really two worlds. I knew it in an intellectual way, but I really experienced it by doing this. We really need to create a connection between these two worlds. We need to build it together. Everything depends on how we build trust."

# A Global View III

Beyond
Multiculturalism in
the United Kingdom

A high official in Paris told me, "Of course, Britain does not have the same sense of national identity that we do." It's a view to which I am certain my British compatriots would take strong exception! But in contrast to the French experience, the United Kingdom has long favored a policy that nurtures multiculturalism and celebrates ethnic diversity. Now, faced with a widening gulf between minority and majority populations, many in Britain question the efficacy of the policy.

Susan and I arrived in London on July 21, 2005, two weeks after bomb attacks killed fifty-two commuters and wounded another seven hundred. As we traveled in from Heathrow, the Underground was disrupted by another four unsuccessful attacks. The head of MI5, the United Kingdom's security intelligence agency, said that the agency and police were tracking two hundred cells involving more than 1,600 individuals. The incidents sparked a vigorous public debate on issues of security, identity, racism, values, and citizenship. The Commission for Racial Equality made news by blocking grants to ethnic minority projects that failed to promote "Britishness" and integration, and its chairman, Trevor Phillips, even suggested that the term "multiculturalism" should be scrapped because it encouraged a tendency toward separateness.[1] Minorities are heavily concentrated in a few cities in the Midlands and in London (where they make up 29 percent of the capital's population). The following year Phillips went further, calling the fragmentation of British society by race and ethnicity "a catastrophe for all of us," and warning that the country was "sleepwalking" its way to apartheid.[2]

The majority of Muslim immigrants entered Britain at the bottom of the socioeconomic ladder. However, most of those involved in the bombings were from middle-class or at least solid working families, so poverty was not the only motivating factor. Second-generation Muslims face particular challenges in a youth culture in the United Kingdom which is dominated by "clubbing," alcohol, and premarital sex.[3] Older Muslims are out of touch with the youth; the traditional hierarchical parent-child dynamic results in a serious generation gap. Thoughtful observers call for dialogue within the Muslim community, giving particular attention to intergenerational understanding. Some leading Islamic thinkers point to the need for Muslims to get out of "intellectual and social ghettos" by participating fully in British life and leaving behind the "us versus them" mentality.[4]

Others say that Britain must make it possible for mainline Muslims—especially young Muslims—to participate in the democratic political process in forums where they can express anxieties and frustration with domestic and foreign policy without being branded as disloyal or supporters of terrorism. Above all, individual white Britishers must realize that cultural integration is a two-way street. Sir Max Hastings, the former editor of the *Daily Telegraph* and the *Evening Standard* says: "I acknowledge an embarrassing truth. In the course of my life I have entertained only perhaps a dozen black guests at parties and never had a Muslim to dinner in my home. The same must be true for many British middle-class people. Until interracial experience finds a path into our own lives, it remains hard to boast that we are contributing much to the assimilation we deem vital to our future."[5]

Traditionally, Britons view immigrants with suspicion. The expansion of the European Union resulted in an influx of eager workers from Eastern Europe—more than five hundred thousand since 2004. The government and employers say they benefit the economy, but public sentiment forced a decision in 2006 to sharply limit Romanian and Bulgarian immigration when those countries joined the Union.

Like the French, many British feel overwhelmed by change. Ironically, many of them are heading for France. The taxi driver who took us from rural Suffolk to the airport told us that he and his wife were planning to move as soon as possible. It was not just the very wet British summer that upset him. "This place is full of asylum seekers," he said. "The country is poor because the government is spending all this money on people from overseas." His sentiments are echoed by many. And when a few of the very people who are being offered refuge (and are supported by generous social services and a national health system) actively encourage violence against the host country—one London-based cleric called the bombers "the fabulous four"—the frustration and alienation are hardly surprising.

The public debate reached new levels of intensity when Jack Straw, the leader of the House of Commons, argued that full-face veils prevented communication and jeopardized British social harmony: "Communities are bound together partly by informal chance encounters between strangers, people being able to acknowledge each other in the street or being able to pass the time of day. That's made more difficult if people are wearing a veil."[6] Prime Minister Tony Blair supported Straw, calling the full veil a mark of separation.

On a more hopeful note, polls showed that most Muslims did not feel that Britain became less hospitable to them following the bombings. A 2006 Pew survey showed that 57 percent of people in the United Kingdom felt that immigration from the Middle East and North Africa was "a good thing." The figure was similar for France. However, when immigrants were asked, "Do you think of yourself first as a citizen of your country or as a Muslim, 81 percent of respondents in the United Kingdom chose Muslim first, in marked contrast with France, where 46 percent said they regarded themselves primarily as French citizens.[7]

The growing number of people from different cultures who make their homes in countries other than their native lands raises important questions about the responsibility of the majority community and that of newer arrivals. Andrew Fuller, a British-born resident in the United States who travels widely for his work with a Christian organization, describes a visit to British colleagues who have lived in Spain for twenty years. They are fluent in Spanish, and their children have grown up in the Spanish school system. Although they are involved in an evangelical "church planting" ministry, they are well integrated in a Catholic-oriented community, assist their community PTA, and participate in a wide range of community activities. They feel themselves more Spanish than British. However, they reported that the English community in Spain now numbers more than 1 million expatriates and is growing at the rate of two thousand a month. Many are refugees from what they consider the high price of housing in the United Kingdom, as well as what they perceive as the high social cost. This is happening at a time when traditional Spanish family life has changed so much that the ethnic Spanish face a massive aging population and resultant population decline in the future.

Fuller writes: "My friends expressed deep concern about the way the influx of Brits is changing the Costa del Sol and making fundamental changes to Spain and society in that region. I also find this very disconcerting since I strongly believe that failure on the part of immigrant communities to enculturate is a primary factor in social disintegration. Placed in the early 20th century this kind of immigration—with its disdain for the local people—would be described as colonial elitism akin to the white presence in Kenya's white highlands or South Africa's Cape Coast."

Westerners are expected to dress modestly in Muslim countries out of respect for cultural norms. Is it outrageous to ask Muslims to reveal their faces out of respect for social sensitivities in the United Kingdom or other European countries? But the British debate about dress misses the real point, since the full veil is usually more of a statement of cultural identity, a reaction to British policies, or expression of grievance rather than a religious expression. Most British Muslims are South Asians and are part of Sunni traditions where the full veil is not required. But many young Muslims do feel alienated and besieged. Condemning the veil may simply increase its political symbolism. Much more important are efforts to establish inclusive and respectful dialogue, develop effective economic development opportunities, and to enable young Muslims to find a way to live their values in a contemporary context.

One leader attempting to do this is Imam Ajmal Masroor, director of Communities in Action, who provides consultancy and support to media and various government agencies on Muslim issues. He is a regular contributor on national radio and TV programs. "We need to get young Muslims to wake up and realize they can become agents of peace. They may be waiting for someone to take their hand and walk with them," he told some Hope in the Cities colleagues. "Islam is here to stay. We can either treat them as foreigners or we can facilitate them to integrate equally." Masroor aims to train one thousand young European Muslims as peacemakers.

Dr. Abduljalil Sajid is another leading imam who speaks out frequently to condemn terrorism and to encourage community building. He has taken part in numerous Hope in the Cities international activities. After September 11, 2001, Sajid, who chairs the Muslim Council for Religious and Racial Harmony and is secretary of the U.K. Ethnic Minorities Representative Council, edited a publication by nineteen leading Muslims articulating an alternative to violence.[8]

Simple hospitality helped change Imam Sajid's own view of the United Kingdom and set him on the path of encouraging interfaith projects. Coming from a gregarious family, he found people private and aloof during his first year in London. An invitation to a home for Christmas led him to get to know a family who lived out values of dialogue and service. Through this interaction with a Christian family, Sajid's own faith found new meaning and practical expression.[9]

One British city that is taking proactive steps to build community is Bradford, home to eighty thousand Muslims, one of the highest concentrations in the United Kingdom. Many of its more than eighty mosques are located in old warehouses, abandoned factories, and disused schools and churches. White flight and housing segregation mean that inner-city schools can be predominantly or 100 percent Muslim, so there is little opportunity for social interaction.

Ishtiaq Ahmed, a spokesperson for the Bradford Council of Mosques, and Dr. Philip Lewis, a university lecturer and advisor to the bishop on interfaith issues, are among the leaders who are responding to the challenge by creating a civic network to build relationships and allay fears. The initiative includes interfaith prayer groups, shared meals, discussion of issues that concern the whole community, and an intercultural leadership course for young professionals of different faiths. The Bradford Council of Mosques encourages mosques to open their doors to different faiths. "Islam is not a private limited company," says Ahmed. "It's a universal, public company, and our mosques should reflect that. Anyone should be able to walk into a mosque, and if they want to pray, they should be able to."

Philip Lewis affirms: "Ordinary people at the grassroots level want to live together, want to talk together. They simply need opportunities, a little enabling."[10]

In Sheffield, Krish Raval is "dedicated to enabling young people to become authentic leaders who integrate their highest values into their everyday lives." An Ethiopian-born British Indian lawyer who studied at Sheffield University and Cambridge, Raval spent a decade developing innovative approaches to training young leadership. His national education organization, Learn to Lead, engages business and nonprofit leaders to impart their knowledge to university students who in turn pass on their newfound skills to younger teenagers, including those who have dropped out of the education system altogether.

As a Hindu, Raval says he has long wanted to expand this training within faith communities. In 2008, with sponsorship from Initiatives of Change and the patronage of prominent leaders of different religious traditions, he launched Faith in Leadership, a program for emerging change makers from diverse faith communities, especially Britain's Muslim youth. Raval says his vision is "a new generation of leadership which is able to rise above the immediate concerns of their particular community and instead work for the common good."

Applicants are selected through a national competition. Raval looks for activists in different faith traditions who are open to being with other faiths, and who want to increase their competency to engage with a new generation. The participants are skilled in youth work and will go into multicultural schools to deliver programs to teenagers. "So you may have a Jewish person mentoring a Muslim kid," says Raval. The program is led by a multifaith team.

Raval envisages "leaders within different faiths who share a common language of leadership and understanding of interdependence." They will also be skilled in communications. "The way you name an issue without alienating people is so important," says Raval. "In year two of the program, we will move into the marginalized areas of the cities where the terrorists are active. We've got to empower the moderates so the government has people to talk to."

### Britain's Hope in the Cities

While much of the current focus is on more recent immigrants to the United Kingdom, Denzil Nurse, a community worker from Huddersfield, sees growing obstacles to the long-established African-Caribbean community. He's not sure that basic racial attitudes have changed very much: "I see another gloss on the same wall." The image of the impartiality of British police was shaken when an official report offered seventy recommendations to address institutional racism following the failure to bring to justice a gang of five white youths who stabbed and killed Stephen Lawrence, an African-Caribbean student, in 1993.

As a person of African-Caribbean descent, Nurse sees the need for African-Caribbean communities to engage, observe, and learn the concept of enterprise development from the Asian communities. "Asians band together to get jobs," he says. "People are using race and religion as a smokescreen to put a career ladder in place. Local authorities say they have people from minority communities. Yes, but what color are they? The racial equality council in Huddersfield has no blacks on it. Most communities have Asians in local politics but very few, if any African-Caribbeans. We have four or five blacks in our local authority where there used to be thirty-four. How can I begin to develop a dialogue between the Asian and the African-Caribbean communities? What part should the local authority play in dissipating the tensions for better cohesive relationships among and between communities?"

At the same time, Nurse believes that the black community has much to learn from how the Asian and Jewish communities have structured wealth creation: "Go to the ant, consider their ways and be wise." Overreliance on grants is a trap for community-based organizations: "I've done a 180-degree turn in my thinking. If you get a grant, it does not pay enough for staff, only volunteers. But if you get a contract as a service provider, you can employ people. We need to get out of the grant mentality into paid employment, from grant dependency to enterprise." Nurse set up a social enterprise, non-profit company to assist grant-dependent voluntary and community groups to identify and package their "products" into deliverable units and to "sell" them to the customer, not supported by grants but through contractual agreements.

Nurse is a leader of a growing Hope in the Cities dialogue project in the United Kingdom that emerged in the late 1990s, based primarily in Liverpool, Nottingham, and London. I talked with Gerald Henderson, one of the coordinators, in his Liverpool home in July 2005.

Henderson came to live in Liverpool after working for seventeen years in Africa: "My experience in Africa touched me and opened my heart. I was never once made to feel unwelcome there. When I finally came back to live in Britain I was quite shaken by the degree of racism, overt and hidden, that I found."

With his wife, Judith, he made several visits to Liverpool in the years leading up to the 1981 riots. They made many friends and decided to make the city their home: "I became involved in community and race relations from the start. Attitudes were pretty confrontational, and I got to know and worked with people who taught me a lot, not least from my mistakes." For Henderson, the critical lesson was "recognizing how fear and control feed confrontation, but also how confrontation feeds fear and control; and how both are linked to some degree to self-interest and lead to breakdown on trust."

Such insights grew from personal experience as he ventured into the arena of Liverpool's highly polarized race relations: "At times I was fearful, not because of what would happen to me but because of what people might think of me: 'What is this middle-class white do-gooder up to?'" He said he had to learn to leave his fear at the door, but also to understand that "giving up control is not giving up responsibility."

He also learned the meaning of privilege: "A few years back I said to someone from the Liverpool black community, 'I understand what you feel.' He shot back at me with considerable strength, 'You will never understand what I feel. Empathize, yes, but feel, no. You have not experienced what I had to go through.' He was right, especially as I was a white person from a privileged background who has scarcely ever been demeaned or excluded because of my race or culture. What he was talking about was not just day-to-day experiences, but the unhealed legacy of history that continues to spawn injustice and discrimination in so many situations." Hearing this kind of pain is not comfortable, said Henderson, "but it has been very necessary and helpful to me."

In response to a question about the underlying challenge in community relations in the United Kingdom, Henderson reflected: "There is so much talk about community cohesion and consultation, but people in the community sense it is just words, and that those in control do not really listen. They go through the actions, but most things have been decided ahead of time. We need to bridge the gap between the person who feels he's not being heard and the person with power and authority who always talks about consultation."

To his surprise, Henderson found himself in partnership with Lawrence Fearon, the son of a Jamaican immigrant, and cofounder of what has been called "the most ambitious grassroots-led community group in Britain." Fearon grew up in public housing in Brent, a borough with the highest concentration of blacks in the United Kingdom. Like others of his peers, Fearon was caught up in a cycle of parties, fighting, women, and petty crime. With little education and facing constant discrimination and police harassment, prospects for young African-Caribbean men like Fearon were slim. Yet in a remarkable turnabout that they describe as a spiritual transformation,

Fearon and his friends Delaney Brown and Leonard Johnson, who were also emerging from prison terms, chose to put their lives on a new course. They raised $2.8 million to buy a former bus station and created a community complex with a gymnasium and squash courts; thirty units for starter businesses, as well as training and seminar rooms; a recording studio; a bar, restaurant, and a hall for four hundred people. Fearon and his colleagues also played a key role in preventing violence when other urban neighborhoods were exploding in 1981.[11]

Fearon and Henderson had both attended the "Healing the Heart of America" events in Richmond in 1993. "The experience at the James River touched me deeply," said Fearon. "I'd never seen an attempt to have an honest conversation as I saw in Richmond. I knew that we had a similar journey to make in the U.K." Gerald and Judith Henderson, who had come earlier to help prepare the conference, were hosted for twelve weeks by Collie and Audrey Burton. Afterward Henderson pondered the deep level of healing and fundamental changes in attitude needed to resolve divisions and causes of conflict. "I think we have sometimes used truths like 'the issue is not color, but character,' as a defense rather than searchlight into our own souls."[12]

Building a partnership between two people of such different backgrounds was not easy: "It took me quite a while to acknowledge how deep within my Anglo-Saxon nature there was a tendency to control, even though I was not consciously aware of it. It came out over issues of communication and demands that were in line with what I wanted to see happen. It was evident in the fact, especially on the phone, that I would interrupt Lawrence in the middle of what he was saying rather than hearing him out. It has been, in part, with Lawrence's help that I have realized that it is not just unconscious racism but deeper factors of control that people like me are unaware of that destroy trust."

Fearon said that at first he had an image of Henderson with his upperclass accent as "someone from the top layer" of British society: "My inferiorities were still very much there. But we've been to places together, and we've taken the step of working as a diverse team. And because we have been together so long, I no longer hear the way he sounds! Doing this together has opened doors to conversations that would not have happened otherwise. It's still a challenge for a black person to speak openly about what they really feel, not just what feels comfortable. I had always thought that if I talked honestly it would seem that I had a chip on my shoulder, but I can do it now in this relationship. It may be painful, but it can be helpful. Also, hearing a white person opening up is so important."

Henderson and Fearon said that they kept short accounts. "We don't allow things to fester," said Fearon. "I like to wrestle it out in the moment. I see confrontation as an opportunity. Gerald is more reserved." Henderson agreed that for him "the temptation is to step back from responsibility to avoid clash. That does not help either. We have to be transparent on these matters because we need to mirror the trustbuilding work we feel called to do in the community."

Another key member of the Hope in the Cities U.K. network is Richard Hawthorne, who runs a family printing business in Nottingham. A quiet, conservative Englishman, Hawthorne has built a web of friendships throughout the city. In the course of a day, a visitor moving though the city with Hawthorne might meet a leading imam, the editor of the newspaper, the president of the chamber of commerce, and a director of human relations.

Hawthorne's humble approach and genuine care for others make him a uniquely trusted member of the community. He was at the heart of creating a partnership that resulted in significant investment in one of Nottingham's poorest areas. His straightforward, disarming approach often defuses tensions. During one difficult meeting, frustration boiled over, and Michael Henry, a black community leader, started to walk out. At that point, Hawthorne began to talk about the need for "honest conversation." Henry found the phrase so riveting that it stopped him in his tracks and he stayed. Hawthorne understands that business leaders must be open. He recalled a meeting with David Campt, the African American race relations consultant, that had prompted a senior businessman to exclaim, "I have realized that I don't feel I need to explain myself, but I expect others to explain themselves."

Phoebe Gill manages Hope in the Cities U.K. and has facilitated numerous dialogues in different cities. "We need training programs for local authorities, police, and fire brigades," says Gill, a consultant in organizational development and human resources, referring to the racist attitudes prevalent in such organizations. "Many minorities leave because of pressure; they were basically forced out."

The Hope in the Cities team has led conversations with Liverpool's black police association. "They feel discriminated against within the police force;

then they also have to deal with the way the black community treats them," says Gerald Henderson.

As in all Hope in the Cities projects, dialogues are led by an interracial team. "We come at this from two levels," says Phoebe Gill, noting the value of drawing on the complementary strengths of the different individuals. "Some people will identify with me and recognize me with my experience and others can identify with Denzil and recognize his experience."

Henderson says that new insights are emerging on all sides as the dialogue projects continue to expand: "A prominent black community leader said, 'I am aware that I and my community are not the only ones who carry pain in this city.' She spoke of the Irish community and some largely white areas in North Liverpool where there is high unemployment. On the other hand, a white participant said that he is becoming increasingly aware of the growing sense of exclusion in minority areas regarding employment and promotion opportunities."

Henderson called one dialogue session "a profound learning experience," which took the group "to a deep level of conversation on questions of exclusion, fear, control and racism. . . . We all agreed that this was the first step on a journey."

An important next step occurred in September 2007, when a group of thirty from the business community and the Black and Racial Minority (BRM) met to talk about how to find common ground from which to work together to transform access to employment in Liverpool. Nurse and Gill facilitated the dialogue, which was sponsored by the city council.

"After six hours of conversation—some of which was uncomfortable, some frustrating, but much enlightening and educative—we came to a place where eleven joint action steps were agreed upon," Gill reported. These will form the basis for new best practices between the communities.

....

In this and the preceding two chapters, we have glimpsed examples of trustbuilding initiatives in Britain, France, and South Africa. These examples demonstrate the potential of the "honest conversation" model. As in Richmond, the challenge is to bring to the table those who are harder to engage but who must be part of the conversation because they can make a difference.

## Creating a Space for Change

In the first part of this book I have shared stories of individuals and groups who are taking courageous steps to heal deep divisions through open and inclusive dialogue, acceptance of personal responsibility, and commitment to reconciliation. I have traced the development of Hope in the Cities in Richmond and similar activities in other communities. In the next four chapters, I explore more deeply the specific tools and methodologies that are proving effective in Richmond and that appear to have universal application. I also include brief case studies from other communities that show how Richmond's particular model relates to other similar models in the constantly expanding community reconciliation movement.

Creating space for change in our communities is an art in which we are all learners. It requires skills of the head and the heart. By identifying and releasing personal "baggage"— in the words of John Coleman—we can create a welcoming environment for others. Through inclusive dialogue, we can hear each other's stories and invite others to share our journey. In acknowledging painful history, we can move toward understanding, shared responsibility, and ultimately forgiveness and reconciliation. Through genuine partnerships and sustained teamwork, we can begin to build trust and to bring about change where it is most difficult and most needed.

# Becoming a Catalyst of Change

The root of what I condemn in others is found at long last in the soil of my own backyard. What I seek to eradicate in society . . . I must first attack in my own heart and life. There is no substitute for this.

—Howard Thurman

I did not do well in science at school, but I remember that in a chemical reaction, the chief characteristic of a catalyst is that it facilitates a reaction between two or more other substances but remains unchanged itself. So perhaps the title of this chapter is misleading, for there is strong evidence to suggest that our personal effectiveness as change agents is strengthened or weakened according to our willingness to see the need for change in our own attitudes, behavior, and relationships.

In *Bread, Bricks, and Belief,* Mary Lean asserts that individual change is the often overlooked factor in community development. Effective social change can start with inner change; in fact, it will be more sustainable if it does. She backs this assertion with case studies ranging from an organization for honest taxi drivers in Rio de Janeiro to farmers overcoming rivalries to increase crop production in India. Lean concludes, "For many, liberation began in areas that might seem far removed from community needs: their personal lifestyles, and habits, their relationships with their spouses, families and neighbors."[1]

Experience also suggests that failure to root social justice efforts on the bedrock of a strong inner life and lived-out values can endanger the most idealistic efforts. The Rev. Canon Robert G. Hetherington, who served for twenty-three years as rector of St. Paul's Episcopal Church in Richmond, reflects on this from the perspective of his experience with the civil rights movement. Hetherington and his seminary classmate Jonathan Daniels were among the students who rallied to Martin Luther King Jr.'s call to support the campaign for civil rights in Alabama in 1965. On August 20, Daniels was killed when he shielded Ruby Sales, a young black woman, from the blast of a shotgun wielded by a white special deputy.

"We were all followers of the philosophy of Harvey Cox," says Hetherington, referring to Cox's influential book *The Secular City*, which argued that
the church should be at the forefront of social change and that God is just
as present in the secular as the religious realms of life. "These were heady
times," recalls Hetherington. "But the forces of darkness were stronger than
we imagined. We thought that if we worked harder we would bring in the
Kingdom of God. People got burned out. We stopped saying our prayers.
We did not renew our spirits. There was a dis-connect."

Charles Marsh, who directs the Project on Lived Theology at the University of Virginia, says that King saw the Montgomery struggle primarily as "a spiritual movement depending on spiritual and moral forces." He
urged his followers to remember that the boycott and its achievements did
not in themselves represent the goal: "The end is reconciliation, the end is
redemption, the end is the creation of the beloved community."[2]

Following threats to his life in January 1956, King confronted his deepest fears and in desperation prayed at his kitchen table to "that power that
can make a way out of no way."[3] In *The Beloved Community*, Marsh writes,
"Faced with the intransigence of white resistance, liberal platitudes failed
him; notions of essential human goodness and perfectibility were not what
the moment required."[4]

Starting in 1960, up to fifty thousand students—many of them white and
privileged—came to the South to live with poor African Americans and to
work with them for reconciliation and justice. Marsh argues that this group,
known as the Student Nonviolent Coordinating Committee (SNCC), possessed a distinctive radicalism that was, in the group's early years, "theo-
logical to the core."[5] The movement pursued a form of discipleship that
was "life affirming, socially transformative, and existentially demanding:
a theology for radicals."[6] Resisting the "cultural paradigm of efficiency," it
made time for "reverie and solitude and for rituals that were refreshingly
unproductive. A certain kind of contemplative discipline was an important
disposition in building community and enabling trust."[7]

Marsh believes that SNCC's retreat from this spiritual basis after 1964
led to its ultimate collapse: "Compassionate action can never drift too far
from its sources without forgetting purpose and mission."[8] The movement
abandoned its principles of nonviolence and interracial partnership, and
"the spirit of wonder, openness, and love gave way to hardened attitudes and
judgments. . . . Ambivalence and increasing hostility towards the church fi-

nally produced conspiratorial evasions on the sources of racial oppression, evasions that demonized whiteness while making concrete reform undesirable and irrelevant."[9]

Many might contest Marsh's conclusions. But he is surely correct when he calls burnout "the activist's occupational hazard." Why has so little attention been given to the role of retreat in the study of the movement? Perhaps, writes Marsh, "because of the difficulty of appreciating the importance of contemplative and moral discipline in social protest."[10]

Hetherington says that, in today's world, "people are strung out." They need to "feed their inner life and nurture mutual accountability for each other."

Personal epiphanies alone will not bring about new social conditions. But social action and institutional change without an accompanying transformation in people, their motives, and their relationships are unlikely to be effective over the long haul. Experts have produced more than enough research papers analyzing the problems of racism, poverty, and exclusion. What is needed now may be simpler but more difficult. As I noted at the start of this book, the most needed reforms in our communities demand political courage and trust-based collaboration that is the fruit of leadership by individuals with the vision, personal integrity, and persistence to call out the best in others and to sustain substantial and long-term efforts.

Hope in the Cities roots its approach to community change in this perspective. Many social movements advocate change in the behavior of others. Hope in the Cities suggests that the best starting point for improving our neighborhoods or cities is to ask whether our own attitudes and actions reflect a spirit of inclusion or exclusion, resentment or forgiveness, egotism or self-giving. Life is a whole. People pay more attention to how we live than to what we say.

David Campt says: "The diversity industry has not done a good job at developing messages about unconscious prejudice. Thus many people think that because explicitly bigoted encounters have diminished, the challenges to inclusion have been solved. Part of the problem is our fault as change agents. We have contributed to the thinking that prejudice and bias are things you 'get past.' Doing this work requires more risk taking by us diversity practitioners because we must own up to our own ongoing struggle against our ingrained lower nature."

Every culture expresses truth differently, and many great humanitarians and pioneers of social justice adhere to no particular faith or reject religion entirely. But in *The World at the Turning*, Charles Piguet and Michel Sentis write:

> We have learnt, in thirty years of working with Buddhists, Hindus, North American Indians, Africans of all beliefs, militant communists, young revolutionaries, powerful capitalists, peasants, politicians, trade union leaders, that hope is not confined to any one temple.
>
> . . . The intimate experiences of the heart and spirit are a reality which can be communicated and which every other human being can respond to, no matter how far removed their expression may be from one's own particular habit of thought.
>
> Of course, this reality has to be stripped of the intellectual and religious verbalizing we normally clothe it in: words, like grand garments on a wasted body, can hide internal poverty. We need to rediscover the one universal language—a life lived out.[11]

## Personal Responsibility

When we find the courage to accept personal responsibility as a basis for change around us, and when we identify attitudes and actions based on feelings of blame and victimization, or a desire to avoid uncomfortable realities of privilege and exclusion, we have taken the first important first step in building bridges.

For Richard Hawthorne, the Nottingham printer, personal responsibility started with a realization that "Britain has recruited people from the Caribbean, Pakistan, and India to do the work we did not want to do, and we were treating them as second-class citizens." Sitting in his car one morning, he felt an inner call to "open my heart to people whom I had kept at arms length."

Five thousand miles from Nottingham, Niketu Iralu, who helped host the Richmond team in the 1988 Indian *yatra*, is exploring the meaning of personal responsibility as a peacemaker in Nagaland, a self-governing state in northeast India, bordering Myanmar. For decades the Nagas have struggled, sometimes violently, for autonomy. Iralu has devoted much of his life to reconciliation efforts. As a tribal elder, he convened a coordination committee to prepare for negotiations between Nagas and the central government. He writes that "the chain of revenge and counter-revenge starting from unhealed hurts is the story inside every conflict. . . . We must all take responsibility for the terrible legacy. . . . Each of us has to recognize where we have ignored the hurt we have caused others."

Yet even a veteran peacemaker has need for new wisdom. In his novel *The Devils of Loudon*, Aldous Huxley writes, "Those who crusade not for God in themselves, but against the devil in others, never succeed in making the world better." The passage jolted Iralu. "I realized with shame," he says, "that I had gone quite far in crusading against the devil in others and received applause and public recognition for this. I felt I was exposing evil and weakening 'anti-social elements.' One day a friend told me that the way I had made my point at a meeting of Naga leaders had deeply embittered a group of people." After careful reflection, Iralu apologized and received a warm response.

At a special ceremony, presidents of twenty-nine Naga tribes on both sides of the Indo-Myanmar border read a pledge: "We will start a process whereby we will truthfully examine the ways and areas in which we may have hurt others so that the needed changes may begin with us, leading to practical steps of restitution to make healing lasting. We will go beyond seeing only where others have hurt us and be ready to see where we too may have provoked them to hurt us, so that forgiving and being forgiven will become possible."[12]

Syngman Rhee, the Korean-born former moderator of the Presbyterian Church (U.S.A.), chose to forgive the Japanese who had occupied his country and the Communists who were responsible for the death of his father. Rhee, who teaches in Richmond and collaborates with Hope in the Cities, was born in what is now North Korea and grew up under Japanese occupation. When he was in fourth grade, the school curriculum was changed; the Korean culture and language were suppressed; and anyone caught speaking Korean at school was severely punished. Even family names were altered. The church was the one place where Korean could be spoken. Later, Rhee's father died in prison under the Communist regime.

One day in 1950, Rhee and his brother escaped, walking for a month through the snow of the Korean winter. He never saw his mother again; she died before he was able to return in 1978. Rhee served with the marines in the South Korean army, then made his way to America, where he studied at Chicago and Yale. He was a campus minister in Louisville, Kentucky, during the civil rights era and marched with Martin Luther King Jr.

Rhee says that the most powerful lesson that he learned from King was the idea that the oppressed have the key to a new beginning: "This touched me deeply, because I considered myself oppressed. I had turned my back on Korea. . . . But the oppressed have the choice of revenge or of forgiving and working for a new society for everyone." This conviction led him to make more than thirty visits to North Korea in efforts to bring about reconciliation with South Korea. "A bridge," he says, "has to touch both sides."

What does responsibility for community trustbuilding mean for me as a British-born, European American male? I can start by acknowledging that every white person, by virtue of the color of his or her skin, carries an invisible knapsack full of passes, secret codes, special provisions, maps, passports, visas, tools, and blank checks that provide access to networks and resources, freedom from surveillance and harassment, and quite simply the ability not to have to think about race at all.[13]

Some years ago we got a call from the police at ten thirty at night saying one of our sons and some friends had been vandalizing mailboxes with baseball bats. One boy had traces of drugs in his car. The police called the parents in. All the boys were white, high academic achievers from middle-class families. The police were kind, the parents were shocked, everyone was polite, and the boys ultimately got off with a severe lecture from the juvenile judge and thirty hours of community service. My wife and I were relieved, but we suspected that if the boys had been a different color, the outcome might have been different.

Bob Armstrong, a prominent member of the white community in Selma, Alabama, says: "I had never heard of the concept of white privilege before I encountered Hope in the Cities. At one point I asked, 'Why does it always have to be about race?' An African American responded gently but firmly, 'Maybe you're not being honest with yourself; maybe it often is about race.' I have never forgotten that moment of truth. It opened my eyes to my own arrogance." As a county district court judge, Armstrong helped to launch an initiative that offers counseling, training, and job placement for young fathers—many of them African American—who pass through child support court.[14]

For Americans in the majority community, responsibility for trustbuilding means challenging those who use fear, prejudice, and internal networks to manipulate public opinion, to block efforts for racial equity, and, above all, to maintain control. It means letting go of deep-seated superiority or indifference.

The Republican mayor of a big city told a conference: "If people say they believe in equal opportunity, then they need to look at issues of housing, land use, education and jobs. It's not fair for people like me to say that we want to get people off welfare and then abandon the schools." James W. Loewen, in *Sundown Towns* (2005), estimates that starting around 1890 and continuing right up until the 1960s, thousands of municipalities, in the North as well as the South, developed a whites-only policy through legal ordinances, banning the hiring of blacks or the renting or selling of houses to minorities, warnings to stay away, and even violence.

For people of minority racial, ethnic, or religious groups, responsibility might require a willingness to challenge those in their communities who exploit poverty and resentment to maintain political power, or who profit from the commercialization of a self-destructive culture. Such black writers and intellectuals as Bob Herbert, Orlando Patterson, and Juan Williams diagnose a poverty of the mind.[15]

"It's time to blow the whistle on a values system that embraces murder, gang membership, misogyny, child abandonment and a sense of self so diseased that it teaches children to view men in their orbit as niggaz and women as hoes," writes Herbert.[16] "If white people were doing to black people what black people are doing to black people, there would be rioting from coast to coast."[17]

Accepting responsibility takes courage. Trustbuilders are prepared to stand alone and risk being misunderstood or rejected even by their own community.

### Building a Personal Tool Kit

How do we nurture inner change, in ourselves and others, so that we become effective agents of healing and hope for divided communities? Certain values and disciplines have stood the test of time and are congruent with all the great faith traditions.

Encouraged by his mentor, Professor Henry Wright of Yale, Frank Buchman, the founder of Moral Re-Armament (now Initiatives of Change), developed a personal tool kit centered on regular early morning times of "listening prayer" in which he wrote down his thoughts. Although silence before the Creator is an age-old discipline, by making it a central tool of his work Buchman pioneered its universal application. The "quiet time," in various forms, has become standard practice for countless individuals and fellowship groups.

The most important space for Susan and me is the first hour of the day, which we spend in deep inner listening. We jot down our thoughts and share them with each other. This is an indispensable foundation for our marriage and our work. It counters fear, peer pressure, and the daily stress of life. It guides decisions about our relationship, our family, our finances, our friendships, and our strategic outreach to the community. The quiet time results in creative action instead of reaction. Jean Brown describes it as a time of *Connection* with the divine or the true self; *Correction* in our motives and behavior; and *Direction* for practical instructions for the day ahead.[18] Every important initiative in the Hope in the Cities movement has grown as a result of obedience to insights gleaned from such daily moments of quiet.

Buchman also came to believe that spirituality cannot be divorced from the highest moral imperatives and survive.[19] Tolerance alone is not a strong enough glue to keep our diverse communities from splintering into competing interests and identities. If there is no objective moral standard, how could anybody claim that one value is better than another? Paradoxically, in recent decades, "as moral relativism grew in strength, so too did a countervailing social consciousness," a desire for shared universal values: for human rights, for rights of women and codes to stop corruption. Relativism is therefore in conflict with widely acknowledged social values of respect, equality, and honesty.[20]

All through history, religious teachers and philosophers have searched for the ultimate values in human behavior, for a moral order that could make the world function as it should. Gandhi called purity of life the highest and truest art. The Prophet Mohammed made selflessness and service to those in need watchwords of Islam. Jesus instructed his followers, "Love your neighbor as yourself."

For Buchman, standards of honesty, purity, unselfishness, and love became a daily benchmark for all aspects of his personal life and public action. Individuals from many faith traditions and cultures have found value in the simplicity of these measures. He drew these principles from a concept originally expressed by Robert E. Speer as a summary of the moral teachings of the Sermon on the Mount and later described by Wright as "the four-fold touchstone of Jesus and the apostles."[21]

Audrey Burton says of her struggle to overcome the wounds of racism and exclusion, "Before, I would have written people off," but by practicing these standards, "I can be around almost anyone and it doesn't set off a time bomb."[22] In the words of John Coleman: "We need to take an inventory of who we are and then be willing to throw away what we don't need. There can be all kinds of baggage: background, education, race, money."[23]

A few years ago, we suddenly lost access to our office database. After hours of fruitless work, the IT consultant threw up his hands in frustration, saying, "I can see the database is there, but something is blocking it." We went to bed full of gloom. Next morning, Susan sat bolt upright in bed exclaiming, "Click the right mouse button!" She headed for the office repeating, "Click the right mouse button" like a mantra. Up popped a menu with an option "remove filter," and with one keystroke the database reappeared as if by magic.

For people of any religion, agnostics or atheists, quiet times in the light of standards mentioned above can help remove "personal filters" that block our effectiveness. For eight years I was in conflict with a colleague. He felt I had failed to support and even undermined him; I felt wrongly judged. It got to the point where we could barely have a conversation. One morning I thought: "What you are feeling does not matter. What does matter is that your friend feels you have wronged him." That day I wrote a short letter asking forgiveness for things I had done that had made it hard for him to trust me. Up until that point, he had avoided entering my house. But a few days later, very graciously and with some courage, he drove two hundred miles to have lunch with me.

It's humbling to acknowledge that I act, sometimes unconsciously, in ways that hurt my friends and colleagues. But being transparent about weaknesses and difficulties can be an unexpected door-opener. People are more much interested in my failures than my successes.

Trust is a fragile bridge we build each day. Honesty about our failures, purity in our motives, unselfishness in our support of others, and love in our readiness to forgive and accept forgiveness: these are building blocks of trust. Trust depends on the authenticity of our lives, our openness, and our willingness to start with change in ourselves.

In the words of Steve Bassett, who wrote the theme song for Richmond's seminal "Healing the Heart of America" event in 1993:

I'll start with my heart,
That's where the future is.
I'll start with my heart,
There's healing when it gives.
I'll start with my heart,
Our differences end in there.
That's what I'll do to get right with you,
I'll start with my heart.

**Making It Practical**

In talking about our family experience and our work in the Richmond community, Susan and I often share a five-point frame of reference that works well for us:

1. LISTEN TO OTHERS AND TO THE DEEPEST THING IN YOUR HEART. Sometimes the easier it is to communicate electronically, the harder it is for us to really hear others and to listen to what is being said—and even more importantly what is not being said. We must create space in our busy lives if we are to really know people and hear their stories. We need regular quiet times ourselves for reflection and discernment. Real listening requires the full attention of the head and the heart.

2. MODEL THE CHANGE WE WANT TO SEE. Do our actions match our ideals? If our behavior was multiplied, would the community be a better place? Are we living values consistently? Are we building unity in our own home? If we can't make it work there, we are unlikely to be effective in the community.

3. ENGAGE WITH THOSE AROUND US. Community building can't be done from the sidelines. Building relationships is the key. For our family, this meant becoming free of desires for insulation or protection. We chose to make our home in a racially diverse neighborhood where people of all backgrounds could get to know each other. When we enrolled our sons

in the public schools, we invested time as a family to make the experience work for them, but also to contribute to the whole school community.

4. RESPOND TO NEEDS AND CHALLENGES. When we truly know people, we break free of stereotypes. There will be wonderful moments of joy and friendship, but we will also encounter conflict and pain. What is our response when things are tough? What do we do with the temptation to run away? How do we relinquish our need to be in control? Are we willing to let go of hurt and allow crises and conflict to take friendship to a deeper level? Healing history is not just about what happened one hundred years ago: it is also about what happened yesterday and what we need to do to put things right in our relationships.

5. RISK GOING BEYOND THE COMFORT ZONE. Building trust often means going toward the thing we fear most. We may fear rejection by others or being misunderstood by our own group. We may fear getting out on a limb, or that we might be getting into more than we bargained for. But it is often the difficult first step that makes something new possible.

**Questions for Personal Reflection**

1. How could your personal work as a change agent be improved by building greater trust with others?

2. Are you modeling the change you want to see around you? If everyone adopted your attitudes or behavior, would the level of trust in your community or city be greater? Are there changes you might need to make in your life in order to become a better trustbuilder?

3. Is there an unresolved hurt or frustration that prevents you from being fully effective in building trust? What are the costs of holding onto it? Is there one step you might take to begin to resolve it?

4. How might you engage with others, respond to a need or challenge, or risk stepping out of your comfort zone?

# From Information to Transformation

······························································································································

Someone once said that the four most frightening words in the English language are, "We've got to talk." It's one thing if you are the person who is saying this, observes Harlon Dalton, "but if you are on the other side, if you are the person who thought things were fine the way they were, or at least you understand that things can be worse, these are scary words indeed. What our partner is saying is that attention must be paid, that respect must be given, and that perhaps power must be shared; that in some significant way the relationship must be altered."[1]

All over the world there are conversations waiting to take place. These "missing conversations" may involve different ethnic, socioeconomic, or religious groups, or people representing divergent political or cultural viewpoints. They may be in the workplace, schools, or neighborhoods.

Most of us can identify with Dalton's comments. Honest dialogue is hard. Often we don't know how to start. We fear rebuff. We fear we will expose ourselves to attack and that we will be blamed. We fear that once we begin the conversation we will not know how to continue. We fear we will say the wrong thing and make fools of ourselves. We fear we will encounter emotions we don't know how to handle.

In *Whose Side Is God On?* Peter Hannon reflects on his experiences of working with Catholics and Protestants in Northern Ireland. Often the motive for dialogue is a desire to talk with the other person or group so that we can learn each other's point of view. This can be helpful where contact has been restricted. But once we know the other person's opinions, he asks, where do we go from there?

Underlying the wish for dialogue is often the hope or the belief that "if only the other side can hear what I have to say they will see how reasonable I am." The trouble, however, seems to be that they say, "We know only too well what you think, and we are not interested, thank you."[2] More information can end up making people even more antagonistic.

Dialogues can become sentimental talk-shops or forums for airing of grievances and personal perspectives, says one observer, casting a skeptical eye on some interracial dialogues in the United States. Implicit is the idea that people can understand each other better by talking, and that from understanding comes healing. "It is when you converse in the context of a relationship that you can sustain something."[3]

It is very difficult for people to talk honestly where there is a history of separation; goodwill alone cannot overcome mistrust and fear. Encounter groups, lectures, or sermons seldom result in useful dialogue. Real dialogue avoids focusing on who is right and who is wrong, but looks for "the kernel of truth in what each person is saying." In the context of race relations in the United States, Christopher Edley says metropolitan communities must give highest priority to developing effective leadership—individuals "who know how to engage people in a constructive discussion about race and how to structure experiences that will change people."[4]

In the Hope in the Cities model of honest conversation, dialogue is more than a tool with which to exchange information. It can lead to transformation in individuals, in relationships, and—if sustained—to change in society. It moves us to action because it touches us at our deepest point of motivation. When we experience dialogue at this level we respond and behave differently. We relate to other people differently and choose different priorities in our lives. Our friendships, our interests, and our worldview are all deeply affected. In honest conversation, isolated people become connected and involved; the frustrated or disillusioned find hope; and the alienated see those on the opposite side in a new light.

Insight, new relationships, and commitment to action: these are fruits of good dialogue. Such dialogues create space where people feel able to express their deepest emotions, listen carefully, and find the courage to shine a spotlight on their own responsibility for change instead of accusing others.

### Sharing Our Stories

Such moments of insight can happen at any time, whether in a formal dialogue, a business meeting, a discussion with family or friends, or a chance encounter. Living responsively to "inner promptings" and having the courage to address the real, often unspoken needs of those around us can make us facilitators of honest conversations wherever we are.

Asking the right question at the right time is crucial. What do we do when people come to us with their complaints and grievances? Do we merely offer sympathy, or do we support them by asking tough questions with love? Offering sympathy may make us feel good and perhaps bolsters our own prejudices or sense of self-importance. But it is easy to encourage a mentality of victimization and blame, which does nothing to empower the other person to become an effective agent of change. If we ourselves are nursing wounds or anger, our tendency may be to sympathize rather than to challenge. What might we need to release ourselves in order for us to help others ask themselves difficult questions?

A willingness on the part of the facilitator to be open about personal mistakes, failures, or fears encourages others. And we can use our personal stories to invite them to join us on our mutual journeys of discovery.

Hugh O'Doherty, a Catholic from Derry in Northern Ireland, is known internationally for his skills in facilitation and leadership training. I heard him admit to a group that when the Good Friday Agreement was signed, he had to confess to a twinge of regret that he would not be able to blame the British any longer.

Sharif Abdullah writes of leading a workshop for the "bluest of blue-collar workers—mostly white males—who were ordered to attend workshops on diversity and change."

> In the middle of a session, Sam, a thin, twenty-something man with blond curls under his baseball cap raised his hand and said, "The white man is an endangered species!" I smiled, said something to humor him and continued on. A few minutes later, Sam put up his hand again and said something similar. I again turned him off.
>
> His hand went up a third time, "You're not listening to me!" I took a breath and said, "You're right. I am not listening. We're going to take a five-minute break and I'm going to center myself so that when we come back, I will be listening."
>
> When we returned, I invited Sam to explain his remarks.
>
> "It's not the colored people who are in trouble. It's not the women who are in trouble. All of us are in trouble! How can I be concerned about someone else when it's my butt on the line? I can't respect a movement that doesn't understand that the whole boat is going down! We can't work for minorities or for women—we've got to work for everyone!"

Abdullah concludes: "No one wants to be pressured, shamed or manipulated into changing for someone else's sake. . . . What catalyzes deep change is an appeal to the heart."[5]

I attended a forum in inner-city Philadelphia where a group of young African American men walked in unannounced and joined the audience. Later we broke into small dialogue groups. My group, which included some of the young men, was led by a professional facilitator. She did her best, but the atmosphere was strained, and people seemed reluctant to open up. Also in the group was a colleague from England, an older, somewhat reserved white man. Suddenly, he turned to one of the black youths and said: "I think I need to be honest. When you all came in this morning, I was scared because you looked so fierce." The young man looked at him in astonishment: "You were scared? How do you think we felt seeing all you people in coats and ties? Our hands were sweaty with fear." Instantly, a bridge was built, and real conversation started.

The role of a facilitator is to offer a welcoming and safe space in which each person feels validated and free to share their stories, as well as their concerns, hopes, frustrations, and visions. One veteran practitioner remarked that the key is "sensible people who will listen." Training certainly helps. But in the end, good dialogue facilitation is more than a technique. It is the product of a way of life. Occasionally we will make mistakes or look foolish. But in my experience, most people are quite intuitive and quickly sense if they are in an environment that is genuine and trustworthy.

### Dealing with Hot Buttons and Unrecognized Wounds

The belief that "we are the solution and that others are the problem" is a major obstacle to trustbuilding and to community change. As facilitators of inclusive dialogue, we may need to park some of our most cherished viewpoints at the door. We should constantly remind ourselves and participants of the difference between debate and dialogue. In debate, participants present information and ideas with the purpose of bringing others into alignment with their own positions. Dialogue involves inquiry, attentive listening, and sharing experiences as well as information and assumptions with the purpose of learning. It is the role of the facilitator to create an inquiring atmosphere.

If any participants feel that they must check their true selves at the door, the dialogue will not be honest. Often those on the political left (I speak as one) are so wedded to their analysis that they make it impossible for those of different views to join the dialogue as equals. A dentist friend of conservative views, who devotes much time to pro bono work, attended a "dismantling racism" training session. He withdrew in frustration because the trainer insisted on group acceptance of a particular social construct and historical interpretation. He was made to feel that his contribution to the community was of no value. A potential ally was lost.

Dr. Bonnie Dowdy, a Hope in the Cities trainer and facilitator, says that if we learn to pay attention, we can feel the physical shift in us when certain types of people talk or certain issues arise. This does not necessarily mean that our tempers flare up. Rather, when our "hot buttons" are pushed, our ability to allow safe space for all perspectives is compromised. Personal un-healed wounds shape how we experience the world and respond to it. They limit our intuitive faculties and our capacity to make room for the experi-ence of others. Dowdy, who is a European American, illustrates this with a personal story:

> While co-facilitating a dialogue, I experienced difficulty in making room for a particular male participant to speak. John is a very successful white business-man who believes he has no racism in him.
>
> I worked hard in the opening two sessions to not respond in a judgmental way and "set his thinking straight," but I could hear *my tone, and the extra en-ergy* behind the comments I offered in response to his statements. I heard the teacher in me setting him straight.
>
> I imagine my responses made him feel that his contribution had little value, that he was part of the problem we were talking about. I was aware enough of the energy he evoked in me so that I spoke to him afterwards, and affirmed his participation in the group. But I still thought *he* was the problem—I just had to learn to manage my frustration better.

Some time later, Dowdy was in a training session when I described my initial reaction to conservatives in Richmond and the realization that this limited the effectiveness of my work. She says:

> At that moment I had an insight that there are certain types of white males who trigger in me some serious personal woundedness that I had not dealt with. To be accepting of all participants in dialogue, I needed to heal the hurt I have experienced.
>
> *My head and my heart connected.* I could see my part of the problem and how my responses did not create trust. Explanations of why I have issues with certain types of white males are no longer an acceptable excuse for my responses. I have

to be honest and say, it is time to take responsibility for my own actions and reactions—to grow up some more.

To be an effective facilitator, one who helps people move from information in the head to transformation of the heart, requires fine-tuning our most important tool, namely oneself.

The task of building just and inclusive communities is too important to be seen as the sole possession of any political worldview. Hope in the Cities is a trusted voice in the Richmond community because everyone feels that in it they find a welcoming space where they can make their best contribution.

## Moving from Enemies to Allies

William Raspberry warns of the trap of failing to distinguish between problems and enemies. He told a group in Richmond that a focus on enemies "diverts time and energy from the search for solutions." A good question to ask is: "If I defeat the enemy in the battle I have engaged, will my problem be nearer to a solution? People respond more favorably to being approached as allies."

Hope in the Cities took this advice to heart in its strategy of "constructive engagement" with the Richmond newspapers. For many years, the editorial policy of the *Richmond Times-Dispatch* and its sister publication, the *Richmond News Leader*, sharply divided its readership. Both newspapers, particularly the *News Leader*, were fervent supporters of Massive Resistance, the protest movement against school integration led by the Virginia General Assembly. A barrage of editorials by James Kilpatrick, the editor of the *News Leader* fueled the discontent.

After African Americans gained control of the Richmond City Council in 1977, the newspapers highlighted conflicts at council meetings, and editorials described the performance of Henry Marsh's majority as "mediocre to poor," marked by "irresponsible fiscal decisions . . . and racist voting."[6] A leader of the Crusade for Voters, a black political organization, spoke for many when he called the press "one of the main catalytic agents causing racial polarization." Another complained of its "plantation mentality."

But throughout the 1980s and 1990s, unseen by the public, a number of reporters and editors were arguing for greater balance in news coverage and more sensitivity to community concerns. Believing that "naming the enemy" does not solve problems, Hope in the Cities set out to build relationships with reporters and editors who were working for constructive change within the institution. Several months prior to the "Healing the Heart of America" conference, HIC leaders met with senior editors to share their vision for Richmond and to enlist the support of the newspaper in communicating the importance of the reconciliation initiative.

Following the event, which the newspaper covered extensively, the reporter Michael Paul Williams arranged for the executive editor, the managing editor, and three other senior editors to meet with a group of thirty citizens to discuss the newspaper's responsibility to the community. Some months later, prompted by Williams and other reporters, the newspaper ran a week-long feature on issues related to racial disparities in the region.

Senior editors took part in dialogues and community forums. And when a front-page photograph of an image of Confederate general Robert E. Lee in a new downtown display of murals inflamed old passions, Louise Seals, the newspaper's managing editor, called on Hope in the Cities to lead twenty editors and reporters on a history tour of Richmond to "sensitize them" to the community.

A special report on Virginia's leading role in the eugenics movement in the 1920s, which resulted in forced sterilization of people suffering from any shortcoming judged to be hereditary—including mental illness, mental retardation, epilepsy, alcoholism, and criminal behavior—and the classification of Native American tribes as black, gave impetus to the General Assembly's decision to pass a resolution of "profound regret" in 2001. And when the city announced plans for a slave memorial, the newspaper ran an eloquent lead editorial in support. Noting that "slaves ranked among Virginia's first families," the editors acknowledged that, until recently, "slavery fell into the category of issues people did not want to talk about. Neither white nor black, it sometimes seemed, longed to confront a painful past. . . . The legacy has not disappeared. Time does not move so swiftly as those who wish to forget history would prefer. . . . A site of appropriate dignity . . . would grant to the slaves as individuals what they were denied in life—their humanity."[7]

On the fiftieth anniversary of the Supreme Court decision on school desegregation, the newspaper featured a history of Massive Resistance that acknowledged the prominent support given that movement by the *Richmond Times-Dispatch* and the *Richmond News Leader* and their "seething advocacy" for segregation. J. Stewart Bryan III, the fourth generation of his family to control Richmond's daily newspapers, approved an editorial that stated: "No man or institution can apologize for the actions of others. But what better moment than the 50th anniversary of *Brown v. Board of Education* for this newspaper to restate its opposition to Massive Resistance, to lament the massive wrong inhering in it, and to laud the Court for removing the last major barrier separating American truths from American ideas?"[8]

Many impartial observers agree that news reporting has become more responsive to community concerns, issues related to racial history, and Richmond's increasingly multicultural population. Shortly before he retired, Bill Millsaps, the executive editor, told me: "I get irate calls from readers every day who say, 'This is not the *Times-Dispatch* I grew up with.' I take that as a compliment."

In 2005, Thomas A. Silvestri took over as president and publisher of the *Times-Dispatch*. For the first time since 1887, a member of the Bryan family is not serving as publisher of one of Richmond's major daily newspapers. Silvestri is a 1997 graduate of Leadership Metro Richmond, a program offering training in leadership skills and experiences of community service to a diverse group of sixty or more citizens annually. He also took part in early dialogues facilitated by Hope in the Cities. Silvestri hired Glenn Proctor, an African American, as executive editor. Proctor was the first person to submit his resume. "At the time I did not know he was black," says Silvestri. "Our initial screening and phone interviews had determined three finalists, and I said, 'We need to do a diversified search.' One of my colleagues said, 'Don't you know Proctor is African American?'"

Silvestri says that politeness can continue to get in the way of meaningful exchange in Richmond: "Glenn Proctor shakes some people up because he says what he means." He also notes that for most people the only contact with the newspaper is with journalists who are out in the field: "We had some unpleasant internal conversations because the reporters have had to deal with all the baggage of the past. Many of them really helped to build back the credibility of the newspaper."

Silvestri has initiated town hall dialogues on affordable housing, immigration, public education, and other key issues. He says, "It's ironic that in a time of Internet connections, we are going back to face-to-face encounters." Silvestri has acted as moderator for more than twenty of these Public Square events. "It's important to welcome everyone and even to invite specific people," he says. "We also share information ahead of time by publishing articles on the topic."

He believes in setting ground rules: "Otherwise people just shout at each other. So we start by saying, 'Here are the questions we want to talk about today.'"

At the first Public Square events, the audience sat theater-style, and people of like mind tended to group together. So Silvestri switched to a square. "People don't know where to sit because I am in the middle. I can look for someone whom I would like to draw out, or turn my back on someone who might want to dominate the conversation."

Silvestri sees the newspaper and its Web sites as "a caretaker of the conversation"—a remarkable turnaround for an institution once known for its prejudicial news coverage and divisive editorials. He keeps his ear to the ground and is open to hearing criticism: "I get some of the best information from people who call to chew me out. I ask them, well, what would you do differently? You disarm them. It's probably just something they want to get off their chest. I had one guy who would often call me early in the morning. Finally his wife came on the phone to say, 'I hope he's not bothering you but I appreciate it so much because otherwise he would be loading it all onto me!'"

## Getting Started

Creating an environment for dialogue requires careful preparation. Care in choosing a site where all feel welcome and secure helps everyone feel at ease. It is useful to ask people where they would be comfortable meeting. Often, a home setting provides a relaxed context, but sometimes a more neutral context is needed. One youth dialogue group in Richmond chose a different site for each meeting; the students got to know different sections of the city and learned to become comfortable in less familiar settings.

Food helps participants relax and relate to each other. But, again, cultural differences are important. When two churches, one predominantly black, the other white, were planning a Sunday afternoon dialogue, the white participants' suggestion of cold sandwiches did not sit well with the other congregation! In choosing menus, it is also important to discover if there are vegetarians in the group and whether religious beliefs forbid certain types of food. Site and menu should not favor one group over another.

Facilitators should help establish some general principles for dialogue at the start. For example, dialogue assumes that each person is there in a genuine search for solutions. While they may disagree—sometimes passionately—all participants should accept that others are on a journey. Everyone is there to contribute and to learn.

Paige Chargois says we are engaged in transformative dialogue:

- When we say things to *reveal our feelings,* instead of *accusing others*

- When we say things to *disclose our own reality,* instead of *controlling another person's reality*

- What we say things that we *really believe,* instead of *what is expected or stereotypical*

- When we say things in such a way that indicates *openness to growth and the future,* instead of speaking only to the *past*[9]

Good dialogue questions should elicit personal storytelling, avoid judgment, and help to cast light on root causes of division or conflict.

*Guidelines for Designing Inclusive and Transformative Dialogue*

- Include everyone, even those whose perspectives you find hard to hear.

- Focus on seeking solutions rather than naming enemies.

- Affirm the best qualities in the other instead of confirming the worst.

- Aim to move through pain and beyond blame to constructive action.

**Questions to Consider in Planning and Recruiting for a Dialogue**

1. What is the underlying conversation that is not taking place? (Focusing on immediate issues, however pressing, sometimes obscures the root causes of problems.)

2. Who needs to be part of the conversation? (If only people of like mind are present, the dialogue will not have much impact.)

3. How might we invite them and engage with them? (Getting the right people in the room, in a welcoming environment, is the most important task in preparing for honest conversation, and it requires intelligent strategies.)

# Walking through History

Dialogue always appeals to people of goodwill. But if it is not founded on
healing wounds of history it will not have much effect.
—Joseph Montville

I sometimes think that we have two kinds of people in Richmond: those
who know too much history, and those who know too little. Both orienta-
tions can pose obstacles to understanding. The first group lives in the past
psychologically, weighed down by memories that color current relationships and expectations for the future. The second group is constantly surprised by—and impatient with—the submerged rocks of Richmond's past
on which seemingly positive initiatives run aground.

One national commentator notes that the companion trait to American
resilience is forgetfulness. But history and memory "provide material for
group myths that are a source of social cohesion because they supply op-
erational codes and a system of ethics," writes Margaret Smith. "History
becomes narrative when it turns into a frame of reference for individuals
and groups in their daily lives."[1] Group identity and maintaining the group
"story" provides psychological security: "Regardless of the material benefits
a person derives from group membership, the person will have a strong psychological proclivity to support certain narratives to keep her own psyche
intact."[2]

Thus how we remember is enormously important. Historical memory
characterized by denial of past wrongs on the part of dominant groups or
an overwhelming sense of victimhood on the part of those who have suffered wrongs produces a cycle of angry accusation and vigorous defense.
The right kind of remembering can build a "common narrative" for a local or national community and can act as a corrective and a guide for the
future.

To those who would say, "Forgive and forget," Nicholas Frayling responds,
"The only way to deal with deep pain and resentment, whether far in the
past or a present experience, is not to forgive and forget but to remember

and repent—or to remember and change." As Anglican rector of Liverpool, Frayling played a prominent role in urging Britain to acknowledge the bitter legacy his country has bequeathed to the peoples of Ireland, both North and South, Protestant and Catholic.[3]

"Like water seeking its own level, the way memory is handled in society will always be an indicator of power relations," writes Smith.[4] Since history is generally controlled by the dominant group, an honest, critical, and inclusive telling of past events is fundamental to any process of community reconciliation.

For minority groups who live with the aftermath of trauma or injustice, the prevailing narrative of the society coincides poorly with their own historical memory. These groups, therefore, live with a twofold curse. First, the substantive ills that they are forced to live with are at least in part the result of their traumatic or unjust history; but second, the very account of that past that has entered the memory of the majority of people in the society erases or obfuscates their trauma. Revising the historical account, therefore, becomes a way to gain visibility for the group and is the first step in gaining more social assistance in dealing with the residual ills.[5]

Sometimes those who perpetrate wrongs also see themselves as victims. Such was the case of Confederates whose resentment against the North's perceived threat to their concept of liberty was stronger than their conscience on the issue of slavery. Following the devastating loss of the Civil War, myths flourished and southern heroes of that conflict attained godlike status, while blacks were further humiliated during one hundred years of segregation. When the sixty-one-foot bronze statue of Robert E. Lee, the hallowed general-in-chief of the Confederate armies, was erected on Richmond's Monument Avenue in 1890, fifty former Confederate generals and more than one hundred thousand people from throughout the South attended the unveiling ceremony.

Eqbal Ahmad writes that people and governments with an uncertain sense of the future "affect distorted engagements with their past. They eschew lived history, shut out its lessons, shun critical inquiry into the past . . . but at the same time invent an imagined past—shining and glorious, upon which are superimposed the prejudices and hatreds of our own times."[6] Groups that are unable to deal in a healthy way with a historical trauma can transmit a mix of fact and fantasy to future generations leading to a "time collapse" in which groups literally believe that the same realities that applied to the past apply today.[7]

Thus history and memory are "containers for grievances." Unaddressed grievances can become powerful tools of mobilization by political leaders. A culture of historical debate "makes it more likely that past injustices will be brought to light and will be addressed."[8]

A "walk through history" enables communities to develop shared narratives that acknowledge the pain, achievements, shame, and pride of all groups. In Richmond before 1993, difficult racial history was either raised as a battleground or closeted. "The process developed in Richmond gave people the courage to deal publicly with it. They did not have to be afraid of being exposed. They could come to learn and to change," says Rev. Paige Chargois. Acknowledgment opens the door for individual and corporate acts of remorse, forgiveness, and repair.

### Walking, Not Marching, through History

A march is a powerful vehicle for protest or for advocacy. Very often it is a statement of group identity, perhaps in opposition to another group. A march frequently focuses on what others should or should not do.

A walk through history is a journey of inner exploration. A march has a destination. In a walk, it is the journey rather than the destination that matters. In a walk, we take in the sights, the sounds, the smells of our surroundings. We observe the changes and what has not changed. A walk jogs our memories by taking us to places of significance in our past. The walk is an invitation, not an accusation. We can say, "Come, join me on this walk of discovery." It is an act of shared memory, grief, mourning, understanding, and even celebration. A march completed is seldom revisited. A walk always yields new discoveries, deeper insights, and different perspectives.

In September 2006, twenty Northern Irish representatives of local government, education, agriculture, business, and the voluntary sector spent a week in Richmond to study the city's approach to reconciliation. Catholics and Protestants remarked on the power of physical contact when they were asked to link hands and walk silently in single file along the historic Slave Trail. In walking through history, "one community was allowed to face its pain, and the other its shame," they said. The absence of graffiti on monuments and memorials—whether Confederate generals, Abraham Lincoln,

or the Slave Trail—startled them. "At home we have to lock our remembrance gardens because the other side comes and vandalizes them."

A group of young professionals from Africa, Asia, and Europe made
similar observations. "In our country, students would have torn down the
statues on Monument Avenue," said a young man from Latvia. But former
mayor Walter Kenney told them he once was invited to the annual memorial service at the monument to Jefferson Davis, president of the Confederate States: "I asked Henry Marsh [Richmond's first black mayor] whether
he had ever attended, and he said he had. I'll never forget that occasion as
long as I live. A woman said to me, 'You are a good mayor; you believe in
diversity.'"

**Hearing the Story from the Point of View of the "Other"**

During a visit to South Africa in 1996, two years after the country's first
fully democratic elections, Walter Kenney, Cricket White, Collie Burton,
and I were received by members of Pretoria's city council in their offices
situated in a new downtown mall. I found myself in conversation with two
members of the executive committee. Pasty Malefo is an ANC member and
former liberation fighter. Johann Du Rand, a former police officer, represents the Freedom Front, the far-right Afrikaner party. Antagonists just
two years before, these men had become friends and partners in working to
meet pressing community needs.

Looking around the room, Johann pointed out another city council
member. "I arrested him one night," he says. "As a young police officer I
was scared to death half the time. But if I had been in Pasty's position as
a black man, I would have been doing the same thing that he was doing."
Pasty responded: "I did some things that I am ashamed of now. But times
have changed." He told me he had been in a house with several ANC leaders
when security forces approached unexpectedly. Their host hid them behind
a panel. They held their breath as the soldiers entered, but it turned out
all the soldiers wanted was a telephone. Pasty said: "I could hear an eigh-
teen-year-old talk with his mother in Cape Town and tell her that six of his
friends had been killed. I knew that he was just a frightened kid, but if he
had found us he would have been forced to shoot us."

I asked how it was possible for them to become friends. Johann said: "We
have learned to talk about these things openly. Yes, I was a police officer;

there's no point hiding the fact. We can even laugh about some of the things now." Pasty added: "We have learned to get beyond race to deal with the needs of the metropolitan area. We may not agree with each other, but we have learned to listen and respect one another."

Learning to look at a history of conflict—whether interpersonal or inter-group—from the perspective of the "other" is a key teaching tool of Hope in the Cities. This does not mean untruths and injustices should be overlooked or justified, but simply that there often exists more than one way of giving a true account of what happened. In working with the group from Northern Ireland, we asked them to divide into pairs. Each person outlined briefly a situation where he or she was in conflict with another family member and then attempted to describe that same conflict from the viewpoint of the other person. We then repeated the exercise around their experiences of sectarian division.

For many, the experience was hard at first. "By telling the other side's story it was as if I was letting my side down and giving credence to the other side's beliefs," reported a woman from Armagh. Another said, "I felt guilty, disloyal to my group." But several also remarked on the feeling of respon-sibility of trying to tell the other side: "You begin to doubt. Have I got this right?"

"I felt liberated from fear of the unknown," said a young man from Bel-fast. "Sometimes when you think about the other side and express it you exorcise your demons. You are liberating yourself. It's more than tolerating; it's respecting, not necessarily agreeing."

### After Acknowledgment

Acknowledgment is only the first step that a person can take to get back on the road to his or her humanity. But it is an essential step. Acknowledg-ment requires an objective understanding of what occurred. Scholars like Philip Schwarz in Richmond ensure that our remembering is grounded in accurate history, not mere sentimentality. The purpose of a walk is to allow people to absorb specific facts in an experiential way and to move from an intellectual understanding to personal engagement. For while facts are es-sential, historical memory has a power of its own. "Facts have emotional components which are attached to our hearts," says Rev. Paige Chargois.

"We need to look within the 'package of pain' because ultimately it's not the facts that challenge us . . . it's the pain we choose not to get beyond."

Following the walk, participants need time to reflect on their experiences. There may be feelings of sadness, embarrassment, or anger. Walk facilitators may help participants to identify those feelings, asking such questions as: What did those feelings indicate to you about your understanding of yourself as a member of a racial/cultural group? What was the physical impact—the hot sun or cold wind? Can you imagine yourself as one of the original participants—a slave owner, a kidnapped African, a guard? What is the legacy of that history today on our relationships, our use of resources, the public conversation on economic development or education? Often trust is built as blacks realize that whites are also affected negatively by history and as whites understand that blacks do not hold them personally responsible.

The walk allows people from different cultures and continents to reflect on the historical context of conflict in their own communities. Sushobha Barve, who led courageous trustbuilding work between Hindus and Muslims following riots in Mumbai in the early 1990s, and heads a dialogue and reconciliation project to heal divisions in Kashmir, spent a sabbatical in Richmond in the fall of 1999. During that time, she joined a four-day retreat with community leaders from eleven cities in the United States and Canada. The group visited some of the sites associated with Richmond's racial history and walked the Slave Trail. Sushobha describes her experience:

> During the time of sharing afterwards, a Caribbean Canadian woman said that the experience of walking the slave trail was too painful for her. She could not understand how people who call themselves human beings could do this to other human beings. While she was speaking, I suddenly thought of India's lower castes that have suffered terrible ill-treatment at the hands of the upper castes—especially the Brahmins, the caste to which I belong. I felt very exposed by the inhumanity of the Brahmins in perpetuating the caste system for centuries.
>
> While these thoughts were going through my mind, the woman was still speaking. "I can never forgive," she said. She felt devastated by the truth that she was confronted with and the pain that it caused her. For the first time I began to feel the pain of what my people had inflicted on other people. Would we be forgiven? It was a full 24 hours before I could give expression to my feelings.
>
> The Caribbean Canadian woman through her pain had exposed a blind spot

in my character, which I had not been aware of. I had always shirked from accepting the full legacy of the ugly caste system. After all, I have been working among the lower castes, and my grandparents and parents had welcomed those from lower castes into our home. This had become an excuse for not accepting the ugly truth about the caste legacy. I felt deeply ashamed for having shut my heart from accepting that legacy. So many of us are unaware of our blind spots. Others' expressions can help us see these and give an opportunity to be different.[9]

Paige Chargois concludes: "By acknowledging the wrong and taking responsibility as a community we begin to be the answer. . . . We can say to each other, 'Not only is the problem in us but the answer is also in us.'"

In the case of Richmond, Hope in the Cities chose to campaign for a community commitment to healthy, integrated public schools as the most significant step in repairing a history of slavery and discrimination that has devastating consequences for today's generation.

Across the United States, numerous communities are learning how to tell their stories through research, public events, and memorials. Here is a sample:

**Farmville, Virginia: An Editor Takes Responsibility**

At the height of Massive Resistance, Prince Edward County closed its public schools for five years, from 1959 to 1964. It was the only county in the nation that completely abandoned public education to avoid racial integration. White students and teachers continued their studies in a newly organized private academy. Meanwhile, African American families frantically searched for alternatives. Some sent their children to stay with relatives in other counties or states, and the Quakers placed about seventy students with host families across the country. But most black students had to rely on courses taught by volunteers in churches. Poor white families also suffered.

Farmville, the county seat, a town of just under seven thousand residents, was the epicenter of the racial storm. In recent years, Farmville residents have worked quietly but persistently to heal the wounds. Blacks and whites who experienced the school closings and the years of separation have come together in public forums to tell their stories. The old Moton High School, where 450 black students were crammed into a space designed for half that number, is now a museum.

Ken Woodley, the editor of the *Farmville Herald,* is a leader in the effort to acknowledge and repair the damage of Prince Edward's segregationist history. Although he was born in Farmville, attended high school in nearby Richmond, and graduated from college just a few miles from Farmville, he first learned about the school closing when he joined the newspaper in 1979. Discussing Massive Resistance was taboo right up to the late 1970s.

In 2003, the Virginia General Assembly, prodded by Ken Woodley and his ally, Delegate Viola Baskerville, passed a resolution of "profound regret" for the closing of Prince Edward County schools. Woodley and Baskerville pushed for more than just remorse. "It's so much better to say, 'I'm sorry and this is what I am going to do about it,'" says Woodley.[10] As a result; the state established a $2 million *Brown v. Board* Scholarship Program for African Americans who had lost precious years of schooling between 1959 and 1964. In July 2008, the Prince Edward County Board of Supervisors voted 7 to 1 to endorse an expression of remorse for the county's exclusionary history and sorrow for how locked doors had "shuttered opportunities" for so many students.

The resolution passed the week before the unveiling of the Civil Rights Memorial at the State Capitol. The memorial pays special tribute to students who walked out of Moton High School in 1951 to draw attention to the inadequate condition of black schools. Later, with the support of Oliver Hill and other attorneys, they helped spark a legal battle that resulted in the 1954 Supreme Court ruling against school segregation.

**Atlanta Remembers**

On September 22, 1906, thousands of whites took to the streets of Atlanta, beating, stabbing, and shooting any African American they could find. In four days of violence, the mobs killed and mutilated at least two dozen blacks and injured many more. The true death toll will never be known because until recently the city had successfully buried the shameful episode.

Nine out of ten Atlantans have never heard of the 1906 riot. As soon as order was restored, the process of forgetting began. The white elite met with selected black leaders, and the two groups agreed to cooperate on the basis of blaming lower-class blacks for the violence and quelling further dissent or public conversation. Two days later, one newspaper declared, "Atlanta is herself again, business is restored and the riot is forgotten."[11]

On the centenary of this defining event, the Coalition to Remember the 1906 Atlanta Race Riot organized four days of history walks, public forums, and dialogues to increase public awareness and to inspire Atlantans to appreciate differences as opportunities to build community.

Starting at Ebenezer Baptist Church and the Martin Luther King Jr. National Historic Site, which opened an exhibit on the riot, a procession drove through the city's downtown to Southview Cemetery and to the only identified gravesite of a victim of the atrocity. Six direct descendants of those murdered, as well as those who resisted courageously, shared family stories and led marking ceremonies. The Atlanta City Council passed a resolution of apology, and state politicians led a walk through the historic district. A panel of distinguished historians traced the origins, key events, and repercussion of the riot. Students wrote articles and produced sketches and videos. Media personalities discussed the role of print and electronic journalism in race relations today. In 2006, for the first time, the story appeared in Georgia's school textbooks.

The *Atlanta Journal-Constitution* gave front-page coverage to the Remembrance events and acknowledged the media's role in provoking the violence. One headline ran, "How Atlanta's Newspapers Helped Incite the 1906 Race Riot."[12]

The inspiration for the Remembrance came from Saudia Muwwakkil, the director of communications for the Martin Luther King Jr. National Historic Site. Southern Truth and Reconciliation, an Atlanta-based consulting organization that responds to groups dealing with the legacy of racial violence, provided some of the leadership for the coalition, which included major universities, religious organizations, local media, and nonprofit organizations.

## Tulsa, Oklahoma: Domestic Terrorism

The Greenwood District of Tulsa, Oklahoma—called "the Negro Wall Street" by Booker T. Washington—burned to the ground in 1921. Over 1,200 homes, as well as businesses, churches, and schools—indeed, virtually every structure in a twenty-two-block area—were bombed, burned, and looted by white mobs in what has been described as the worst act of domestic terrorism in American history.[13]

On May 30, 1921, a young white elevator operator named Sarah Page alleged that Dick Rowland, a successful black shoeshine man, had attacked her. Rowland was arrested on a charge of rape. The next morning, the *Tulsa Tribune* ran an editorial and a front-page article entitled "To Lynch a Negro Tonight." A crowd of angry whites appeared at the county courthouse demanding that Rowland be lynched. A small group of about sixty black veterans of World War I arrived to protect Rowland. A struggle ensued, and a shot was fired that set the riots in motion. The "official" death toll of African Americans was thirty-six, but the *Tulsa Race Riot Report* claims this is a low-ball estimate. The more likely figure is anywhere from one hundred to three hundred. Bodies were thrown into mass graves in a city cemetery.

Despite immediate responses of shock and sympathy for the victims and even commitments to "rehabilitation" and "reparations" by the Tulsa Chamber of Commerce, such sentiments soon faded.[14] The mayor even attributed the riot to lawlessness among the black community. Insurance companies did not honor a single claim. As in Atlanta, the desire to forget quickly took precedence. It took fifty years before the restoration of public memory began thanks to the black-owned *Oklahoma Impact*, which in 1971 published a cover story, "Profile of a Race Riot." Widely read in the black community, it was ignored by whites. A decade later, Scott Ellsworth, a doctoral student of John Hope Franklin, published his thesis, *Death in the Promised Land: The Tulsa Race Riot of 1921*, which opened the way for hundreds of studies.

White silence is understandable although not excusable. But the story of Greenwood was equally unknown to most African Americans born after the events. Black parents and grandparents talked little around their own dinner tables about the riot and the fact that black residents had resisted courageously. "Some said they kept quiet because they could not know if such a riot might erupt again. Others said that they did not want to discourage their children from believing that with hard work they could build a bright future in spite of enduring white racism."[15]

In 1997, the governor of Oklahoma, the mayor of Tulsa, and the Oklahoma legislature agreed to an official inquiry and formed the Tulsa Race Riot Commission. After four years of investigation and heated negotiations between members of the biracial, bipartisan commission, the report called for reparations to riot survivors and to the black community as a whole for school segregation, disenfranchisement, and lynchings. Specifically, the commission recommended direct payment of reparations to survivors of the race riot and their descendants, college scholarship funds, establishment of an economic development enterprise zone in the Greenwood District, and a memorial inclusive of the reburial of any human remains found in the search for unmarked graves of riot victims.

The state legislature set up a structure in the education department for awarding scholarships to descendants of victims, and the governor authorized $750,000 for a public memorial. However, the lawmakers got bogged down in debates over reparations. As of 2009, the city government had taken no action.

In the absence of government action, John Gaberino, a leading businessman, announced that he would raise $1.5 million for awards of five thousand dollars to survivors and young descendants. The Center for Racial Justice convened the Tulsa Reparations Coalition, which is pressing for implementation of the commission's proposals. In 2005, the Harvard law professor Charles Ogletree Jr. and the attorney Johnny Cochran filed suit on behalf of riot survivors in federal district court. The suit failed, the decision was upheld by the 10th Court of Appeals, and the U.S. Supreme Court declined to hear further appeals.[16]

## The Wilmington Coup of 1898

Wilmington, North Carolina, was the only major port under the control of the Confederacy during the Civil War. It made an astonishing recovery from the ravages of that war, becoming a regional railroad center and shifting exports from naval stores and cotton to cotton, lumber, peanuts, and fertilizer. The economic revival attracted immigrants from Europe, freed slaves, and poor white tenant farmers. A small but significant black middle class prospered. By 1897, African Americans owned nearly 14 percent of businesses in the city.[17]

But tensions grew as white workers began to feel that blacks were advancing at their expense and as the United States entered a deep depression in 1893. Things came to a head in 1898, when the Democrats ran a vicious, and successful, white supremacy campaign to unseat a government made up of white populists and black Republicans.

The day after the election, a public meeting endorsed a series of resolutions called the "White Man's Declaration of Independence," which stated,

"We will no longer be ruled, and will never again be ruled, by men of African origin." Their special target was Alex Manly, editor of the *Daily Record*, the nation's only African American daily newspaper. Manly had dared to suggest that some alleged "rapes" of white women were actually consensual relationships. The Declaration demanded that Manly leave town or be forcibly expelled. A committee of prominent white citizens presented the Declaration to chosen representatives of the African American community. When they did not respond quickly enough, a mob of two thousand whites destroyed the *Daily Record* offices. White groups roamed the city, attacking and killing African Americans. In all, about twenty died.

Although the newly elected Democrats were not due to take office until the spring, the committee forced the city administration to resign, installed one of their members as mayor, and expelled any Republican politicians who had not already fled from the city. Thus Wilmington experienced what may be the only coup d'état in the history of the United States.

As in the case of Atlanta, Wilmington "forgot" about the riot for a century. But in 1998, the 1898 Centennial Foundation coordinated broad-based community efforts to remember the victims of the coup and the subsequent exclusion of many African Americans from the city's economic life.

Public forums, museum and library exhibits, and dramas brought Wilmington's hidden history to light. Four hundred people took part in small-group dialogues in homes, churches, and offices. Black and white business leaders held forums to encourage inclusive partnerships. A working group on black economic development focused on heritage-based tourism. Research conducted by students on significant historical sites provided material for a publication for an African American Heritage Trail.

One thousand people attended a symposium, which opened with the unveiling of a historic marker honoring Alex Manly. Citizens launched a "People's Declaration of Interdependence" to repudiate the earlier "Declaration of Independence." Scholars contributed to publish *Democracy Betrayed: The Wilmington Race Riot of 1898 ands Its Legacy* (1998). A state commission urged the government to repay descendants of those victimized by the riots and recommended state-funded programs to support local African American businesses and home ownership.

On November 8, 2008, after a decade of work by community leaders and city officials, a memorial park was dedicated near the site of the worst rioting. Marguerite S. Shaffer, coordinator of the Graduate Program in Public

History at the University of North Carolina Wilmington (UNCW), writes that public art and monuments "have the power to define and unite a community through both physical and symbolic meaning. . . . [T]hey have the potential to become sacred spaces signifying the character and values of a diverse community."[18]

Leaders of the Wilmington initiative say their aim is to acknowledge the past and to "assume personal responsibility to make our community one where economic justice and racial harmony flourish."[19]

## Northerners Discover Their Complicity

On October 10, 2003, the city of Duluth, Minnesota, unveiled a memorial to three African Americans lynched there in 1920. The great-great-grandson of one of the mob leaders was on hand to offer his apologies to the descendants of the victims. A teacher in Washington state, he had discovered the grisly story while researching family history.

The New York Times noted that the Duluth memorial is "part of a national journey that began in the 1990s, when scholars and museums began to pull back the covers on a shameful and horrific period" between the 1880s and 1930s, when "thousands of black Americans were hanged, mutilated, burned alive or dragged to death while huge crowds looked on."[20]

Like the unveiling of the memorial in Minnesota, the discovery of graves in New York shatters the long-held assumption that the legacy of slavery and racism is a southern problem. The original African Burial Ground is believed to have contained the remains of ten to twenty thousand people. Four hundred were discovered accidentally during the construction of an office building in Lower Manhattan. Forty percent of the skeletons belonged to children, most of whom died of malnutrition. "In the mid-nineteenth century, slavery was the way America breathed," write Charles Johnson and Patricia Smith in Africans in America.[21]

Katrina Browne was astonished to discover that her Rhode Island ancestors were prominent slave traders. Poring over a family history sent by her grandmother, she stumbled on the ugly truth. Browne can trace her family back seven generations to Mark Anthony DeWolf, of Bristol, Rhode Island, the father of the largest slave-trading family in U.S. history. More than ten thousand Africans made the hellish passage across the Atlantic in the holds of DeWolf-owned ships. Over three generations, from 1769 to 1820, the family built a fortune on the trade. Sixty percent of U.S. slave voyages were launched from Rhode Island. Browne was appalled: "Everything about it was contrary to my image of my family and how we had been raised. It also shattered my image of the North."[22]

Browne contacted two hundred family members, inviting them to join her in a journey of discovery. Most did not respond. But nine agreed to join her in retracing the slave triangle between the homes and factories in Rhode Island, the slave forts in Ghana, and the DeWolf plantations in Cuba. The result is Tom DeWolf's memoir of the journey, *Inheriting the Trade*, and a documentary film by Browne, *Traces of the Trade: A Story from the Deep North*, which premiered on public television in 2008.

"To tell the story of the DeWolfs, you have to tell the story of the ship-builders, the sailmakers, the rum makers, the blacksmiths who made the chains and the locks, and the people who bought shares in the slave ships. . . . [I]t's important to set the record straight about New England's complicity," says Browne.[23]

As an Episcopalian, Browne thinks the church should take responsibility for its involvement in slavery. The growing understanding that northerners benefited as much from slavery as southerners strengthens the hand of those arguing for an apology and even reparations. Browne showed an early cut of her film to the General Assembly of the Episcopal Church in 2006 and to the Union of Black Episcopalians. The church issued a formal apology, promised to battle racism, and launched an investigation into its links to slavery and whether the church should compensate black members. The timing was significant as 2007 marked the four-hundredth anniversary of Anglicanism in the United States and the two-hundredth anniversary of the ending of the transatlantic slave trade.

### A Triangle of Hope and Reconciliation

The process of acknowledgment of history and commitment to a shared vision for the future reached a climax in Richmond in March 2007 with the completion of the third leg of a "Reconciliation Triangle" between the United Kingdom, West Africa, and the Americas.

At the height of the slave trade, Liverpool ship owners financed 40 percent of the European ships involved. Ships from Liverpool made five thousand Atlantic crossings. One hundred Liverpool ships transported 28,200

Africans in 1771 alone. Ships took manufactured goods to Africa in exchange for slaves to provide a workforce in the West Indies, and then carried coffee, chocolate, sugar, tea, and cotton back to Britain. Three out of five Africans taken to Jamaica endured the voyage on Liverpool ships. Carvings of African heads still adorn the city hall, and streets bear the names of merchants enriched by the triangular trade. When slavery was finally outlawed, the British government paid plantation owners £20 million in compensation, equivalent to two-fifths of the national budget. John Gladstone, father of one of Britain's most famous prime ministers, William Gladstone, received £93,526 in compensation. Freed slaves did not receive compensation. They were obliged to work as apprentices for their former masters for six years.

In 1994, Liverpool took steps to acknowledge this history by opening a gallery on transatlantic slavery at the Maritime Museum. (Thirteen years later, this was expanded greatly as the International Slavery Museum.) On December 9, 1999, in its last formal act of the millennium, the city council passed a resolution of "unreserved apology" for Liverpool's role in the iniquitous trade and the residual effects of slavery on its communities of African descent. The council committed itself "to work closely with all Liverpool's communities and partners and with the peoples of those countries which have carried the burden of the slave trade."[24] The Lord Mayor, Joseph W. Devaney, said that in apologizing the city sought neither forgiveness nor absolution. "It is my belief that Liverpool can only be truly forgiven after a process of reconciliation through action has taken place," he said. The council committed to such action, with full participation of Liverpool's black communities, to combat racism and discrimination and to recognize and respond to the city's multicultural inheritance and the many talents of its people.

Canon Nicholas Frayling spoke in the Council Chamber before the unanimous vote. Commending the council members, he told them, "The only way to bring about lasting reconciliation is to face the pain of history with courage, and then to change."

Later that month, President Mathieu Kerekou of the Republic of Benin convened an international gathering for representatives from the African Diaspora as well as from former slave-trading countries in Europe and the Americas. Paige Chargois traveled from Richmond. Lord David Alton of Liverpool presented a statement by the leaders of Liverpool's city council.

Benin had actively participated in the slave trade for almost three hundred years. Seeking to heal the deep divides in his own country and beyond stemming from this history, Kerekou apologized for his ancestors' prominent role in selling fellow Africans to slave traders: "We owe it to ourselves never to forget, to acknowledge our share of responsibility in the humiliation."[25] In April 2000, a delegation from Benin, including four government ministers, joined in a ceremony of racial healing on the banks of the James River in Richmond, where they repeated their president's apology.[26]

From these encounters, the vision of a "Reconciliation Triangle" linking Liverpool, Benin, and Richmond emerged. A symbol of the new relationship came in the form of a fifteen-foot-tall bronze sculpture by Liverpool artist Stephen Broadbent. Entitled *Reconciliation*, it depicted two figures in close embrace. Liverpool donated a full-scale replica of the sculpture to Benin. Upon seeing it during an official visit to Liverpool with Richmond's vice mayor, Rudolph McCullom, Paige Chargois immediately declared that the project must include the Americas. Following her report to the Slave Trail Commission, Councilman El-Amin secured city funds for a second copy to complete the triangle in Virginia. According to Kerekou, the three statues would be "a physical and symbolic representation of a process bringing together in an expression of repentance, forgiveness and reconciliation, the descendants of those that profited from the evil trade, those on the continent from which they were taken and those now living in the place to which many slaves were taken."

Ten years of coordinated efforts by Hope in the Cities teams in Richmond and Liverpool, working with both city governments, played an essential role in facilitating the Reconciliation Triangle project. In August 2005, a delegation of twelve from Liverpool, including Broadbent and representatives from Liverpool Hope University, witnessed the unveiling of the Benin statue. Rev. Sylvester "Tee" Turner from Richmond represented Hope in the Cities and Richmond's Slave Trail Commission. He was joined by Lawrence Fearon from the U.K. Hope in the Cities team. Fearon said: "The visit to Benin meant much to me because of the diverse group that shared the journey. It was an important step to healing the wounds of the past and developing relationships of trust."

On March 30, 2007, five thousand people celebrated the unveiling of the Richmond statue in the presence of the ambassadors of Benin, Gambia, Niger, and Sierra Leone and a delegation from Liverpool. Richmond's Slave Trail Commission created a landscaped plaza near the former slave market where kidnapped Africans and their descendants were torn from their families and "sold down the river" to southern plantations. Water flows over a map depicting the transatlantic slave trade triangle. An inscription acknowledges the suffering of millions of Africans who were transported from their homeland, concluding, "Their forced labor laid the economic foundations of this nation."

Just one month earlier, the Virginia General Assembly had become the first state in the nation to offer a formal apology for slavery. As Virginia marked the four-hundredth anniversary of the first English colony at Jamestown, House and Senate lawmakers voted unanimously to express "profound regret" for the involuntary servitude of Africans and the exploitation of Native Americans. Virginia's governor, Tim Kaine, told the crowd at the unveiling that the state's apology was appropriate, since Virginia had "promoted . . . defended . . . and fought to preserve" slavery. Within the year, Alabama, Maryland, North Carolina, New Jersey, and Florida followed Virginia's example.

A more personal apology occurred at a city council meeting when council vice president Delores McQuinn, who chairs the Slave Trail Commission, introduced a resolution of support for the March 30 event. A member of the public, Silver Persinger, surprised everyone with an emotional confession that his family had owned 301 slaves: "I would like to take this opportunity to apologize on behalf of my family. . . . It's a small act of reconciliation, but I hope it's meaningful." Visibly moved, McQuinn accepted Persinger's apology, saying that he had shown "what this reconciliation and this statue is all about."[27] Later, as she addressed the expectant crowd under a brilliant blue sky, she recalled her enslaved great-grandfather. When his son asked to see the records of his family, the plantation owner burned them before his eyes. "If I stand here today, I cannot be a hypocrite," said McQuinn. "I too must extend forgiveness from the depth of my heart and soul."

Ambassador Segbe Cyrille Oguin of Benin, acknowledging his country's involvement in the "shameful deeds" of the slave trade, called the ceremony "a blessed completion" of a triangle of new relationships between Benin, Richmond, and Liverpool. The *Richmond Times-Dispatch* headlined its front-page story "A Monument to Reconciliation."[28] But the *Richmond Free Press* warned its readers not to "violate the spirit" of the statue by ignoring the call to justice. The newspaper highlighted the keynote address of Dr. John Kinney, dean of the School of Theology at Virginia Union University, who challenged his listeners: "Today is not a conclusion. Today is a day of commitment."[29]

Some might legitimately question the value of erecting monuments. Lawrence Fearon says he and his colleagues in the United Kingdom recognize that genuine and lasting repair of the slave trade's legacy of trauma and mistrust requires a change of minds and hearts: "That requires dealing with the root causes of racism, exclusion, frustration, and injustice, and the denial and sense of victimhood which are linked to it."

The vision of the Reconciliation Triangle extends beyond symbolism. Organizers see an opportunity to develop educational and economic links and to promote cultural heritage. St. Paul's Episcopal Church is initiating a microlending project with Ghana. Educators in Richmond hope to link students from public and private schools with their peers in Benin and Liverpool. Liverpool students helped design panels for the base of the sculpture, and a citywide contest engaged hundreds of Richmond students in writing on the theme of reconciliation. An inscription on the base of the sculpture reads, "Acknowledge the past; embrace the present; shape a future of reconciliation and justice."[30]

Wounds caused by racial, ethnic, or religious conflict pose a huge challenge to community cohesion everywhere. Healing these wounds is important for Richmond, and for America, and it is essential for the world. Acknowledgment is the first step toward true dialogue and acts of repair.

**The Characteristics of the "Walk through History"**
**and Process of Acknowledgment**

Each community will develop its own approach to acknowledging its specific history, but an effective process involves an accurate, respectful, inclusive public telling of the story. Experiences in Richmond and other communities demonstrate that a walk through history establishes an agenda for healing by:

- Allowing the conscience of large numbers of people to be mobilized;

- Liberating all parties by breaking the cycle of guilt, denial, and resentment; and

- Enabling people of different backgrounds to take ownership of shared history.

History acknowledged can provide creative energy for the restoration of broken relationships and the reform of unjust systems.

**Questions to Consider in Developing a "Walk through History."**

1. What is the unacknowledged and/or unhealed history that divides your community?

2. What resources are available to research this?

3. What shared experience could bring people together to claim a shared history?

# Networks of Trust

Pearls are formed around points of irritation.
—billboard in Sydney, Australia

"One stick does not make a strong fire," says Syngman Rhee. "If we are going to carry on a vision for justice and peace we must learn to be a team. However brave and talented I may be, without a container or framework, compassion and commitment can become wrongly directed."[1]

Creating a strong container is the hardest and often most neglected component of social change initiatives. Yet it is a more decisive factor in sustaining a healthy movement than charismatic leadership, technical expertise, or even funding.

Team life is paradoxical. We enjoy working with groups when they are effective, and we overcome challenges to reach productive outcomes. The energy and creativity generated by good teamwork is deeply satisfying. But we also know the "frustration, hostility, compromise, slowness or periods of 'stuckness' that do punctuate life in groups."[2] So while we may complain of being overworked, many of us, if we are honest, actually prefer working alone and doing things our way rather than enduring the stress of including others who bring a different approach.

Nonetheless, the task of building healthy, inclusive communities is beyond the capacity of any one individual or even one organization. We benefit from working with people who challenge our assumptions and viewpoints, or who have different styles. We need the skills, insights, and knowledge as well as the different cultural perspectives that others bring.

The market is saturated with books on team development, many of them excellent. I would simply observe that building effective diverse teams and partnerships—especially in the context of racial, class, and cultural divisions—is easier in theory than it is in practice. "Bringing change in a community is like weaving an oriental rug," says T. K. Somanath of Richmond's Better Housing Coalition. "People want instant change, but it takes a long time."

What does the Hope in the Cities experience tell us about teambuilding? What does it mean to be a team? How do we create Syngman Rhee's container that holds us accountable to one another and that draws out the best of everyone?

The broad movement for reconciliation in Richmond is the product of intentional and constant focus on developing genuine partnerships and networks of trust. In this context, teambuilding draws on all the values and skills discussed in the previous three chapters. It means having the courage to start a change process in our own lives; it requires open dialogue with those who are different from us; and it issues in public actions to acknowledge broken relationships and commitments to work together to restore for historic wrongs.

The stories in this book illustrate two aspects of team development. One builds diverse but close-knit core groups of activists, dedicated to specific tasks. The second nurtures communitywide networks of people carrying forward different enterprises, but connected by common values and a common vision. These *implicit* networks may be as important over the long term as the *explicit* teams engaged in a particular project.

## Building an Explicit Team

### Who Is the Team?

The membership of the Richmond Hope in the Cities team was not decided by a particular leader, but emerged organically as people expressed their commitment to further involvement in the process. Often this resulted in surprising people becoming part of the team. The questions asked in the chapter on dialogue—What conversation is not taking place, and who needs to be part of the dialogue?—are essential diagnostic tools for revealing underlying issues and identifying key players to be invited into the group. It is a sign of health if the core group contains people of different views, backgrounds, and experiences. Conversely, if most members of the core group represent one social stratum or hold identical political opinions, their efforts will easily be marginalized.

Welcome and expectancy are important keys to building diverse teams. It is remarkable how eager people are to support you when you express a genuine need. In welcoming others, I make myself vulnerable and expose my weaknesses and shortcomings. I make space for others who may have more creative ideas or bolder convictions, and perhaps may hold views that challenge my comfort level. In welcoming others, I expect that they will change and grow just as I change and grow.

The team is waiting to be discovered. The most exciting realization for me has been that everywhere there are individuals who—perhaps unknown to themselves—have the potential to give inspired leadership. Our most important task is to be aware of this reality and to try and live in such a way that each person can make his or her distinctive contribution.

When Susan and I arrived in Richmond we had no way of knowing that Collie and Audrey Burton would be our neighbors and would become our closest allies. And when a business leader found he was welcomed without judgment by the fledgling Hope in the Cities team, he surprised grassroots activists with his commitment to racial justice. As we stepped outside of our comfort zones, we discovered unexpected partners.

In Pasadena, John and Denise Wood followed a strategy of "listening to the community" and "caring for the care givers." The leaders of the Dayton Dialogues took time to build a broad-based steering committee drawn from business, education, and grassroots organizations. Both the Pasadena and Dayton efforts were distinguished by patient, deliberate relationship building with specific individuals.

In Richmond, we identified four stages in building a team to address community divisions.

## The Core Group

The first steps in creating a core team will vary. In some cases, a major public event provides a context to identify individuals who are interested in being part of a sustained process. More often a smaller group comes together to build relationships and agree on a course of action. Whatever the sequence, the process described in the previous chapters is predicated on building a committed core group of from six to fifteen people. This group is the "guardian" of the process. Although the group will build partnerships with many other organizations and engage in a variety of public activities, it must devote priority time to ensuring that all of its members understand and commit to the fundamental guiding principles of honest conversation.

## Internal Dialogue

In order to unite around a shared set of values and strengthen relationships, the group should conduct its own internal dialogue such as I have described earlier. A group dedicated to connecting divided communities must take time to understand how personal attitudes and behaviors are shaped by the cultural, ethnic, religious, or political environment. Honest, internal dialogue is not a one-time event but a constant necessity in maintaining the team. I cannot stress strongly enough the importance of this "inner work" by the core group.

Tee Turner, who became Hope in the Cities Richmond program director, distinguishes between teams that are "issues-driven" and teams that are driven by "relationship building": "Teams that are issues-driven often have no expectation beyond the task. It can lead to an attitude of 'What's in it for me?' rather than 'What's in it for the other person?' Through relationship building you learn about the person, their concerns, their strengths, and how they can make their best contribution."

Sometimes people are not prepared for the difficulties and disappointments they encounter in working with people with whom they thought they shared a common vision of community. It is often easier to love the dream than the actual people they are asked to work with. Because they will disappoint and even hurt one another, the members of the core group must practice the art of forgiveness.

## Wider Support

As the group clarifies its shared values and vision and becomes more confident in its relationships, it reaches out to others in the wider community. This may take the form of exploring partnerships with organizations that have similar goals of building just and inclusive communities, and of intentional efforts to build relationships with business, government, and religious leaders. Broad-based support among leaders of different racial/ethnic and religious groups, as well as across the political spectrum, will help others recognize that the process cannot be pigeonholed as partisan but represents an effort to bring people together across traditional divides. Groups in several cities have used "A Call to Community" to build broad support.

*Public Action*

Public events play an important role in capturing people's imagination, generating media attention, and recruiting more people to join community change initiatives. Newfound allies and supporters may wish to cosponsor a visiting guest speaker, a walk though history, a town hall meeting, or a breakfast forum.

There are three essential elements to the public event: First, it shows that people across racial and ideological lines can hold up a common vision of a more united community. This can be demonstrated by the participation of diverse people, or by the sharing of a common platform by people representing historically divergent perspectives. Second, the event should have some participatory component that allows those who attend to feel that they have contributed. In Oregon, hundreds of people sat in the House chamber and signed their names in support of the proclamation. Third, the event recruits people for the next step. Large public events can be excellent chances for the core group members to discuss their experiences of dialogue, new perspectives, and personal decisions, and to interact with others in the community.

We can imagine the four stages outlined above as a constant cycle of internal team building, strategic outreach, and public engagement. The core group continues to grow and strengthen as more people are drawn into the process of honest conversation and reconciliation actions.

**Team Maintenance**

A team dedicated to bridging social divisions goes though several stages of development. As Niki Toussaint concludes from her experience with Oregon Uniting, a team needs managers as well as entrepreneurs and visionaries. It needs administrators and nurturers, innovators and reality-checkers, activists, thinkers, and influencers. An effective team recognizes and appreciates the different strengths and talents of each member. Good team leaders ensure a good balance of skills and aptitudes.

Take an inventory of personal team-building styles. Do conflict or divergent ideas energize me or shut me down? Is leadership shared? Is it free of paternalism? In what way does my culture influence my team-building style? A longtime African American colleague surprised me by saying, "I sometimes feel that you withhold your true feelings as a means of maintaining control." It had never occurred to me that what I regarded as normal Scottish reserve might be interpreted by someone of another culture as a control mechanism.

A few years ago, I wrote a note to a colleague pointing out places where I thought our teamwork could be improved. The next day I received a four-page response from this person, taking strong exception to what I had written and strongly questioning my motives. I was outraged. My immediate temptation was to hit the reply button and send back an equally self-righteous message. Luckily I have learned that overnight reflection on such matters can be useful. The next morning it became clear to me that I should call this colleague and offer to go to her home. When I got there I found a completely different person. There was warmth, there was welcome, there was honesty and vulnerability. The next day I received a one-line message: "What a journey!"

The most important role of the core group is to model relationships within the group that reflect the kind of changed relationships that it is advocating to the larger community. Participants must be prepared to share their mistakes and their ongoing struggles. Here are some tips for maintaining healthy teams:

1. Put people before projects. Commit to each other. Build relationships that will last beyond the life of any particular activity. Spend time together, not just at work, but enjoy social time. Invite the team into your private space—your home. Play and celebrate together.

2. Share responsibility and avoid reliance on one person. Be sure everyone in the team is clear about his or her role. Use diverse cochairs to lead meetings or make presentations. (Hope in the Cities made an informal rule always to make public presentations or conduct key interviews as interracial teams.)

3. Hold each other accountable to the principles of honest conversation and personal responsibility. Be aware that the tensions and conflicts within the larger community are always present within the team/network that is attempting to bring change.

4. Deal with issues as they arise openly and directly. Unaddressed issues fester and divide. Work on challenging relationships; difficulties can be growth opportunities.

5. Share risk. Don't ask a colleague of another racial, ethnic, religious, or political background to take steps of courage without an equivalent readiness on your part. (For example, by associating with white Americans in dealing with sensitive issues, African Americans sometimes risk misunderstanding by their peers. Whites must be willing to take similar risks with their peer groups.)

6. Hold fast to vision and mission. But welcome new ideas. Each team member, even the newest, has a contribution to make. Everyone brings something to the table.

7. Establish short- and medium-term goals as well as lofty visions. People need to see success in small areas.

8. Be generous with one another. Allow each other the right to make mistakes. Recognize that we are all on a journey.

## Supporting Implicit Networks

In communities where formal networks have failed, the role of informal networks—not linked by any particular organizational structure, but linked by intangible threads of relationships, shared understanding, and selfless care for the "other"—becomes increasingly important. These implicit networks are the glue that holds the community together. In a city like Richmond where traditional political and business mechanisms are unable to move beyond racial or cultural barriers, these implicit networks provide the moral and spiritual support for courageous initiatives. Implicit networks look for allies, often in unexpected places. They challenge existing divisions and mental models. And they are willing to be "silent partners," ready to support the hopes and needs of others without any public credit or monetary advantage. "Tea is not sweetened until the lump of sugar is dissolved," said a wise man. Trustbuilders do not stand out for their own glory.

On a Saturday afternoon at Richmond Hill retreat center, Dominion CFO Tom Chewning tells a group of community leaders that he valued the support that he felt from these implicit networks during his campaign to put the Ashe statue on Monument Avenue. So deeply does he feel this connection that he has taken an hour in the midst of a family wedding to share his experiences with the group. "I realized that we needed a conspiracy of good people" to make it happen, he says of the Ashe project. "This was not a question of consensus; it was a question of leadership. I went to the people who are the opinion leaders and said, 'I want you to know that we will do this in a dignified way. I hope you will help, but at least respect.'" Even so, many people with whom he had close relationships were upset and turned a cold shoulder, but, he said, "That's the price you pay."[3]

People like Audrey and Collie Burton, who have also paid the price of criticism or misunderstanding by their peers, are part of Chewning's support network. They have encouraged countless others to follow visions for a reconciled community. When Glen and Lavetta McCune launched their dream of the One Voice Chorus—now more than one hundred strong and involving sixty congregations—Audrey served enthusiastically as its founding president. "Without Audrey we probably would not be here," McCune told a downtown audience in the fall of 2006.

Audrey also supported Martha Rollins, a white businesswoman and neighbor whose church had been involved in dialogues. For many years Rollins, who owns an antique store in the city's West End, had dreamed of starting a furniture restoration business as a way of teaching skills to ex-offenders and people in recovery from drug abuse. "Audrey introduced me to the neighborhood in Highland Park," on Richmond's North Side, Rollins says. "I said, 'Oh no, I'm not going to Highland Park. It's not safe there.' But God opened my heart in different ways." The result was Boaz and Ruth, a program that is rebuilding lives and restoring economic vitality to the community.

Through Audrey Burton, Rollins met Ellen Robertson, the founder of Highland Park Restoration and Preservation Program (HPRAPP), a community development corporation that has enabled hundreds of families to buy their own homes. Robertson says: "Audrey was doing consulting for HPRAPP. As part of that she created a roundtable for women in executive positions who needed a place to exhale. We would put out white linen and fine china; we would talk, cry, and bond. We decided not to form an organization, but lots of initiatives came from it. That was where I met Martha Rollins."

Robertson, who now serves on Richmond's city council, held a lease on an old firehouse that she offered to Rollins as a location for a business. At first Rollins hesitated, but in 2002 she took the plunge, and Boaz and Ruth was born. Seven years later, the budget of this faith-based initiative had grown from $15,000 to $600,000. Boaz and Ruth nurtures business skills and also cross-cultural connections. "This is about growing the social fabric rather than strictly the exchange of the dollar,"[4] says Robertson, a former Hope in the Cities board member.

Alex Wise also appreciates the support of the implicit network. When he came to Hope in the Cities to share his vision of a Civil War center, the board cleared its agenda and devoted an entire meeting to the subject. At first many African Americans were skeptical, if not downright hostile, to the idea of giving further prominence to the war. For two hours they cross-questioned Wise as he explained the significance of including the black experience in the museum. In the end, the board voted unanimously to support the vision, and one African American member, a former NAACP official, offered to accompany Wise in approaching other organizations in the community. Wise describes the meeting as a turning point in the life of the project: "It made it possible." Several board members served as community advisors and facilitators.

**Being Present**

The strength of an informal network is seen in the willingness of individuals to be "present" for each other, whether or not they have any formal role to play. At countless community occasions, large or small, certain faces are always to be found.

The former rector of St. Paul's, Robert Hetherington urges us, "Never underestimate the power of showing up." One day he received a call from a blind man who had been on the periphery of St. Paul's ministry for many years. "He wanted to set up an appointment and come and see me," says Hetherington. "Coming to St. Paul's was hard work; he had to ride three buses. I wondered what he had in mind to make such a tremendous effort. He told me he wanted to thank me for showing up at his mother's funeral fifteen years ago. You could have blown me over with a feather."

Hetherington recalls that he had attended the service at the funeral home, although he had no role to play: "The Baptist preacher preached a sermon about hell and damnation. I did not think his words were very pastoral. After the service, I met briefly with my blind friend and told him and his family that we would keep his mother in our prayers. That was it. He came all the way, riding three buses just to thank me for showing up."

Jim Ukrop also believes in showing up. As a practical businessman, he gets frustrated with the process of dialogue, but he continues to be a presence at every effort for partnership building and reconciliation. When asked what keeps him coming back to the table, he responds: "It's the way you create a knowledge base. I am impatient. I get in peoples' faces. I said something to someone the other day, and I need to write and apologize. But I do believe in showing up. I see so much injustice and the country becoming more unequal."

Ukrop, whose grandfather came from Slovakia in 1900, chafes at the confining social climate of functions where "everyone looks alike and talks alike and the only conversation is about hunting, fishing, and vacations." He warned one establishment figure, "You can build a wall around your country club but you are not going to be able to keep your grandchildren behind that wall."

Richmond Hill is one place where informal networks are nurtured. Reflecting on the organic movement occurring in Richmond, Ben Campbell says: "It's been a pretty different experience here from other places where people dealt with racial and sociological conflict with a lot of shouting matches, political posturing, and heavy conversations which never really changed anything. Here people end up wanting to be found in the same place. They are placing themselves astride a gradually widening gulf and see their future as common rather than separate. I just got an e-mail from someone I don't know saying we need to have a meeting about a certain issue, and when I looked at the list of eight to ten people, I knew every one of them. In this movement we are part of, people are held by a sense of intentional mutuality more than any particular outcome."

### An Environment for Change

Implicit networks nurture an environment in which change can occur; they support risk takers; they enable good things to happen. The debate over whether Richmond should change its electoral process to allow a popularly elected mayor divided the city for years. Proponents asserted that Richmond needed a leader who could represent the whole community, not just one district. Opponents feared loss of political power for the black community, since the more affluent, largely white, districts were likely to attract a heavier voter turnout. A former U.S. congressman (and Richmond mayor), Thomas Bliley, and former governor Douglas Wilder (himself a likely mayoral candidate) formed a commission to hold public hearings and to recommend changes in the city's charter. Dr. John Moeser, an expert on urban studies and a veteran Hope in the Cities board member, tells how he unexpectedly found himself playing a pivotal part in bringing the matter to a successful conclusion.

Ernie Brown, an entrepreneur who founded the Bank of Richmond, called Moeser one day. "John, I've been thinking how we could break through the stalemate," he said. Brown's idea was that in order to win, a candidate must secure a majority of votes in at least five out of the nine electoral districts. He suggested getting together with Melvin Law, the former chairman of the school board, and Marty Jewell, a community activist. Someone approached Sa'ad El-Amin, an outspoken and sometimes controversial member of the city council. The meeting took place in El-Amin's home. John said he was somewhat apprehensive, but "in the spirit of Hope in the Cities, I felt I needed to be there." At the first meeting, Brown posed his idea, but the group agreed it needed to find out more about the voting pattern. Moeser agreed to do the research to discover whether without Brown's proposed system whites would have an unfair advantage.

Moeser then testified before the Wilder-Bliley Commission: "I was roasted by Doug Wilder at the public hearing. He thought the plan was crazy. My point was that it would protect African Americans, and I knew that any plan for electing a mayor-at-large would have to get a sign-off from the Justice Department, which was biased against at-large mayoral arrangements because they tended to discriminate against poor voters."

A little while later, Paul Goldman, Wilder's political advisor, called Moeser: "He asked me to meet him at the Strawberry Street Café. Goldman was warming to the plan and wanted me to testify at a second hearing. I said, 'No way, after the beating I got the first time.' But I decided to go ahead, and this time there was a completely different reception. I think they realized that it was the only way."

Moeser became the public face for the new policy, which the Justice Department approved. In the election, Douglas Wilder swept all nine districts and all but two or three precincts to become Richmond's first popularly elected mayor.

In contrast to the prevailing culture of self-promotion, implicit networks allow Richmonders to support each other's visions in the spirit of "living to make the other person great."

....

**Questions to Consider in Building Effective, Diverse Teams
and Networks**

1. How might I enable the visions of others to grow? How might I help them to do their best work?

2. Is there a person who might welcome my support?

3. Who are the particular people or organizations in the wider community who are well intentioned, and are doing potentially important work, but who are not sufficiently connected to be fully effective, or who lack emotional support? How might I help them?

# Building Capacity, Assessing Progress

The qualities and skills described in the preceding four chapters form the core of Hope in the Cities' integrated approach to capacity building. A careful analysis of successes and failures of racial reconciliation and dialogue efforts in Richmond and those of its partner organizations in other cities confirm the need for community leaders at all levels who are willing to be deeply honest with each other and who have adequate knowledge, superior facilitation skills, and the intuitive ability to keep diverse groups engaged.

Intensive training programs in Richmond led by an experienced faculty of trainers and practitioners are supplemented by leaders from academic institutions, business, and nonprofit organizations who share real-life experiences of a city working to build new relationships. Participants come from across the Richmond region as well as from other cities. They are often highly committed individuals who are already engaged in a range of community activities. A typical class of thirty includes people of diverse socioeconomic backgrounds as well as ages. The program intentionally mixes grassroots organizers, corporate employees, formerly incarcerated individuals, youth leaders, and university faculty, as well as people of different faith traditions and political viewpoints. For some the first encounters are a shock. When one participant introduces himself as "a registered Republican," an African American activist exclaims, "I don't think I've ever met a Republican before!"

The class begins with everyone claiming their personal values and then slowly and tentatively testing each other's tolerance and acceptance. As they start to wrestle with the idea of personal responsibility and personal change leading to community change, emotions come to the fore. "I want action, and I'm tired of silly games and relationship building and getting to know each other!" complains one young woman on the first morning. "My community is in crisis and I need to help it change *now*!" By the next day, the group has found its pace and cohesion. "I'm still impatient, but I think

I am beginning to see how this can help me," says the woman who wanted change *now,* "and I plan to stay and learn all I can."

"It's comforting that it's okay to be in turmoil, to be very, very uncomfortable—that's part of the process. And it is not up to the facilitator to fix that," says a recently retired corporate executive.

A senior staff member with a major health care provider was initially tempted to dismiss the approach as too simplistic. But he says, "When you start to apply it, you realize its power." An ordained minister, psychologist, and executive coach, he has experienced many leadership programs, "but they lack fire because they are missing this element." "I came to this with pencil sharpened, ready to learn all the skills. But the tools we need to fix the problems out there are tools you invent from the inside out." His experience in the program led to a career change and the creation of a new center for leadership and spirituality.

Another participant wrote in his personal evaluation: "My professional work as a public theologian and university chaplain has exposed me to most of the principles in the program, but not all the practices. Outcomes included renewal of my practice of centering prayer. I became more forthcoming with my spouse about my needs." The principal of an elementary school in one of Richmond's poorest neighborhoods said, "I have added a period of reflection to my day."

"I came thinking I knew a lot already," said a professional facilitator from Ohio. "I facilitate difficult dialogues. But I learned that I still carry stereotypes and assumptions which get in the way. I was struck by what was said in the first module about the power that is in me to be an agent of change. That was transformational for me. It is shaping my life. I learned what it means to really step out in faith."

A distinctive feature of the program is the interaction between people of different income levels. A young woman who works for affordable housing in Washington, D.C., arrived so frustrated by the injustices she saw in that city that she felt ready to "blow something up." Later she told her classmates: "I have realized that I have been very angry and very hurt. I've been hurting everyone else outside of me because of that. I've learned not to put people in boxes, and I've learned to listen, and I've learned to be honest. . . . I swore I was the best person on this whole planet with the biggest heart, but I was hurting so bad that I was just trying to protect myself from all of you.

... I can now be successful in the things I want to do because I will attempt to no longer shut people out."

A white male asked how he should start: "Should I just go into a public housing area and start knocking on doors and introduce myself as a white man who wants to get involved?" Later he claimed the beginning of real friendships with African Americans and was excited at the prospect of participating in a multiracial team that would impact Richmond in a positive way. Black participants shared similar sentiments. "When I came here on Friday, I didn't have any white friends," said one, "Now I do."

A self-described "community strategist" says: "A lot of money goes to people who have master's degrees and Ph.D.s to study the community, organize, and build capacity. But these degrees don't help without patience and wisdom." Encounters with what she calls Richmond's "plantation mentality" and the withdrawal of resources based on class and race made her angry. "What I learned from the program was better listening skills so that I can see beyond what affects me personally in order to move toward the need of the whole community. You have to create some space to pierce the consciousness."

A young Muslim American wrote: "I very quickly saw that this was really going to bring me closer to some core value that was in my religion. The Prophet Muhammad and all the great prophets talk about loving humanity and loving other people . . . not just loving those who were good and who were doing things exactly the way you wanted. It was about loving other humans, period. And I don't think I really did. . . . I've been isolated in a way, working within my own community. This program kind of shocked me into recognizing how deeply connected I am to many other people who are so different in so many different ways."

The director of the human relations commission from a major city described his training in Richmond as "a life-changing experience." Now a member of the city council, he says he learned that "before we can move past any 'ism' we must first admit we have it in us."

The alumni of Richmond's training programs actively support each other in developing projects, defusing crises, facilitating dialogues, and exchanging information. Two were elected as members of the school board. Plans built on the foundations of methodologies developed by Hope in the Cities are emerging to expand Richmond's ability to support community leaders locally, nationally, and internationally through the creation of a "center for community trustbuilding."

## A Multilayered Process

Richmond's story continues to unfold. This book can mention only a few of the many heroic trustbuilding initiatives undertaken by countless individuals and organizations. Something is stirring. Hearts have been moved; consciences have been activated; unexpected partnerships are emerging. The movement cuts across traditional boundaries. A web of new relationships is growing. But the real work has only just started. The coming decade will show whether these relationships result in the growth of a much more equitable and inclusive community.

According to Viola Baskerville, Hope in the Cities has gone to a deeper level of community conversations: "In the past dialogues were helpful, but now the conversations seem to be stripping away years of unwillingness to talk earnestly about race, politics and economics. It's about time!"[1] Baskerville became Virginia's state secretary of administration in Governor Timothy Kaine's cabinet.

Tom Chewning believes Richmond is "on the cusp of what makes us a real community." He says, "I am able to have dialogue with people that I couldn't have had before." He advises Hope in the Cities to "stick to the work of building trust."

The reader may ask whether "talk" has really changed anything in Richmond. I hope that the stories and case studies in this book show that formal dialogue is just one step in the process of honest conversation. Honest conversation is a multilayered process involving personal encounters, informal discussions around dinner tables, walks through history, acts of restitution and forgiveness, team development, nurturing of networks, as well as structured dialogue. All of these may be happening simultaneously or concurrently. For many hundreds of Richmonders, honest conversation has permanently affected their lives and work.

Mark Hierholzer, the CEO of ChildSavers, a clinic serving mental health and developmental needs of children, says he is "one of the less visible but very real beneficiaries" of the movement. When he joined the clinic, he found himself working for the first time with a predominantly African American community: "To be honest, I struggled with how to approach the issues of racism and racial prejudice openly with people, and this made me very uncomfortable. My experience at Hope in the Cities was the first time I had ever experienced the opportunity to openly discuss issues of race and racial feelings. It was a very liberating experience. I found myself able to address these issues openly with people in my work. I was a better person for it, and my work also benefited."

Independent researchers Amy Hubbard, Leonda Keniston, and Julie Honnold conducted surveys of dialogue participants in Richmond, Dayton, and Portland. They conclude that formal dialogues generally do not result in specific community action. In postdialogue surveys, both blacks and whites indicated a shift from external concerns to internal relationships. Both blacks and whites ranked making new friends across racial lines as the most important factor in their dialogue-group experience. "The demands of the dialogue focused their attention on their relationships with one another, a necessary precursor for any possibility of working together to evolve." "This is not to say that participants do not engage in social action, but they seem to understand the primary goal of the dialogue is to build relationships, reconcile differences and foster mutual and self understanding."

Many black respondents came to "teach" and not to make friends but ended up doing both. And although blacks were more likely to drop out of dialogues, those who persisted reported an even higher "very positive" experience than whites.

"For critics, lack of clear action planning would seem to confirm their belief that dialogue does not lead to action in the community and may in fact limit and constrain political action. While we share these concerns, we believe that making that assumption would be a mistake for the following reason: Sociologists have argued that mobilization of people into social movements occurs along social networks." Following successful dialogue, participants are "much better positioned for involvement in cross-racial community action" because of their greater knowledge about community affairs and their personal connection with people linked to organizations. Survey respondents listed numerous community activities and discussed regular ties with community action and civic organizations. They will no doubt bring their new perspectives to their community work and spread the dialogue message throughout the community.

The sheer numbers of people involved are becoming an "enlightened pool of individuals ready to be mobilized." It is certain, the researchers conclude, "that social networks are being formed, communication is flourishing, and relationships are being built." This provides a framework for "sound democratic practices that are bringing people together and if this is the primary goal . . . then it has been successful."[2]

Harold Saunders, chairman and president of the International Institute for Sustained Dialogue (an offshoot of the Kettering Foundation), acknowledges that anyone who engages in dialogue work lies awake at night asking, "What does this add up to?" He writes, "Over the last 15 years . . . a number of people in foundations wanted a numerical, objective, hard-results statement, a bottom-line kind of answer, and I have to say that I don't know of a single social change program that lends itself to that kind of evaluation." Saunders says sustained dialogue creates spaces where people can try to relate to each other differently: "We are engaged in a process of change the likes of which are not too familiar to people who use conventional social science paradigms for understanding and judging."[3]

**Where Are We Now?**

In 2007, James Crupi, who had conducted a study of Richmond in the early 1990s (see chap. 6), returned to issue another report card on the region. While praising significant progress in several areas (reduced crime, a strong nonprofit network, some cooperative ventures, and improved race relations), he observed that metro leaders had not accomplished several critical tasks. Among them were moving from tactical to strategic thinking and action, and "resolv[ing] long-standing historical and cultural attitudes that serve to undermine trust among area leaders and prevent bold, needed initiatives."[4]

Spurred on by Crupi's recommendations, political and business leaders agreed to develop a vision for the future development of the Richmond region. Chamber of Commerce president and CEO James Dunn called it a significant step: "For the first time, the entire region will come to the table and work together." Robert Grey, a leading African American lawyer, said the process would be built on "inclusiveness, transparency, engagement, accountability and sustainability."[5]

Yet progress is slow. Richmond's leaders must realize that we will sink or swim together and begin to "start behaving like a real region—a community of shared interests—instead of self-interested parties."[6] For the process to succeed in fully engaging all sectors of the community, honest conversation and acknowledgment of historic wounds will be necessary. Courageous and far-sighted leadership is called for. Risks must be taken.

But Sheryll Cashin, author of *The Failures of Integration: How Race and Class Are Undermining the American Dream,* told a gathering of five hundred civic leaders in 2004: "You are way ahead of a lot of other communities. . . . Ten years of honest talking and building trust across boundaries of race and class. That's what the nation needs to be doing."[7]

Jack McHale, a former Chesterfield County supervisor and chair of Hope in the Cities, 2005-8, believes a good foundation has been laid for regional cooperation. He says local elected officials must now begin to build the trust between each other that will allow them to come together and "start dealing with the tough issues," taking a regional approach to one major problem a year for the next four years. They should begin "substantive and serious discussions regarding multi-jurisdictional cooperation" and sell to their constituents "the idea that regional cooperation can benefit all of us, not one or the other."[8]

As I conclude this narrative of Richmond's journey, I have asked some of the city's most dedicated local change makers: What gives you hope, and what do you see as the greatest challenges?

Business leader Jim Ukrop says, "In spite of dysfunctional government at the regional level, in spite of political leaders who are followers, we are making amazing progress." He attributes this mostly to the leaders of the nonprofit community—people like T. K. Somanath of the Better Housing Coalition and Jim Dunn, who retired in 2008 after many years as the president and CEO of the Greater Richmond Chamber of Commerce. "We have a community with soul," Ukrop continues. "We have not torn down our neighborhoods. We have the river. There is so much we have not taken advantage of.

"Our timing is right if you look at the emerging national trends. In the 1980s, 10 percent of people aged twenty-four to thirty-five lived within three miles of downtown. In 2000, it was 30 percent. In the 1980s, I could not imagine my kids would want to be downtown. But they said, 'Dad, that's where the energy is.' That's when the light bulb went on in my head. Young people choose a place, not a job."

But Ukrop is impatient: "Our public policy needs to go beyond civil rights. In many ways, public policy has hurt people. I am a competitor. I want to see our city be known as a place where people can say, 'They are doing things right.' A place where we have innovative public policies, and equal justice for all. Where unity is created by celebrating each person. Where economic wealth is shared proportionally by the diversity of our community. That takes interaction."

Many of those I interviewed emphasized persistent economic disparity as the region's biggest unmet challenge. Community activist Lillie Estes says, "There is a tremendous disconnect between what people earn at the minimum wage and what it takes to live." Councilwoman Ellen Robertson says most of the economic development is benefiting middle- and upper-income groups: "We're not building integration yet." John Moeser agrees: "Tax abatement led to major restoration, but it was not coupled with strategies to provide affordable housing."

Moeser says: "The Hope in the Cities movement has changed the lives of many people. They are doing things they would never have done before. But structurally we are still where we were in the 1970s. We need one or two leaders, especially in the corporate community, who will have the courage to start a process of reform." He believes there is no perception of crisis. "Those who are not directly impacted by injustice can go about their lives without seeing the threat. Those who are suffering are too busy just trying to survive to do much about it."

Jane Talley, who worked for thirty-five years in family and children services, sees an urgent need to heal the relationship between African American men and women. Slavery required the "undoing of the black male," says Talley. "If we don't get this healing with each other, we can't heal with other people. Public policy—especially welfare policy—is hugely damaging to black men because there is no support for married couples. When I speak to men, they stand up and cheer. For the first time, they have understood why things are the way they are. It's like reading a book and for the first time seeing your own story."

At Richmond Hill, Ben Campbell takes the long view: "If you had asked me fifteen years ago whether six hundred people would show up for a breakfast about integrating our school system, I would have said, no way. It is possible that within the next few years we may see such a marked improvement in our schools that we can say Richmond has turned the corner.

It will have to do with how the leadership of the metropolitan city views the enterprise much more than test scores."

Campbell says the growth of the Better Housing Coalition illustrates the possibility for collaborative action: "We've put the best resources into an intentional, interclass, interracial, interjurisdictional enterprise, with support of corporate and political leaders." As an example of a vibrant network, he calls Leadership Metro Richmond, with its diverse alumni of over 1,700 from twenty-nine annual classes, "a remarkably radical phenomenon." Finally, he turns to the newspaper: "The changes at the *Times-Dispatch* are extremely important. There's been a dramatic change with the new publisher and editor. I've just been at a meeting with Glenn Proctor [the executive editor] with five or six black intellectuals in the room. Even Ross Mackenzie [the archconservative editor of the editorial page] was asking questions about regionalism because he thinks it's important." Campbell describes the reconciliation movement in Richmond as "a revolutionary activity of some magnitude."

In 1996, Audrey Burton told a gathering of national leaders about her path to healing: "There was a time when I used to wonder who could I blame? Why was I so angry at so many of my brothers and sisters who are not of African American descent? Why was I so angry at some of my brothers and sisters who began to collude and condone the behaviors of people who had negative attitudes and behavior?

"And so I had to look at my own belief system. The spirit of this nation cannot change unless the spirit of the people changes. I had to be honest about myself. Every time I sat at the table with my brothers and sisters of European descent I wondered what was going on in their minds. What are they going to say that is going to cause me to become unraveled? And now I am a healed and empowered African American who is proud to be in this country. I can stand up and quietly say with love and compassion, 'What is it that we need to sit down and talk about and how do we do this in a way that will bring healing not only for me but also for you?'"[9]

A decade later, Audrey Burton says: "Hope is spiritual and social. It's not just futuristic. It is a powerful word and concept. The more we say it, the more we become it. This is an identity for us. We become hopeful in a spiritual sense, and we apply this identity in the social fabric of this community."

### The Challenge of Honest Conversation for America

The journey begun with Richmond's first walk through history on that steamy June afternoon in 1993 will not end until we have created a new American community that builds on honest acknowledgment of the past to create the will for a future of inclusion and opportunity. This cannot be done on the cheap, and it will not be comfortable. But the needs of our communities are too urgent for us to allow historic wounds and fears to continue to divide us. We need honest conversation.

A starting place might be an acknowledgment by white Americans that history provides little reason for black communities to trust the motives of white leaders. They might say: "It is true that in many communities we resisted integration and then abandoned the system and placed our children in suburban or private schools. We constructed highways that tore the heart out of established African American neighborhoods. We contributed to the concentration of poverty by concentrating public housing in specific inner-city neighborhoods and refused them in the suburbs. We participated in the disinvestment of the city."

How might members of the African American community begin the conversation? They might say: "For too long we have nursed historical grievances, played the racial guilt card, and been reluctant to acknowledge progress made. We have often blamed others while neglecting to care for our own communities and abandoning our young people to drugs and violence. We have allowed some of our leaders to put political power and patronage before the health of the community."

Both black and white could say: "We have remained silent when we should have spoken out. We have been resistant to change."

These would be difficult, courageous things to say. But a frank acknowledgment of the underlying sources of distrust might encourage the process of truly honest conversation.

America's story is complex and interwoven. It defies easy stereotyping. By honoring each other's stories and accepting shared responsibility for change, we can heal the wounds of this country and forge something of incalculable value for a world torn by conflicts rooted in historical grievance and competing identities.

The pioneers of honest conversation described in this book are people of courage and imagination. They are, in the words of Mari Fitzduff, the

Northern Irish peacemaker, leaders who can transcend the needs of their own group and who are willing to risk becoming "strangers in their own land." Remember, she says, "the strangers on the edge are the only people who can see the future as well as the past, the global as well as the local."[10]

We are all on a voyage of discovery. We can accompany each other on the journey, and we can live so that our communities become places of hope and opportunity, where the contribution of each person is valued.

We can become trustbuilders starting in our own home, our own neighborhood, our own city.

# Epilogue

......................................................................................................................

October 7, 2006

A crowd has gathered again at the Tredegar Iron Works for the opening of the American Civil War Center. Torrential rain lashes the walls of the old building, flooding the plaza; the One Voice Chorus sings "Wade in the Water" as the guests make their way to the entrance in ankle-deep water. But spirits are not dampened; the weather simply adds to the drama of the occasion, and the crush of people in the lobby creates an intimacy and sense of connection between attendees as they strain to follow the proceedings.

State and local officials are on hand, as well as former Republican governor James Gilmour and John Snow, the U.S. secretary of the treasury, who reads a message from the White House. The architects and builders have skillfully used the original structure to create a 10,000-square-foot exhibition, In the Cause of Liberty. The museum is radical in its ambition. Most striking, writes a historian in the *Wall Street Journal*, is "the evenhandedness with which three perspectives—North, Confederate and African American—are explained."[1]

James McPherson, the Pulitzer Prize–winning Civil War historian and advisor to the museum, says it is a "bold departure" from the romanticized portrayals of the war. "I felt most strongly about being open, not using any coded language to talk about slavery and the war aims." "I hope it will get African Americans of the present day to take a fresh look at the Civil War in a way that engages them and gets rid of the notion that this was done for us, or to us," says another historian, Charles B. Drew. Liberty, in other words, was not just a gift of the North but an achievement by African Americans themselves.

S. Waite Rawls III, the executive director of the Museum of the Confederacy, tells the *Washington Post* that one of the most important and undertold stories is that of African Americans during the war: "The basic mission of Tredegar is extraordinary in what they are trying to do."[2] His museum is one of thirty institutions that have provided artifacts for the exhibit. John

Motley, a retired African American business executive from Connecticut, donated a large collection of black memorabilia. As chairman of the center's board, he asserts, "This is the right idea, this is the right time, this is the right place."[3]

Not everyone is pleased. "It puts villains on the same plane as American heroes, Lincoln and Douglass," says Raymond Boone, editor of the *Richmond Free Press*. But John Fleming, a distinguished African American historian and vice president of museums at the Cincinnati Museum Center, takes a different view. Although the Confederate goals would have kept blacks in slavery, "I came to understand why they fought for home and liberty, as they understood it. That was a big jump on my part."[4]

"How much such a place is needed," says Councilwoman Ellen Robertson, praising its "dedication to making sure that the balance is respected and that the whole truth is being told in a balanced and respectful way. . . . I felt it compelling that the City of Richmond be a strong supporter." State Secretary of Administration Viola Baskerville, one of the prominent African American elected officials who gave key support to Wise as advisor and advocate, tells the inaugural crowd, "Several years ago when I was first asked to describe this project, three words came to mind: conflict, challenge, and change." Baskerville saw early on that "the beauty of the Tredegar project is that now African Americans can begin to understand that we weren't just acted upon, but that we contributed to our own freedom."[5]

The Richmond's Children's Choir sings "Amazing Grace." Alex Wise, whose vision launched the enterprise, is deeply moved and struggles through tears to begin his remarks. Motley puts an arm on his shoulder. "This was a living intellectual center long before we ever had a building," says Wise. "We claim this building to tell how the war shaped our history."

One former skeptic calls it "the fulfillment of what I thought was an impossible dream: all the stories told at the same time with respect and dignity."

The event is more in the nature of a Richmond family gathering than a formal ceremony. And, indeed, an unusual reunion is taking place outside of the official activities. In the previous three years, Alex Wise has discovered the descendants of William Henry Grey, the son of his Confederate ancestor and a slave woman.

One Saturday afternoon in January 2004, his cell phone rang. A woman

calling from Texas introduced herself as Starita Smith. After a few pleas-
antries, she said, "I think we may be related."

Wise's story of his ancestor, Governor Henry A. Wise, told in the first
chapter of this book, was spotted on the Hope in the Cities Web site by
someone who passed the word to Smith's cousin Leslie Edwards, a former
Tuskegee airman living in Cincinnati. After her call with Alex Wise, Smith
sent him a photograph of William Henry Grey, the reputed son of Henry
A. Wise; it shows a strong likeness to the governor's oldest son, Jennings.
William Henry Grey was the ancestor of W.H.G. Carter, the founder of
the first black Unitarian congregation in the country; Leslie Edwards and
Starita Smith are his descendants. Later that spring, Wise traveled to Dallas
to meet the extended Carter family. Wise says: "We broke bread, ate ribs,
drank beer, and talked a good deal. . . . The meeting meant enough to Leslie
Edwards, now in his eighties, that he rode the twelve hours from Cincinnati
to Dallas, then turned around after dinner and took the bus home."

On this October day in Richmond, ninety of the Wise-Grey-Carter family are on hand to continue their discoveries. Alex Wise says, "One huge
lesson of the Wise-Grey-Carter story for me is that we have to stop demon-
izing each other based on race and look at one another as mutually connected human beings."

In his prayer of dedication, Ben Campbell names the center "a place of
hope . . . where we can feel what is underneath us, the wounds we do not
know, the hatreds we do not fully acknowledge, the pains that yet must be
healed . . . a place where we can, with one another, find a renewed city for
generations."

"The storm is passing over," sings the children's choir, and the rain eases
up.

America is at a crossroads. One road leads to community; the other to the chaos of competing identities and interests. We have all hurt one another, often unconsciously, in ways we would never intend. We need each other. We need to eradicate the scourge of racial division. We must demonstrate that our diversity is our greatest strength and that out of this diversity is rising a new American community. We can offer hope to a world torn by divisions of every kind.

We invite everyone to join us in a renewed commitment to an American community based on justice, reconciliation, and excellence. The original promise of this country, that out of a rich diversity of peoples a great nation would rise, has only partially been fulfilled. This unique experiment remains incomplete because the promise of equal opportunity and dignity for all has not been fully realized. Much of the distrust, resentment, and fear in America today is rooted in our unacknowledged and unhealed racial history.

For many of us, race determines where we live, where we send our children to school, and where we worship. Because racism is deeply embedded in the institutions of our society, white individuals are often insulated from making personal decisions based on conscious racial feelings and do not experience the daily burden that their brothers and sisters of color have to carry. We must change the structures which perpetuate economic and racial separation. But no unseen hand can wipe prejudice away. The ultimate answer to the racial problem lies in our willingness to obey the unenforceable.

The new American community will flow from a spirit of giving freely without demanding anything in return. In the new American community, when any one individual is injured, exploited, or demeaned, all of us will feel the pain and be diminished. It will be a place where hearts can put down

---

"A Call to Community," Initiatives of Change, 23 May 1996; and Corcoran and Greisdorf, *Connecting Communities.*

roots and where each feels accepted and at home. Some painful memories cannot be erased. But forgiving is not forgetting; it is letting go of the hurt.

To build this new American community, we must empower individuals to take charge of their lives and take care of their communities. In cities across America, bold experiments are taking place. Citizens have initiated honest conversations—between people of all backgrounds—on matters of race, reconciliation, and responsibility. They have chosen to move beyond blame and guilt, beyond hatred and fear, deciding to face the past with courage and honesty. They are demonstrating that through honesty, a willingness to embrace each other's painful experiences, and with God's power to change us, the wounds of the past can be healed and our nation become one community.

This approach calls us to a new concept of partnership and responsibility. It means:

- Listening carefully and respectfully to each other and to the whole community.

- Bringing people together, not in confrontation but in trust, to tackle the most urgent needs of the community.

- Searching for solutions, focusing on what is right rather than who is right.

- Building lasting relationships outside our comfort zone.

- Honoring each person, appealing to the best qualities in everyone, and refusing to stereotype the other group.

- Holding ourselves, communities, and institutions accountable in areas where change is needed.

- Recognizing that the energy for fundamental change requires a moral and spiritual transformation in the human spirit.

Together we will share our lives and the resources God has given us to make America a community of hope, security, and opportunity for all.

NOTES

Chaper 1. A City in Recovery

1. L. D. Wilder, "Entrenched Racism Has Hampered State's Growth," *Richmond Afro-American and Richmond Planet,* 29 January 1983.

2. Unless otherwise stated, all quotes of participants in this event are taken from transcripts provided by the speakers.

3. Donald Shriver, *Honest Patriots: Loving a Country Enough to Remember Its Misdeeds* (Oxford University Press, 2005), 139.

4. Ibid.

5. Presentation to Hope in the Cities board, 16 October 2003.

Chapter 2. Repairing the Levees of Trust

1. Neil Peirce and Curtis Johnson, *Boundary Crossers* (James MacGregor Burns Academy of Leadership, 1997), ii.

2. *The Changing Racial and Ethnic Composition of U.S. Public Schools* (Pew Hispanic Center, August 2007).

3. Gary Orfield and Chungmei Lee, *Historic Reversals, Accelerating Resegregation, and the Need for New Integration Strategies* (UCLA Civil Rights Project, August 2007).

4. Trevor Phillips, "A Burning Issue for Us All," *Observer* (London), 6 November 2005.

5. Peregrine Worsthorne, "I've Lived to See the End of the Britain That I Loved," *Daily Telegraph,* 18 March 1999.

6. Charlayne Hunter Gault, National Public Radio, 10 June 2008.

7. Charles Piguet and Michel Sentis, *The World at the Turning* (Grosvenor, 1982), 3.

8. Robert Corcoran and Karen Elliott Greisdorf, *Connecting Communities* (Initiatives of Change, 2001), 50.

9. *Breakthroughs,* Initiatives of Change newsletter, December 2003.

10. Peirce and Johnson, *Boundary Crossers,* iii.

11. David Rusk, *Inside Game/Outside Game* (Brookings Institution Press, 1999), 59.

12. Shriver, *Honest Patriots,* 140.

Chapter 3. Catalysts of Change

1. Tom Campbell, Cassandra Wynn, and Bill Miller, "Old Leadership Not Swayed," *Richmond Times-Dispatch,* 22 September 1981.

2. Ibid.

3. Margaret Edds, "The Path of Black Political Power," *APR Reporter* 8, no. 3 (1985), Index.

4. Campbell, Wynn, and Miller, "Old Leadership Not Swayed."

5. Edds, "The Path of Black Political Power."

6. Collie Burton quoted in "Political Clout Seen as Start," *Richmond Times-Dispatch*, 21 September 1981.

7. Virginia's cities are independent, i.e., they do not belong to any county.

8. Tom Campbell, Cassandra Wynn, and Bill Miller, "Knowledge of Other Group Seen as Key to End Polarization Here," *Richmond Times-Dispatch*, 25 September 1981.

9. Ibid.

10. Patricia Morris, *Promises Kept: A Study in Organizational Development, Housing Opportunities Made Equal in Virginia* (HOME, 2001).

11. Tom Campbell, Cassandra Wynn, and Bill Miller, "Refusal Rates Run High in Racial Views Poll," *Richmond Times-Dispatch*, 23 September 1981.

12. Michael Henderson, *All Her Paths Are Peace: Women Pioneers in Peacemaking* (Kumarian Press, 1994), 79.

13. "Move Beyond Blame and the Politics of Difference to Work for Solutions," Hope in the Cities newsletter, December 1993.

14. Robert Corcoran, *The Courage to Change: A Story from Richmond, Virginia*, videofilm, 1985.

15. Letter to city council members, 14 March 1977.

16. Sydney Cook and Garth Lean, *The Black and White Book* (Initiatives of Change, 1979).

17. Garth Lean, *Frank Buchman: A Life* (Constable, 1985), 500.

18. Corcoran, *The Courage to Change.*

19. Ibid.

20. See Douglas Johnston and Cynthia Sampson, *Religion, the Missing Dimension of Statecraft* (Oxford University Press, 1994); and Lean, *Frank Buchman: A Life.*

21. Gary Robertson, "A Definitive Lesson in Social Grace," *Richmond Times-Dispatch*, 30 June 1998.

22. Corcoran, *The Courage to Change.*

23. Richard Ruffin, "Richmond—A Model City?" *New World News* 26, no. 8 (January 1978), published by Moral Re-Armament.

24. Karen Elliott Greisdorf, *Healing the Heart of America*, videofilm (Cornerstone Productions, 1993).

25. "A New Leadership," *News of Moral Re-Armament*, November 1983.

26. Henderson, *All Her Paths Are Peace*, 77.

27. Corcoran, memorandum, 13 February 1984.

## Chapter 4. Influences

1. Corcoran, *The Courage to Change.*

2. Peter Hannon, "Liverpool's Leading Authority on Chaos," *For a Change,* November 1987, published by Moral Re-Armament.

3. Ibid.

4. Alfred Stocks, from the transcript of a speech in Caux, Switzerland, August 1986.

5. Ibid.

6. Interview by Bob Azurdia, BBC Radio Merseyside, 26 March 1986.

7. Stocks speech.

8. Ibid.

9. Gerald Henderson Papers.

10. Stocks speech.

11. Henderson Papers.

12. Stocks speech.

13. Corcoran, *The Courage to Change.*

14. Mary Jane Walsh, "City Concerns, Country Life: Howe Todd Works on Richmond's Future, from Restoring the Canal to Healing Racial Divisions," *Style,* November 1993.

15. "Richmond Launches Out," *Breakthroughs,* Initiatives of Change national newsletter, December 1986.

16. Rajmohan Gandhi to the author, 18 June 1987.

17. *For a Change,* 1 April 2000.

18. Corcoran and Greisdorf, *Connecting Communities,* 3.

## Chapter 5. Long-Distance Runners, Prophets, Bankers, and Builders

1. Basil Entwistle, *Making Cities Work* (Hope Publishing House, 1992), 2.

2. Ibid.

3. Ibid.

4. Katherine Calos, "World According to Woods: Hinges Are Key to Doors," *Richmond News Leader,* 29 May 1991.

5. John and Denise Wood, paper presented at "Making Creative Connections" workshop, sponsored by Unitas, the Ecumenical Center for Spirituality, Montreal, 12 November 1995, 3.

6. Denise Wood, *Experiencing Pasadena: The Needs, Promises and Tasks of an American City* (All Saints Episcopal Church, Pasadena, 1984).

7. Wood, *Making Creative Connections,* 5.

8. Ibid, 8.

9. Margaret Smith, "Pasadena's Long-Distance Runners," *For a Change,* November 1987.

10. The bank's founder, Maggie Walker, was the daughter of a former slave and grew up in Richmond. In 1903, she founded the St. Luke Penny Savings Bank

(later Consolidated Bank and Trust), becoming the first woman to lead a financial institution in the United States.

11. Mary Lean, "Repairing the Carpet of Community," *For a Change*, December 2003.

12. *Report of the National Advisory Commission on Civil Disorders*, Kerner Commission (U.S. Government Printing Office, 1968).

13. Corcoran, *The Courage to Change*.

14. Greisdorf, *Healing the Heart of America*.

**Chapter 6. Breaking the Silence**

1. Hugh Thomas, *The Slave Trade* (Simon and Schuster 1997), 568.

2. Selden Richardson and Maurice Duke, *Built by Blacks* (Richardson, 2007), 10.

3. Robert Harold Gudmestad, "The Richmond Slave Market, 1840–1860" (master's thesis, University of Richmond, 1993), 107.

4. Charles Johnson and Patricia Smith, *Africans in America: America's Journey through Slavery* (Harcourt Brace, 1998), 87.

5. Ibid., quoting from Michael Mullin, ed., *American Negro Slavery: A Documentary History* (University of South Carolina Press), 99–100.

6. Shriver, *Honest Patriots*, 132.

7. Michael Paul Williams, "Unity Walk Taken in Friendship," *Richmond Times-Dispatch*, 19 June 1993.

8. Mike Brown, "Healing the Heart of America," *For a Change*, August–September 1993.

9. Walter Kenney, address at Brooklyn Borough Hall, N.Y, 26 May 1994.

10. Greisdorf, *Healing the Heart of America*.

11. Conference report, Initiatives of Change, 1993.

12. Greisdorf, *Healing the Heart of America*.

13. Margaret Edds, "Richmond Conferees Strive to Bridge Racial Gap," *Virginian-Pilot* and *Ledger-Star*, 19 June 1993.

14. Walter T. Kenney, Grace E. Harris, and Harry Jacobs to Richmond regional leaders, 24 February 1993.

15. Public conference invitation, Initiatives of Change, 1993.

16. Brown, "Healing the Heart of America," *For a Change*, August–September 1993.

17. Corcoran and Greisdorf, *Connecting Communities*, 49.

18. Ibid, 50.

19. Ibid.

20. Greisdorf, *Healing the Heart of America*.

21. Corcoran and Greisdorf, *Connecting Communities*, 42, 43.

22. Ibid.

23. Ibid.

24. Richard Ruffin, "Walk from Past to Reconciliation," *Richmond Times-Dispatch*, 25 July 1993.

25. Richmond City Council, 28 March 1994, Resolution 94-R91.

26. Ibid., 13 July 1998, Resolution 98-R102-107.

27. Jeremy Lazarus, "Gov. Kaine Pardons Gabriel Prosser," *Richmond Free Press*, 30 August 2007.

28. Michael Paul Williams, "Markers Fill Holes, Open New Paths," *Richmond Times-Dispatch*, 7 April 2006.

29. Richardson and Duke, *Built by Blacks*, 10.

30. Michael Paul Williams, "VCU, Wilder Ignore Duty to History," *Richmond Times-Dispatch*, 5 June 2008.

31. Governor L. Douglas Wilder, the nation's first elected black governor, worked with Ashe to launch Virginia Heroes and was a proponent of a Monument Avenue site for the statue.

32. Stephen Salpukas, "Monumental Effort," *Style*, 7 January 1997.

33. "Monument," *Richmond Hill Update*, August 1995.

34. James A. Crupi, *Back to the Future: Richmond at the Crossroads*, 1993.

35. Deborah Kelly, "Regional Summit May Have Gotten Its Second Wind," *Richmond Times-Dispatch*, 5 February 1993.

36. *Richmond Free Press*, 31 December 1993.

37. Randolph Smith, "The Changing of the Regional Guard," *Richmond Times-Dispatch*, 28 November 1993.

38. Randolph Smith, "Chavis Seeks Merger of 3 Governments," *Richmond Times-Dispatch*, 18 June 1993; Bill Wasson, "Consolidation Call Receives Mixed Reviews," *Richmond Times-Dispatch*, 19 June 1993.

39. Gordon Hickey, "Backers Hope for Growth Sharing," *Richmond Times-Dispatch*, 31 December 1996.

40. Corcoran and Greisdorf, *Connecting Communities*, 81.

41. Jeff Caldwell and Harry Kollatz Jr., "What Are We Afraid Of?" in "Richmonders and Race," special report, *Richmond Magazine*, November 1998.

42. Kenney, Brooklyn Borough Hall, N.Y., 26 May 1994.

43. "Monument," *Richmond Hill Update*, August 1995.

44. Christopher Edley, "In Confederate Capital, Shared History Leads to New Solutions," *USA Today*, 27 February 1997.

**Chapter 7. A Call to Community**

1. Michael McQuillan, Hope in the Cities report, 1996.

2. The White Citizens' Councils were set up to oppose integration in the South.

3. "Recapturing the Power of Community: Honest Conversations in Cincinnati," Hope in the Cities newsletter, April 1995.

4. Greisdorf, *Healing the Heart of America*.

5. Chicago City Council, 9 February 1994.

6. Hope in the Cities newsletter, November 1995.

7. Ibid.

8. "The National Launch of 'A Call to Community,'" Hope in the Cities newsletter, 23 May 1996.

9. William Raspberry, "A Nation of Poor Listeners," *Washington Post*, 23 October 1995.

10. http://clinton1.nara.gov/White_House/EOP/OP/html/ut.html.

11. "The National Launch of 'A Call to Community.'"

12. Bill Bradley, speech, Cooper Union, New York City, 20 April 1999.

13. Bill Bradley, speech, National Press Club, 9 February 1995.

14. "The National Launch of 'A Call to Community.'"

15. Ibid.

16. Ibid.

17. Hope in the Cities newsletter, Summer 1997.

18. Ibid., Winter 1996–97.

19. See David Schoem and Sylvia Hurtado, eds., *Intergroup Dialogue, Deliberative Democracy in School, College, Community, and Workplace* (University of Michigan Press, 2001), 7–10.

### Chapter 8. One America

1. http://archives.clintonpresidentialcenter.org/?u=061497-remarks-by -president-at-uc-san-diego-commencement.htm.

2. *Interracial Dialogue Groups across America: A Directory* (Center for Living Democracy, 1997).

3. *Pathways to One America in the Twenty-first Century—Promising Practices for Racial Reconciliation* (U.S. Government Printing Office, 1999).

4. *One America Dialogue Guide: Conducting a Discussion on Race* (U.S. Government Printing Office, March 1998).

5. *Pathways to One America in the Twenty-first Century.*

6. In 1790, the value of America's slaves was estimated at $140 million, twenty times the budget of the federal government.

7. Even the *Statue of Freedom* atop the dome was cast by a Maryland slave.

8. "Forward on Race—Together," and "Justice and Reconciliation," *Philadelphia Inquirer*, 20–21 May 2001.

9. Randall Robinson, *The Debt: What America Owes to Blacks* (Dutton, 2000), 107.

10. Ibid, 216.

11. Shelby Steele, *A Dream Deferred* (Harper Collins, 1994), 33.

12. Ibid, 23.

13. Taunya Lovell Banks, "Healing the Divide," *Baltimore Sun*, 6 February 2005.

14. Bill Bradley, *Time Present, Time Past: A Memoir* (Knopf, 1996), 373–74.

15. www.pm.gov.au/media/Speech/2008/speech_0073.cfm.

16. Chris Rice, *Reconciliation Wednesday for Leaders*, e-mail service (Reconcilers Fellowship, 28 May 1997).

17. Andres Tapia, "The Myth of Racial Progress," *Christianity Today*, 4 October 1993.

18. Rice and Perkins told their story in *More Than Equals* (InterVarsity Press, 1993). After Perkins's death, Rice explored their friendship in a memoir, *Grace Matters* (Jossey-Bass, 2002).

19. Faith and Politics Institute report, n.d.

20. Maggie Potapchuck, *Steps Toward an Inclusive Community: The Story of Clarksburg, West Virginia: A Tool for Assessing Your Community's Inclusiveness* (Joint Center for Political and Economic Studies, 2001).

**Chapter 9. Reaching Out**

1. Natchez report, Hope in the Cities survey, 22 May 1997.

2. Unification Committee minutes, 25 January 1999.

3. Natchez report and Hope in the Cities report to W. K. Kellogg Foundation, June 2000.

4. Natchez report to Hope in the Cities, 24 October 2000.

5. The first black history parade in Natchez was held in 1997, and the museum relocated in 1998.

6. The first black mayor of Natchez was Robert Wood, who built the city's first black school in 1871. He was part of the short-lived "black and tan" revolution that took place eight years after the Civil War, when African Americans won half of Mississippi's state offices.

7. Mike Brunker, "Race, Politics, and the South," MSNBC.com, 17 August 2004.

8. U.S. Census, 2007.

9. Michael Henderson, *Forgiveness: Breaking the Chain of Hate* (Arnica, 2003), 74.

10. General Laws of Oregon, 1843–1872, Oregon State Archives.

11. "Day Acknowledges Bigotry," *Salem Statesman Journal*, 22 April 1999.

12. Henderson, *Forgiveness*.

13. Ibid, 75.

14. HR3 floor speech quoted in Henderson, *Forgiveness*, 78–79.

15. Ibid, 80.

16. Ibid, 75.

17. *Directions Northwest*, Moral Re-Armament regional newsletter, Spring 1999.

18. For detailed descriptions of Oregon's Day of Acknowledgment, see Henderson, *Forgiveness;* and Shriver, *Honest Patriots*.

19. Anita Rasmussen, speech at Metropolitan Richmond Day, 18 November 1999.

20. Osker Spicer, "Day to Acknowledge Racism Grows into Year of Awareness," *Oregonian*, 23 April 2000.

21. The mission of Uniting to Understand Racism (UUR) is to advance racial

justice and reconciliation through honest dialogue, acts of reconciliation, and education. UUR works with local businesses, schools, government, and nonprofit organizations to help raise awareness of unexamined racist attitudes and to encourage proactive change.

22. Marjorie E. Loyacano, *A History of Race Relations in the Miami Valley*, ed. Margaret Peters and Fred Bartenstein, undated publication for Dayton Dialogue on Race Relations (Carillon Historical Park).

23. "Dayton Launches Call to Community," Hope in the Cities newsletter, 1 February 2000.

24. Corcoran and Greisdorf, *Connecting Communities*, 61.

25. Geoffrey Pugh, memorandum on Race and Reconciliation Collaboration Meeting, Dayton City Hall, 30 April 1999.

26. Hope in the Cities report to W. K. Kellogg Foundation, October 2000.

27. John Gullion, "Salaam Says Foundation for Change of Heart Has Been Set," *Selma Times-Journal*, 1 August 2004.

28. These included Randy Ross, New Jersey Office of Bias Crime and Community Relations; Jim Snow, George Mason University Institute for Conflict Analysis and Resolution; Melissa Wade, Study Circles; Michael Wenger, Network of Alliance Bridging Race and Ethnicity; and Tamra d'Estree of Denver University. With Heierbacher's leadership, the first NCDD conference took place in 2002.

29. Michael Paul Williams, "Racial Issues Simply Too Big for Small Talk," *Richmond Times-Dispatch*, 1 December 1997.

30. Hope in the Cities report to W. K. Kellogg Foundation, 5 October 2000.

**Chapter 10. Family Choices**

1. Richmond public schools Web site, www.richmond.k12.va.us/.

2. *Milliken v. Bradley* (1974).

3. Orfield and Lee, *Historic Reversals*.

4. Virginia Department of Education, *Student Membership and Free and Reduced Lunch Report*, September 2004.

5. Richmond public schools Web site, www.richmond.k12.va.us/.

6. Virginia Department of Education Web site, http://www.doe.virginia.gov/.

7. Justice Sandra Day O'Connor, *Grutter v. Bollinger*, 2003.

8. Scott E. Paige, *The Difference: How the Power of Diversity Creates Better Groups, Firms, Schools, and Societies* (Princeton University Press, 2007).

9. Richard Kahlenberg, *All Together Now: Creating Middle-Class Schools through Public School Choice* (Brookings Institution, 2001).

10. Clara Silverstein, *White Girl* (University of Georgia Press, 2004), 56.

11. Ibid, 35–36.

12. "Memories of Busing in Richmond," online exhibition by Richmond History Center, www.richmondhistorycenter.com/busingtimeline.asp.

13. Silverstein, *White Girl*, 86.

14. Ibid, 96.

15. Greg Pokusa, "Judges Panel Honors the Late Judge Robert Merhige," *Juris Publici* (University of Richmond Law School) 34, no. 8 (24 October 2005).

16. "Clustering of White Pupils Stirs Richmond Furor," *New York Times*, 9 December 1992.

17. Richmond public schools Web site, www.richmond.k12.va.us/.

18. "Neighborhood Rediscovers School," *Richmond Times-Dispatch*, 1 April 1991.

### Chapter 11. If Every Child Were My Child

1. Data from Richmond public schools Web site, www.richmond.k12.va.us/.

2. "He has shown you what is good. What does the Lord require of you but to do justice, and to love kindness, and to walk humbly with your God?" (Micah 6:8).

3. *Changing the World One Relationship at a Time*, Micah Initiative Report, St. Paul's Episcopal Church, 2 March 2002.

4. Zachary Reid, "Walker Sets Admissions Review," *Richmond Times-Dispatch*, 20 June 2008.

5. Claudia Wallis and Sonja Steptoe, "How to Bring Our Schools out of the 20th Century," *Time*, 10 December 2006.

6. Don Cowles, "If Every Child Were My Child: Racial, Economic Disparities Threaten Public Education's Promise," *Richmond Times-Dispatch*, 1 November 2004.

7. Edward L. Glaeser, Matthew Kahn, and Chenghuan Chu, *Job Sprawl: Employment Location in U.S. Metropolitan Areas* (Center on Urban and Metropolitan Policy, Brookings Institution, May 2001).

8. Hope in the Cities proposal to the Community Foundation, Richmond, Va., 5 July 2000.

9. Michael Paul Williams, "Dialogues: Turning Talk into Action," *Richmond Times-Dispatch*, 11 June 2001.

10. Hope in the Cities evaluation documents.

11. Ibid.

12. Greisdorf, "The City That Dares to Talk," *For a Change*, 1 February 2002.

13. Ilana Shapiro, *Training for Racial Equity and Inclusion: A Guide to Selected Programs* (Aspen Institute, 2002), 60–61.

14. *Plessey v. Ferguson* was the infamous 1896 Supreme Court decision that condoned separate and equal education.

15. John Moeser, from transcript of remarks at Metropolitan Richmond Day, 2005.

16. Kahlenberg, *All Together Now.*

17. Ben Campbell to *Richmond Times-Dispatch*, 10 September 2007.

18. Jonathan Kozol, *The Shame of the Nation: The Restoration of Apartheid Schooling in America* (Crown, 2005).

19. Sheryll Cashin, *The Failures of Integration: How Race and Class Are Undermining the American Dream* (Public Affairs, 2004), 79.

20. Orfield and Lee, *Historic Reversals*.

21. Don Cowles, "Laboratories of Democracy: Why Won't Metro Richmond Integrate Its Schools?" *Richmond Times-Dispatch*, 9 November 2005.

**Chapter 12. Muslims and Christians**

1. The dialogues in this chapter are not reproduced from transcripts. However, the participants quoted agreed to allow me to include their comments here.

**Chapter 13. A Global View I: South Africa**

1. www.sairr.org.za/

2. Fanie du Toit, *Cape Times* (Cape Town, South Africa), 7 April 2005.

**Chapter 14. A Global View II: France**

1. Frédéric Chavanne, "Dialogue with Muslims," trans. Benjamin Brinton, *Changer International*, Winter 2006.

2. Transcript from "Tools for Change" conference, 19 July 2006, Caux, Switzerland.

3. www.iofc.org/node/25475 (first published in *Changer International*, trans. Lindsay Collinge, March–April 2007).

4. Laurent Klein and Mehrézia Labidi-Maïza, *Abraham, réveille-toi, ils sont devenus fous!* (Les Editions de l'Atelier/Les Editions Ouvrières, 2004).

**Chapter 15. A Global View III: The United Kingdom**

1. Tom Baldwin and Gabriel Rosenburg, "Britain 'Must Scrap Multiculturalism,'" *Times* (London), 3 April 2004.

2. Richard Woods and David Leppard, "Are We Sleepwalking Our Way to Apartheid?" *Sunday Times* (London), 18 September 2005.

3. Russell Razzaque, "I Ran from the Extremists, but Some of My Friends Entered a Parallel Universe," *Independent*, 30 July 2005.

4. Tariq Ramadan, "We Muslims Need to Get out of Our Intellectual and Social Ghettos," interview by Paul Valley, *Independent*, 25 July 2005.

5. Yasmin Alibhai-Brown, "Cultural Integration Is a Two-Way Street," *Independent*, 1 August 2005.

6. BBC interview, 6 October 2006.

7. Pew Research Center poll, April–May 2006.

8. *Why Terror? Is There No Alternative?* (Caux Books, June 2004).

9. Abduljalil Sajid, *A Journey of Discovery: A Muslim Encounters Initiatives of Change* (Caux Books, 2007).

10. Esme McAvoy, "Building Community: Bradford's Story," Initiatives of Change Web site, www.iofc.org.

11. For the full story, see Mary Lean, *Bread, Bricks, and Belief* (Kumarian Press, 1995).

12. Letter to author, 1 July 1993.

### Chapter 16. Becoming a Catalyst of Change

1. Lean, *Bread, Bricks and Belief,* 12.

2. Martin Luther King Jr., "The Role of the Church in Facing the Nation's Chief Moral Dilemma," 1957, 3: 136, Papers of Martin Luther King Jr., King Center, Atlanta.

3. Martin Luther King Jr. and Clayborne Carson, *The Autobiography of Martin Luther King, Jr.* (Grand Central Publishing, 2001), 77.

4. Charles Marsh, *The Beloved Community* (Basic Books, 2005), 33.

5. Ibid., 89.

6. Ibid., 90.

7. Ibid., 92.

8. Ibid., 90.

9. Ibid., 115–16.

10. Ibid., 80.

11. Charles Piguet and Michel Sentis, *The World at the Turning: Experiment with Moral Re-Armament,* trans. Ailsa Hamilton (Grosvenor, 1982), 3.

12. Niketu Iralu, "Who Will Break the Chain of Hate?" *For a Change,* 1 August 2004.

13. Peggy McIntosh, "White Privilege and Male Privilege: A Personal Account of Coming to See Correspondences through Work in Women's Studies," working paper 189 (Wellesley College Center for Research on Women, 1988).

14. "Honest Conversation Opened His Eyes," *Breakthroughs,* Initiatives of Change newsletter, Winter 2008.

15. Juan Williams, *The Phony Leaders, Dead-End Movements, and Culture of Failure That Are Undermining Black America—and What We Can Do About It* (Random House, 2006).

16. Bob Herbert, "Blowing the Whistle on Gangsta Culture," *New York Times,* 22 December 2005.

17. Bob Herbert, "A Triumph of Felons and Failure," *New York Times,* 24 August 2006.

18. Jean Brown, *A Serious Guide to Remaking the World* (Caux Books, 2007).

19. Lean, *Frank Buchman: A Life,* 77.

20. Rushworth Kidder, "Rape, Relativism, and Respect: Duke University's Dilemma," *Ethics Newsline,* newsletter for Institute for Global Ethics, 10 April 2006.

21. Robert Speer, *The Principles of Jesus* (New York: Fleming H. Revell, 1902). See also www.aabibliography.com/principles_of_jesus_robert_speer.htm.

22. Corcoran, *The Courage to Change;* Henderson, *All Her Paths Are Peace,* 73.

23. Corcoran, *The Courage to Change.*

### Chapter 17. From Information to Transformation

1. Harlon Dalton, speech, National Press Club, 23 May 1996.
2. Peter Hannon, *Whose Side Is God On?: By an Enquirer in Northern Ireland* (printed by University Press, Belfast, n.d.), 24.
3. Felicia R. Lee, "The Honest Dialogue That Is Neither," *New York Times*, 7 December 1997.
4. Report of the conference "Linked Future: Building Metropolitan Communities," 27–28 January 1997, program of the Carter Center.
5. Sharif Abdullah, *Creating a World That Works for All* (Barrett-Koechler, 1999), 106–7.
6. "Ten More Years?" editorial, *Richmond Times-Dispatch*, 6 May 1980.
7. "Slave Memorial," editorial, *Richmond Times-Dispatch*, 8 February 2000.
8. "Brown & Interposition," editorial, *Richmond-Times-Dispatch*, 16 May 2004.
9. Corcoran and Greisdorf, *Connecting Communities*, 74.

### Chapter 18. Walking through History

1. Margaret Smith, *Reckoning with the Past* (Lexington Books, 2005), 14.
2. Ibid, 26.
3. www.iofc.org/en/programmes/hic/newsroom/reports/.
4. Smith, *Reckoning with the Past*, 8.
5. Ibid, 15, 16.
6. Eqbal Ahmad, *The Conflict Within*, 15 February 1998, www.geocities.com/CollegePark/Library/9803/eqbal_ahmad/conflict.html.
7. Vamik Volkan, *Bloodlines* (Farrar, Straus and Giroux 1997), 58.
8. Smith, *Reckoning with the Past*, 13–14.
9. Sushobha Barve, "Seeing the Differences, Seeing the Similarities," Hope in the Cities newsletter, vol. 1, no 2 (July 2000).
10. "Interrupted Educations to Be Made Whole after 50 Years," VOANews.com, 29 September 2005. For a full history see http://go.vcu/peeples.
11. Shaila Dewan, "100 Years Later, a Painful Episode Is Observed," *New York Times*, 24 September 2006.
12. Jim Auchmutey, "How Atlanta's Newspapers Helped Incite the 1906 Race Riot," *Atlanta Journal-Constitution*, 17 September 2006.
13. Barbara Palmer, "Stanford Alumnus Seeks Reparations for Survivors of Deadly 1921 Race Riot," Stanford University News Service, 16 February 2005.
14. Tulsa Chamber of Commerce Board, quoted in *The Tulsa Race Riot Commission Report*, 159.
15. Shriver, *Honest Patriots*, 147.
16. Shriver says Tulsa presents a particularly good case for reparations since there is strong evidence that local authorities and members of the National Guard aided and abetted the rioters: "What a government *permits* or *authorizes* by ac-

tion or inaction of its officers has implications for the continuing liabilities of that government *transgenerationally*" (ibid., 149).

17. Margaret M. Mulrooney, "The 1998 Coup and Violence," *Centennial Record,* December 1989.

18. Ibid.

19. Ibid.

20. "A Lynching Memorial Unveiled in Duluth," editorial, *New York Times,* 5 December 2003.

21. Johnson and Smith, *Africans in America,* 338.

22. *Providence Journal,* 17 March 2006.

23. Ibid.

24. Special meeting, Liverpool City Council, 9 December 1999.

25. Quoted by Lord David Alton of Liverpool, House of Lords.

26. Rex Springsteen, "We Cry for Forgiveness," *Richmond Times-Dispatch,* 30 April 2000.

27. Michael Paul Williams, "A Power in One Man's Reconciliation," *Richmond Times-Dispatch,* 16 March 2007.

28. Gary Robertson, "A Monument to Reconciliation," *Richmond Times-Dispatch,* 31 March 2007.

29. "Message: Don't Violate Statue," *Richmond Free Press,* 5–7 April 2007.

30. The Episcopal Diocese of Virginia is pursuing a "triangle of hope" with Liverpool and West Africa to reverse the impact of slavery on current and future generations. In June 2007, five bishops from Liverpool, Virginia, and Ghana walked Richmond's Slave Trail as part of events marking the four-hundredth anniversary of the presence of the Anglican Church in the Americas.

### Chapter 19. Networks of Trust

1. Lecture to Connecting Communities Fellowship Program, Richmond, Va., 2004, www.hopeinthecities.org/node/22919.

2. Kenwyn K. Smith and David N. Berg, *Paradoxes of Group Life* (Jossey-Bass, 1987), 4.

3. www.hopeinthecities.org/node/22919.

4. Greisdorf, "Harnessing the Power of Boaz and Ruth," *For a Change,* 1 August 2006.

### Chapter 20. Building Capacity, Assessing Progress

1. Greisdorf, "The City That Dares to Talk," *For a Change,* 1 February 2002.

2. Amy Hubbard, Leonda Kenniston, and Julie Honnold, evaluation reports to Hope in the Cities and Dayton Dialogue on Race Relations, October 2000 and September 2004.

3. "A Conversation with Harold Saunders," *Carnegie Reporter* (Fall 2005).

4. www.grcc.com/files/Putting_The_Future_Together_FINAL.pdf.

5. Emily C. Dooley, "Looking Ahead in Our Region," *Richmond Times-Dispatch*, May 9, 2008.

6. Michael Paul Williams, "No Vision, No Heart, No Chance," *Richmond Times-Dispatch*, 20 November 2008.

7. Rob Corcoran, "A Commitment to Every Child," *Breakthroughs*, Initiatives of Change newsletter, November–December 2004.

8. Jack McHale, "In Chesterfield's Defense," *Style*, 20 February 2008.

9. "The National Launch of 'A Call to Community,'" Hope in the Cities newsletter, 23 May 1996.

10. Mari Fitzduff, lecture presented at "Tools for Change" conference, 19 July 2006, Caux, Switzerland, www.iofc.org/node/24494.

## Epilogue

1. Andrew Ferguson, "A Museum Divided," *Wall Street Journal*, 13 October 2006.

2. Jacqueline Trescott, "The Blue and Gray and Black," *Washington Post*, 7 October 2006.

3. Gary Robertson, "Civil War Center Takes Shape," *Richmond Times-Dispatch*, 23 April 2005.

4. Trescott, "The Blue and Gray and Black."

5. Cindy Brown Austin, "The Missing Piece," *Hartford Courant*, 4 August 2002.

# INDEX